Islam and Postcolonial Narrative

John Erickson examines four major authors from the "Third World" – Assia Djebar, Abdelkebir Khatibi, Tahar Ben Jelloun, and Salman Rushdie – all of whom have engaged in a critique of the relationship between Islam and the West. Erickson analyses the narrative strategies they deploy to explore the encounter between Western and Islamic values and reveals their use of the cultural resources of Islam, as well as their intertextual exchanges with other "Third World" writers. Erickson argues against any homogenizing mode of writing labeled "postcolonial" and any view of Islamic and Western discourses as monolithic or totalizing. He reveals the way these writers valorize expansiveness, polyvalence, and indeterminancy as part of an attempt to represent the views of individuals and groups that live on the cultural and political margins of society.

JOHN ERICKSON is Professor of French and Francophone Studies at the University of Kentucky. He is founder and editor of *L'Esprit Créateur*. He has co-edited three volumes of critical essays and published two books: *Nommo: African fiction in French*, and *Dada: Performance, poetry, and art*. He has published numerous essays on comparative literature, modern European literature, and "Third World" writing.

Islam and Postcolonial Narrative

JOHN ERICKSON

CAMBRIDGE
UNIVERSITY PRESS

PUBLISHED BY THE PRESS SYNDICATE OF THE UNIVERSITY OF CAMBRIDGE
The Pitt Building, Trumpington Street, Cambridge, CB2 1RP, United Kingdom

CAMBRIDGE UNIVERSITY PRESS
The Edinburgh Building, Cambridge CB2 2RU, UK   http://www.cup.cam.ac.uk
40 West 20th Street, New York, NY 10011–4211, USA   http://www.cup.org
10 Stamford Road, Oakleigh, Melbourne 3166, Australia

First published 1998

Printed in the United Kingdom at the University Press, Cambridge

Typeset in 9/13 pt Lexicon (*The Enschedé Font Foundry*), in QuarkXPress® [TAG]

A catalogue record for this book is available from the British Library

ISBN 0 521 59423 5 hardback

To SUZANNE

Contents

Preface

This book looks at oppositional narratives of four contemporary Muslim authors writing in languages of European provenance. In the study of these narratives I endeavor to bring out their specificity and divergences that inveigh against our seeing the authors as each setting out to do the same thing in the same way. I am interested rather in the commonality of their aims, which emerges in their categorical rejection of the hegemonic and totalizing forces of institutionalized thinking that impinge on human individuals and minorities who deviate from the well worn paths of conformity.

In terms of narrative, I am particularly interested in the ways these authors have each set about to fashion a specific, localized idiom, while under the ideological shadow of the dominant discursive structures of their respective societies. Though invariably their writing is marked by a dissenting, contestatory mode, it is marked as strongly by the rich profusion of beliefs and practices of the Islamic and Greco-Roman–Christian traditions and the diverse secular ideas and customs upon which they have drawn. I find it as important to see how they have used these riches as to look at how they have expressed their divergences.

Of the authors I study, three write in French and come from the North African littoral: Abdelkebir Khatibi and Tahar Ben Jelloun from Morocco and Assia Djebar from Algeria. The fourth author, Salman Rushdie, comes from the Indian continent and writes in English. I shall on occasion speak of the writings of these authors as postcolonial, but the individualized character of their writings prevails against any misguided attempt to enclose them within an undifferentiated grouping or system of reference.

Postcolonial is a useful term to apply to writing only insofar as it refers to writers emerging from varied cultures and circumstances, who have experienced analogous structures of domination imposed in the past by colonizing powers and shaped in the present by those same or other external powers, or by indigenous (neo-colonist) powers. The writers I call postcolonial seek, each in her or his own way, a space of writing that sets itself apart from those structures of power.

Many onlookers have regarded such writers as writing on the periphery, but their voices are more and more being heard. We can ascertain the efficacy of what they say as much by the often brutal attempts to suppress them, whether in Algeria or East Timor, as by the growing awareness of readers that they speak to some of the most important issues of our time – having to do, above all, with the relation between human individuals and minority groups and the societies that govern them.

I write out of the conviction that these voices, coming from elsewhere than that place where most of my readers and I are situated, say profoundly important things to us if we are willing to listen. Much of the most significant writing of our time comes from beyond the often arbitrary discursive boundaries set by the dominant political–social powers in Europe, on the North American continent, or in other regions of the world. What Roland Barthes has said of the Moroccan Abdelkebir Khatibi – that identity in his writing is of such a pure metal that it comes to be read as difference – applies to all of the writers I choose to look at. Their difference, or differences, for they address us through distinctly different timbres, have much to say to us about our own differences. For we are all located elsewhere with relation to others.

Critically, my own approach leans heavily on authors and commentators conversant from birth with the Islamic faith and the forms it has variously taken in far-flung areas of the world, as well as on other authors and commentators from so-called Third World regions who have undergone first-hand experience of colonialism or of the hegemonic structures it has left in place in numerous countries that have gained nominal independence. Many of my sources are thus "foreign" to the European or North American readers but "indigenous" to the subject at hand, that is, to the condition of postcoloniality wherever it might be found. All translations are mine when no source is given. In several instances I have modified the translation to convey nuances I felt had to be brought out.

I wish to give special thanks to Ross Chambers and Laurence Porter for their exceedingly helpful suggestions in regard to early versions of the present work; to Jean-François Lyotard for his encouraging reading of my manuscript as well as his enriching and ever-expanding thought that has over the years inspired me to conceptualize the world differently; and to Assia Djebar and Abdelkebir Khatibi for sharing ideas with me that have left their important mark on the formulation of my work. Several other persons, who have read parts of this study or my essays, have also left their imprint in some shape or form on my thinking. In some instances, these persons have contributed unknowingly to what has gone into the present book. Among them, I wish to mention in particular R. Lane Kauffmann, Hussam Al-Khateeb, Edouard Glissant, Françoise Douay-Soublin, Lilyan Kesteloot, and Evelyne Accad. I hasten to add, however, that their ideas have sometimes grown unrecognizable owing to my idiosyncratic adaptation of them. Additionally, my close collaboration as general editor with guest editors of special issues of *L'Esprit Créateur* devoted to postcolonial topics has opened up to me many valued avenues of discursive exchange. Among those guest editors are Eric Sellin, Elisabeth Mudimbe-Boyi, and Ali Behdad. Particular thanks go to anonymous readers whose wonderfully perceptive and constructive readings of an earlier version of this book have helped me to straighten out many inconsistencies, focus my subject much more effectively, and deal more discerningly with its many complexities.

Last of all, I want to express heartfelt apologies to my Abyssinian Trotsky, who often, after keeping patient vigil over his empty bowl while I tussled with ideas, felt called upon to sprawl over the manuscript pages on my desk. He slowed me down on occasion but gave measure to overly concentrated thought by restoring me to the needs of my less prosaic if no more real surroundings.

My work was supported in part by research grants from the National Endowment for the Humanities and Louisiana State University. I was also able to pursue essential research and engage in a valuable exchange of ideas as NEH Visiting Scholar in Residence at the University of Minnesota, Morris; as Visiting Favrot Chair at Rice University and participant in the wonderfully stimulating Rice Circle; and as resident lecturer in the Centre des Etudes Francophones at the Université de Paris IV–Sorbonne during the spring of 1993.

Some chapters of this book have drawn on material, revised and expanded, from certain of my essays published in literary reviews and as chapters in edited collections. I wish to thank the following publishers for permission to use this material:

"Writing Double: Politics and the African Narrative of French
Expression," Special issue on African Literature and Politics. Ed.
Claire Dehon. *Studies in Twentieth Century Literature*. (Winter 1990):
101–22.

"Veiled Woman and Veiled Narrative in Tahar Ben Jelloun's *Sandchild*,"
of which an earlier version appeared in *boundary 2* 20.1 (1993):
47–64, copyright © 1993, Duke University Press.

"*Metoikoi* and Magical Realism in the Maghrebian Narratives of Tahar
Ben Jelloun and Abdelkebir Khatibi," in *Magical Realism: Theory,
History, Community*. Eds. Lois Parkinson Zamora and Wendy Faris.
Durham: Duke University Press, 1995. Copyright © 1995, Duke
University Press.

"Women's Space and Enabling Dialogue in Assia Djebar's *L'Amour, la
fantasia*," in *Postcolonial Subjects: Francophone Women Writers*. Eds.
Mary Jean Green, et al. Minneapolis: University of Minnesota
Press, 1996. Copyright © 1996 by the Regents of the University of
Minnesota.

Permission to quote materials excerpted from texts published by the following persons and publishing houses are also gratefully acknowledged:

Alfred A. Knopf for Salman Rushdie, *Midnight's Children* (1982).

Dorothy S. Blair for her translation of *Fantasia: An Algerian Calvacade* of
Assia Djebar. London: Quartet Books Limited, 1989; Portsmouth,
New Hampshire: Heinemann, 1993.

The Boston Museum of Fine Arts for permission to reproduce as a
jacket illustration the painting of a "Pensive Poet," *c*. 1630.

The University of Chicago Press for Ross Chambers, *Room for Maneuver.
Reading (the) Oppositional (in) Narrative*. Copyright © 1991 by the
University of Chicago.

The Continuum Publishing Group for excerpts from "Living On:
Border Lines" by Jacques Derrida, trans. James Hulbert, in Harold
Bloom, et al. *Deconstruction and Criticism*. Copyright © 1979 by The
Continuum Publishing Company (published under the imprint of
Seabury Press).

Cornell University Press for *Language, Counter-Memory, Practice. Selected
Essays and Interviews by Michel Foucault*. Ed. Donald F. Bouchard
(1977), and Françoise Lionnet, *Autobiographical Voices* (1989).

Editions Denoël for Abdelkebir Khatibi, *Maghreb pluriel* (1983); and *La
Mémoire tatouée* (1971).

Assia Djebar for *Femmes d'Alger* (1980); *L'Amour, la fantasia* (1983); "Le
point de vue d'une Algérienne sur la condition de la femme
musulmane au 20e siècle," in *Le Courrier de l'UNESCO*

(August–September, 1975); and "Fugitive, et ne le sachant pas," in
L'Esprit Créateur (Summer 1993).

Editions Fata Morgana for Abdelkebir Khatibi's *Amour bilingue* (1983).

New Directions Publishing Corp. for Jorge Luis Borges, *Labyrinths.
Selected Stories & Other Writings*. Eds. Donald A. Yates and James E.
Irby et al. Copyright © 1962, 1964 by New Directions Publishing
Corp. Reprinted by permission of New Directions.

Oxford University Press for W. Montgomery Watt, *Mohammed. Prophet
and Statesman* (1961). By permission of Oxford University Press.

Presses Universitaires de France for Abdelwahab Bouhdiba, *La
Sexualité en Islam* (4th edn, 1986). Copyright © 1975 by Presses
Universitaires de France.

Quartet Books Ltd for Dorothy S. Blair's translation of *Fantasia: An
Algerian Calvacade* by Assia Djebar (London, 1989).

Random House, Inc. (Pantheon Books) for the US, Canada, and Open
Market rights to Salman Rushdie, *East, West. Stories*. Copyright ©
1994.

Readers International for Abdellatif Laâbi, *Rue de retour*. Trans.
Jacqueline Kaye (1989).

Routledge (London) for Homi Bhabha (ed.), *Nation and Narration* (1993).

Salman Rushdie for *The Satanic Verses* (Viking Penguin, 1989);
Midnight's Children (Alfred A. Knopf, Inc., 1980); *Imaginary
Homelands* (Granta Books, 1991); *East, West. Stories* (Pantheon Books,
1994); *The Jaguar Smile* (Penguin, 1987); "A Pen Against the Sword. In
Good Faith," *Newsweek*, February 12, 1990.

Editions du Seuil for Tahar Ben Jelloun, *L'Enfant de sable*. Copyright ©
Editions du Seuil, 1985, and *La Plus Haute des solitudes. Misère affective
et sexuelle d'émigrés nord-africains*. Copyright © Editions du Seuil,
1977, 1985; Edouard Glissant, *Le Discours antillais*. Copyright ©
Editions du Seuil, 1981; and Tzvetan Todorov, *Poétique de la prose*.
Copyright © Editions du Seuil, 1971.

Penguin Books USA Inc. (Viking Penguin Inc.) for rights in the US and
the Philippines: *The Satanic Verses*. Copyright © 1988 by Salman
Rushdie; *The Jaguar Smile*. Copyright © 1987 by Salman Rushdie;
Imaginary Homelands. Copyright © 1991 by Salman Rushdie.

Penguin Books Canada for rights in Canada: *The Satanic Verses*.
Copyright © 1988 by Salman Rushdie.

The Wylie Agency (London) for rights in the United Kingdom and
Open Market rights: *The Satanic Verses*. Copyright © 1988 by Salman
Rushdie; *Imaginary Homelands*. Copyright © 1991 by Salman
Rushdie.

Introduction: creating new discourses from old

A rediscovered country offers itself as what it is,
without closure or totality.　　　ABDELKEBIR KHATIBI, *Amour bilingue*[1]

You have always had this scrupulous reverence
for the dignity of the other, whoever he may be.

ABDELLATIF LAÂBI, who spent eight and
a half years in a Moroccan prison for "crimes of opinion"[2]

This study examines postcolonial narratives of four major Muslim authors of fiction from diverse origins and backgrounds, who have elaborated counterdiscourses in European languages.[3] It focuses on the problematics involved in developing such counterdiscourses while staying within the frame of the linguistic and cultural "systems" of the power structures within and under which these authors have written. While their narratives vary too greatly to suggest a single model of oppositional writing, the tendency and emphasis of their writings give evidence of a common aim – to refute totalizing, universalizing systems and reductive processes, in whatever society or form they may be found, which threaten to marginalize individual and minoritarian dissent, and to create a dominant cultural discourse that is univocal.[4]

My personal experience leads me to emphasize narratives by French-speaking writers from the Maghreb (North Africa), more particularly from Morocco (Tahar Ben Jelloun and Abdelkebir Khatibi) and Algeria (Assia Djebar). I have also chosen to study the writing of Salman Rushdie, who, while brought up in the Islamic tradition in the Middle East and writing in English, shares with his French-speaking counterparts knowledge and experience of Muslim beliefs and practices, and offers another model of the postcolonial writing of authors versed equally in European culture and diverse cultures in countries where Islam is the primary system of faith.

The late Kateb Yacine, perhaps the foremost North African writer in French, speaks of the refusal of some postcolonial writers to become "domesticated," that is, to submit unquestioningly to the structures of power that frame them in. It is just such writers and their diverse responses that interest me:

> In our Arabic tradition, there are some poets who have refuted even the message of the Prophet. People believe them to be proud, but it is not true. It is a matter rather of a total confidence in the word as word and the refusal to become domesticated. There is the true poet. He is someone who does not claim to make of his word something that domesticates men and that teaches them to live, but on the contrary someone who brings them a freedom, a freedom often uncomfortable moreover. I believe that the true message of the poet lies in this. It is not the fact of saying to the people that you must do this or you must do that; it is precisely to break all frames that have been placed around them so that they might bound back.[5]

The "true poets" to whom Kateb refers hold in common an attempt to forge a non-totalizing, alternative discourse that achieves a freeing of difference and serves as a model for those ("the people") who suffer the constraints of unforgiving social–cultural bonds. These "true poets" all live under threat of repression, as in the extreme cases of the many writers and intellectuals assassinated by unknown Algerian extremists,[6] as well as in that of the death sentence (*fatwa*) handed down on Salman Rushdie. Nonetheless, it is an oversimplification to view the resistance of these postcolonial writers ("poets") described by Kateb as signifying unqualified refutation of the "message of the Prophet," for, far from all being set on rejecting Islam and Muhammad, most reject only the dictates imposed by Islamic extremists. Nor is it valid to see them as uncategorically rejecting the religious and social beliefs and practices of the Western cultures in which they have been schooled, for it is only the hegemonic tendencies of those cultures and their discourses, and the ideologically driven aspects of their languages, that they resist.

The writers I am about to study are, to varying degrees, believers in the Islamic (Sunni) faith system and, moreover, draw willingly and strongly upon Western culture, literature, and thought. But, in strikingly different ways, their writings refute or clash with certain of the strictures imposed in the name of the Word – of the Qur'ān, the Sunna or collections of Traditions (sayings and stories) of Muhammad, and the manner in which Ijma', the consensus underlying Islamic practice and belief, is interpreted (particularly by the Shi'a branch of Islam) – as well as those strictures imposed in the name of the magisterial discourses of Western society. In sum, these are the strictures imposed by those commentators and lawgivers in Islam and in the West who have variously sought to control and even to deny the word (in small letters) to errant individuals and (Djebar argues) particularly women.

Though the generalizing of difference is something that a study of narratives emanating from diverse cultures cannot fully avoid, the last thing I wish to do is to put forth a monolithic concept of an imaginary creature called "*the* postcolonial author." My more modest intention is rather to treat the question of *difference* in its manifold varieties, past and present, as they may be found in the specific postcolonial discourses I shall examine and the postcolonial critical commentary I shall call upon.

I have chosen to characterize the narratives I discuss and their authors as *postcolonial*. In recent years, many critics and commentators, sensitive to the hierarchical implications inhering in the term "Third World," have sought other terms to refer to non-Western culture – such as "emergent" or "developing," which conveniently ignore or slight the long and rich cultural and linguistic heritage preserved and handed down for centuries through indigenous languages and oral literatures.[7]

All such terms imply that the non-European world occupies a less advanced position on a scale of social development or that its development is incomplete – as emphasized by the participle ending of words such as emerg*ing* and develop*ing*, used by the Westerner to characterize them. Conversely, such terminology suggests that the Western cultures are at the apex or center of human and social development and thus represent what the non-Western cultures work towards. The same holds for the adjectives "Anglophone," "Francophone," "Hispanophone," and "Lusophone," used to identify countries outside the "mother" country, where European-derived languages are spoken. By their prefixes, these terms put a premium on the language and culture of the "mother" country: metropolitan England, France, Spain, or Portugal. They valorize the political and economic interests of the "mother" country and gloss over the significant cultural/linguistic differences existing between the non-metropolitan countries and the Metropole as well as between themselves.

Roland Barthes, in discussing official phraseology used to designate African countries, speaks of it as serving purposes other than those of communication. "It is a language charged with bringing about a coincidence between norms and facts, and with giving to a cynical 'real' the certainty of a noble moral... a writing one could call cosmetic because it aims at covering up the facts with language noise, or... with the adequation of a linguistic sign" ["C'est un langage chargé d'opérer une coïncidence entre les normes et les faits, et de donner à un réel cynique la caution d'une morale noble... une écriture que l'on pourrait appeler cosmétique parce qu'elle vise à recouvrir les faits d'un bruit de langage, ou... du signe suffisant du langage"].[8] Official phraseology in this context is a code without relationship to its content (or even to a contrary one), whose primary purpose is one of control and the legislation of social and linguistic behavior. A code of intimidation.

The term "postcolonial" is of very recent coinage. The word "colony" from the Latin *colonia* was used to denote "a public settlement of Roman citizens in a hostile or newly conquered country" (the *Oxford English Dictionary*). The word made its appearance in modern languages in fourteenth-century French. Its modern sense is observed in Latin and Italian writers of the sixteenth century. The word *colonie* was solidified in the French language in the seventeenth century to denote a territory dominated and administered by a foreign power. The connotation of economic exploitation came to the fore in the eighteenth century. The end of the nineteenth century, notably with Marxist criticism of the system of colonization, introduced into French the word *colonialisme* (1902) and *colonialiste* (1903). In 1960, the word *néo-colonialisme* appeared, preceded by words indicating the presumed end of the colonial system (*décolonisation*, 1952). The word "postcolonial" is of such recent origin that neither the *OED* nor the *Grand Robert* make mention of it.

Critics and commentators have tended to employ this term indiscriminately to denote non-Western cultures that have gained nominal independence, though the majority of these cultures, often administered by surrogate neo-colonialist regimes, remain under indirect control by the same political and economic forces that ruled under empire. Notably few former colonies, particularly in Africa, have wrested a true measure of independence from the West and its surrogates, as such critics as Jean Ziegler have continually argued with formidable statistical and documentary evidence.[9]

I shall use the term "postcolonial" only for those cultures that have attained a measure of self-autonomy or for narratives in which we observe a counterdiscourse expressive of an agonistic position consciously undertaken against the controlling norms of dominant discourses, whether of European or non-European origin. It is not an anomaly, therefore, to find postcolonial narratives by writers on the order of Ben Jelloun from countries ruled by neocolonial despots such as Hassan II of Morocco. Indeed, one can make the case that different narratives by the selfsame author may be characterized as postcolonial (for example, Ben Jelloun's *L'Enfant de sable*) and orientalist or non-postcolonial, that is, strongly submissive to the literary norms of Western culture (for example, Ben Jelloun's *Nuit sacrée*).

When I speak of a postcolonial author and her or his discourse, I do not intend to set in place a new organizing principle of discourse, or to impose anything like a fixed meaning or a unified "non-Western" outlook which, as Salman Rushdie reminds us in *The Jaguar Smile*, is simplistic.[10] Nor do I seek to disinter the traditional notion of the author as a unifying factor of a discourse with reference to whom we can explain its genesis and coherence. On the contrary, I am mindful of the existence of a multiplicity of discourses by non-Western authors, more particularly a number of them that interact and bear resemblances to each other in their contestatory mode, in their condition(s) of possibility, but which are discontinuous and often conflictual if not contradictory.

Postcolonial theory in many of its formulations has tended, on the one hand, to elide cultural and national particularity between non-Western nations under the umbrella category "postcolonial." On the other hand, others of its formulations have tended to view ethnic and cultural groups as discrete entities characterized by a theoretical polarity existing between the so-termed West and the non-Western, the colonial and the postcolonial, etc. Urged on by a need to pronounce differences between adversarial contenders, postcolonial theory often overemphasizes disparities and fails to take into account the negotiation that has transpired between different countries and different cultures.

This situation provides a partial answer as to why I have chosen to study the narratives of the four authors I have mentioned. Far from having entered into a purely adversarial relation with colonial and neo-colonial entities, these authors have negotiated between them – between European culture and language and their own mother tongue(s), between Islamic teachings and their awareness of secular concerns that extend beyond or outside of the Qur'ān. The writings of these four authors exemplify in varied ways the exchange that usually transpires between non-Western writers, the former colonial occupiers, and the present neo-colonialist or traditionalist forces in power.

While very much interested in the articulation of national, cultural, or ethnic particularity in the works of Muslim writers and thinkers, I am keenly interested as well in how they appropriate Western (Judeo-Christian) or Islamic beliefs and practices while elaborating a third, distanced position lying "elsewhere" – that is, between the hypothetical extremes of the "pure" hegemonistic power structures of Western and Islamic cultures, on the one hand, and a "pure" non-Western, non-Islamic oppositional mode, on the other. Both extremes are imaginary constructs in the case of the authors I study.

Nothing approaches "pure" in these contestatory or, more accurately, these give-and-take relationships. Paradoxically, the only "pure" category seems to be that of the mixed or *métissée*, as Khatibi and the Martinican author and critic Edouard Glissant call it – the bastardized, the culturally diluted. The term transcultural has been used to describe the dilution of one culture by another. Obversely, the prefix "post" of *post*colonial, in suggesting a departure from or a step beyond, unfortunately scants the notion of transference between or interpenetration of cultures (colonial, Western, non-Western, neo-colonial, Islamic, popular Arabo-Berber culture, etc.).

I have often asked myself the question whether my own subject position, of someone schooled in the rational discourse of European–North American culture, can elude colonizing (im)positions. I believe it is possible in function of my studies in discourses of the Western other (the eristic thinkers of the classical age and their descendents), of the transculturation that my own thought and perceptions have undergone in the approximately seven years I have lived in non-Western cultures, as well as of the intellectual and cultural maturation of my thinking that has been influenced by contact with non-Western cultures. The *pensée métissée* (unraveling thought) underlying my own intellectual and emotional development has given me a sense of non-Western otherness, of that betweenness essential to a "feel" for the interchange between peoples and ideas of different cultures.

When I speak as I will of the important "freeing of difference" occurring in the discourses of various postcolonial thinkers and writers, that freeing must be understood as a composite difference that emerges from a mingling of various intellectual metals into a "new" substance that partakes of this/that, past/present, self/other. As Khatibi has written, no pure beginning exists; all beginnings are but crossroads of previous beginnings, and those of others, *ad infinitum*. From the starting-point, however – the particular beginnings of the narratives I study, or the specific beginnings of the authors' intellectual and emotional positioning – the beginnings we shall meet with may be thought of as preliminary steps in the conscious and intentioned production of meaning, as Edward Said has defined it.[11]

The works I shall study do not represent original departures, but a combination or mixing (*métissage*) of preceding endeavors (of the author and of other authors, cultures, ideas, and positionings) and a new combination that speaks to the desires and convictions of the author and like-thinkers.

As I will argue throughout, the authors I study, far from attempting to bring about a simple poetics of reversal, a dialectical move to replace one system or frame of power by another, offer new and powerful dynamics of narrative engaged in an unending polymorphous and polyphonic mixing.

The question of language

Owing to the fact that the writers I have chosen to study set out to write their own cultural midground into existence through a language originating in a foreign culture, the problematics of that utilization are of paramount importance.

The Moroccan writer and activist, Abdellatif Laâbi, speaks of the use of a European-originated language in this way: "Provisionally making use of French as an instrument of communication, we are ever conscious of the danger into which we risk falling, which consists in utilizing that language as a means of cultural expression" ["Assumant provisoirement le français comme instrument de communication, nous sommes conscients en permanence, du danger dans lequel nous risquons de tomber et qui consiste à assumer cette langue en tant qu'instrument de culture"].[12]

Every language, as is implicit in the danger mentioned by Laâbi, carries with it an ideological register that directs the way the user formulates his or her thoughts and legislates the conditions of acceptable expression in accord with the specific requirements of that culture from which the language emanates.

A characteristic of language that offers an opening onto a solution, however, is its aleatory character, its unpredictability and proclivity to escape us owing to what Michel Foucault calls its "fearful materiality."[13]

To master the aleatory character of language, institutionalized discourse has smoothed the rough edges of speech, sought to purge it, on the one hand, of the unexpected and, on the other, of any blatant apparition of the totalizing intent of institutions themselves. On the contrary, numerous postcolonial writers who, as the Argentinean author, Julio Cortázar, has described them, "work the limits,"[14] have seized precisely on the potential of discourse for disruption, its dangerously exhilarating tendency to explode, by exposing its sharp edges, uncovering its asperities, introducing into it the unexpected and uncontrolled.

The semiotic enterprise is central to the tactics devised by the postcolonial writers we shall treat. Lucy Stone McNeece mentions two important features of Abdelkebir Khatibi's unorthodox and idiosyncratic use of language: the fact that self-knowledge and knowledge of others derives from our relation to signs that function differentially and in various ways in diverse cultures; and that, however much we believe we use language to create meaning, language in fact inscribes meaning upon us.[15]

Tahar Ben Jelloun speaks of how "Each society possesses a screen on which appear the authorized signs. Everything lying outside these signs is condemned. For our society, the totality of these signs is a book" ["Chaque société a un écran où apparaissent les signes autorisés. Tout ce qui est en dehors de ces signes est condamné. Pour notre société l'ensemble de ces signes est un livre"].[16] The book he refers to is the Qur'ān, which delimits what subjects and discursive forms are valid, but the same process of authorization (legitimation) operates in the fundamental authoritative texts of all societies (those in the Islamic sphere as well as those of Western societies, all of which govern by the authority of multiple texts). Islamic cultures, like Western cultures, differ markedly in terms of the texts and practices by which they govern.

Most English sources depict the Shari'a (the Islamic legal system) as deriving from four sources or principles at work in formulating Islamic legal practice: (1) the Qur'ān, from which has derived a body of doctrine as well as rituals, practical duties and laws, elaborated and mediated by (2) the Sunna (the way or example of the Prophet, based on "hadith" or the Traditions, the moral sayings and stories of Muhammad's actions), (3) "analogy" (qiyas), and (4) Ijma' (consensus, or the principle expressed by Muhammad that "My community will never agree in an error," which holds that beliefs and practices historically held by the majority of Muslims is true).[17]

The interpretation that appears to be emerging very recently among

(Sunni) Muslim scholars is that there are rather two major sources of law (the first two: the Qur'ān and the Sunna), and that the second pair may provide modes of "interpretation" among certain communities at certain periods, but are by no means universally accepted, at least in the relative weight they are accorded in reaching decisions regarding the establishment and interpretation of the legal code. It is for that reason of course that there exist differing schools of law (madhahib).[18]

For just such reasons, the very diversity of cultural – social, juridical, and political – practices by which various Islamic cultures around the world govern makes it impossible to speak of Islam in monolithic terms, just as the reference to cultural practices subsumed under the rubric of the "West" covers a multitude of social, juridical, and political variations.

It is by the power of the sign that societies, despite their variations, process information so as to regulate and organize the manner in which individuals perceive and "know," the ways in which they interpret and map their environment prior to acting and as the basis for their actions.[19] All societies arrogate the power of the sign to themselves through a system of collective mapping, a system of exclusion, limitation, and appropriation, to use Michel Foucault's terms, that imposes strategies to attenuate or assimilate all adversarial discourses. The function of discourse, as scholars such as Pierre Bourdieu and Richard Terdiman have observed, derives less from a need to communicate than from a desire to promulgate through specific mechanisms of determination a system of representation that asserts and stabilizes the beliefs and values of the culture and seeks to control the meaning of that discourse.[20]

The projects of the writers I shall look at operate in a diversity of ways to reseize control of the signs that the dominant linguistic and cultural systems have appropriated in order to restore a system of reference that speaks to their desires and the cultural specificity of their perceptions. Salman Rushdie urges the need to repossess the wells of language that have been poisoned by the "vocabularies of power."[21]

Translating a foreign language

In utilizing a language deriving from a Western culture as a lingua franca to articulate one's needs, perceptions, and desires – a language infused with the ideology of that culture that has been a major factor in the development of relations of power and dominance in the cultures it has invaded and colonized beyond the boundaries of Europe or North America –

postcolonial writers at first glance appear to be restricted to two choices:
(1) accepting European linguistic hegemony through complete acquiescence to or ignorance of the ideological implications of that discourse or,
(2) taking a position of overt opposition to it through radical exterioriza-
tion. The first choice is untenable for postcolonial writers seeking to
articulate their difference from the master discourse, but the latter falls
into a snare laid by the magisterial discourse itself, for the position of
oppositional exteriority amplifies and reinforces the discourse of power
by emphasizing its dominance. The two choices lead to assimilation and
appropriation. Only a third choice would appear to avoid the pitfall: that
of silence.

Is it possible, however, to conceptualize yet another modality offering
a more effective field for contestation and change?

Certain writers from non-European cultures, availing themselves of
the discourse of the European Other, of a foreign culture with its own
means and modes, have developed diverse countertactics that reposition
narrative discourse. They have devised ways to dismantle its ideological
infrastructures that legislate the permissible conditions of truth, so as to
rescaffold and reconfigure it, and to replace its absolute Truth that
brooks no variations with countervailing local and specific "truths."

They have succeeded in creating, as Khatibi describes it, with specific
reference to Maghrebian writers utilizing a European language, a new
space for their writing by radically inscribing themselves in the "interval" between identity and difference:

> That interval is the scene of the text, what it puts into play. In
> Maghrebian literature, such an interval – when it becomes text and
> poem – imposes itself through its radical strangeness, that is, through
> writing that seeks its roots in another language, in an absolute
> outsidedness.
>
> [Cet intervalle est la scène du texte, son enjeu. Dans la littérature
> maghrébine, un tel intervalle – quand il devient texte et poème –
> s'impose par son étrangeté radicale, c'est-à-dire une écriture qui
> cherche ses racines dans une autre langue, dans un dehors absolu.][22]

In locating themselves in that space between identity and distance of
which he speaks, Khatibi is referring, on the one hand, to the absolutistic
Sameness or tendency towards similitude of the dominant language that
works towards assimilation of all its speakers (of whatever language, of
whatever culture) and, on the other, to their (the Maghrebian writers')

radical alterity to the European culture that has formed the ideological supports of the language.

That "other language," that discourse of "radical strangeness," that "absolute outsidedness" marks the work of several postcolonial writers who have filled the otherwise silent void of non-communication between the former Western colonizers and the former colonized with voices from the outside proclaiming their presence as Other.

The process is less one of strict oppositionality, however, than of a positive complementarity. In his book *Maghreb pluriel*, Khatibi also describes how the assumed foreign language, interiorized so as to become an effective form of writing, transforms the mother tongue of the speaker by structuring it and carrying it away towards what he terms the untranslatable. It is not simply a matter, however, of one language adding itself to the other or effecting a pure juxtaposition with it. On the contrary,

> each one *signals* to the other, calls on the other to maintain itself as
> outside. Outside against outside, that foreignness (strangeness): what
> a language desires (if I dare to speak thus) is to be singular, irreducible,
> rigorously other. I think that ... the translation functions according to
> that intractability, that unceasingly receding and disruptive
> distancing. And, in effect, all Maghrebian literature of so-called
> French expression is a narrative of translation. I don't say it is only
> translation; I emphasize that it's a question of a narrative that *speaks in
> tongues*.
>
> [chacune *fait signe* à l'autre, l'appelle à se maintenir comme dehors.
> Dehors contre dehors, cette étrangeté: ce que désire une langue (si
> j'ose parler ainsi) c'est d'être singulière, irréductible, rigoureusement
> autre. Je pense ... que la traduction opère selon cette intractabilité,
> cette distanciation sans cesse reculée et disruptive. Et en effet, toute
> cette littérature maghrébine dite d'expression française est un récit de
> traduction. Je ne dit pas qu'elle n'est que traduction, je précise qu'il
> s'agit d'un récit qui *parle en langues*.]   (186)

It is obvious that, in regard to a foreign language, Khatibi uses the word translation not in the narrow sense of a mere rendering of linguistic and cultural equivalents of one language into another language, but rather in the strong sense of the transformation of that language into a vehicle for the re-vision and reworking of its foreign linguistic and cultural values and their reinscription into a new context of value reflective of the indivisible union of two languages (the assumed language and the mother tongue), two cultures (French and Maghrebian). The result, which I shall take up at length in my chapter on Khatibi, is the creation of what he calls a *bi-langue* (a double or bi-language, from the adjective bilingual), which is "rigorously other," forever distanced, unseizable, and unappropriable by either Islamic or European magisterial (dominant) discourses. The *bi-langue* is the basis for an "écriture métissée," an unraveled and unraveling writing (*Maghreb pluriel* p. 181). The binary linguistic and narrative model of traditional translation (that displaces one language with another) gives way to an antinomical linguistic and narrative structure in which former opposites coexist, cohere in a new voice.

Characteristics of some postcolonial discourses

In the following chapters, I focus on individual narratives by the four authors I study: *L'Amour, la fantasia* (*Fantasia: An Algerian Calvacade*) of Assia Djebar, *L'Enfant de sable* (*The Sand Child*) of Tahar Ben Jelloun, *L'Amour bilingue* (*Love in Two Languages*) of Abdelkebir Khatibi, and *The Satanic Verses* of Salman Rushdie. The narrative discourses of the four writers are marked by storytelling, influenced by oral folk tradition of the Middle East and North Africa. They present small narrative units working locally to replace directly, and refute indirectly (usually), the canonical master narratives of European thought concerned with the legitimation of knowledge. The latter are grounded, as critics have reiterated, in universal philosophic categories that have constituted the logocentric tradition descending from Aristotle, through the Scholastics, through Hegel, and down to such modern day theorists as Lukács, all of whom have valorized the concept of "totality."[23]

The discourses I study tend also to emphasize a dialogic relationship extending outside the text, between the empirical author and reader, as well as operating inside the text between the narrator (implied author) and narratee (implied reader), the narrator and characters, and between characters themselves. The oftimes fusion of author and narrator, as in Djebar's narrative, or even author/narrator and character, as in Khatibi's narrative, redound with a sense of autobiography. All four authors foreground a preoccupation with a metalinguistic dynamic (writing about writing) and dramatize the difficulty of assigning identity – of author, narrator, characters, and, by implication, of self in general. This dialogic operation reverses the conventional direction of narration by producing narration as an outcome of dialogic exchange, in lieu of the imposition of narrative structures fixed in advance that determine the direction to be taken by speech events. In such dialogic narrative, speech events produce further speech events that result in narrative as their byproduct.[24] The underlying aprioristic structures of conventional narrative are as a consequence detotalized. Dialogic exchange explores, moreover, a plurality of propositions and positions; it works against closure and finality; it is atemporal and irreducibly polyvocal, and presents propositions and understandings in essentially non-linear, synthesizing sequences.

Through story-telling and dialogic exchange, Ben Jelloun, Djebar, Khatibi, and Rushdie engage in "language games" such as those Ludwig Wittgenstein has described.[25] The effect is to delegitimize the master narratives, whose pre-existing rules regulated the sequence and unfolding of speech events: dialogue no longer follows the script laid down by narrative but includes that script (rules and codes) within it. Wittgenstein asks whether there are not situations in which we play with language and make up the rules as we use it. He asserts that there are even situations where we alter rules as we go along.[26] As the narratives I discuss unfold, as the author organizes smaller narratives within the greater narrative, the reader often comes away with the impression of improvisation. Khatibi tries on different endings for a selfsame narrative; Ben Jelloun rewrites his narrative extensively through different and often contradictory story-tellers. Both writers alter the rules and appear to make up new ones as the occasion calls for.

Another way to make up the rules as one goes along lies in the example of *The Thousand and One Nights* with its creation of endless stories through such an enabling device (or disabling device from the standpoint of the patristic Sultan) as the embedded 602nd tale (invented by another story-teller, Borges – see the chapter on Ben Jelloun) that returns us to the beginning story and consequently involves us in an infinite circular progression. In Ben Jelloun's *L'Enfant de sable, The Thousand and One Nights* serves, in fact, as an explicit source text from which he boldly borrows characters.

Instead of the metanarrative (the ideological, philosophically based narrative) at the heart of the grand narratives of European cultures, which aprioristically and implicitly refers back to preconceived principles that, tautologically, "prove" the validity of the story-line (argument), many postcolonial texts tend to manage knowledge through the phenomenon of language as event, that is, language concerned with the pragmatics of its own execution. The conceptualization of event as non-referential, as non-reducible to a unified consciousness or a historical progression, results in difference being conceived not as complementary

and constitutive of a more general concept or order, but as "pure" event –
what Michel Foucault hypothesizes in speaking of that which would
occur if thought "conceived of difference differentially, instead of search-
ing out the common elements underlying difference."[27]

The postcolonial discourses of Ben Jelloun, Djebar, Khatibi, and
Rushdie do not predicate a dialectics of resistance and revolution, but
simply refuse to accept unquestioningly the principles (ideology) of the
master discourses of various Islamic societies and of the European societies in whose languages they write – much in the manner that Foucault
formulates it:

> The freeing of difference requires thought without contradiction,
> without dialectics, without negation; thought that accepts
> divergence; affirmative thought whose instrument is disjunction;
> thought of the multiple – of the nomadic and dispersed multiplicity
> that is not limited or confined by the constraints of similarity.
>
> ("Theatrum Philosophicum," p. 185)

In their description of the effects of this freeing of difference, Gilles
Deleuze and Félix Guattari, in L'Anti-Oedipe, contrast the potentially differential discourse of non-Western writers and the magisterial discourse
of the colonizer, in whose system Oedipus symbolizes par excellence control and which thrives on dialectical reasoning and binary polarities:

> Unconscious revolutionary investiture is such that desire... blends
> the self-interest of the dominated and exploited classes and releases
> fluxes capable of breaking at once all segregations and their Oedipal
> applications, capable of hallucinating history, of making races
> delirious and of setting continents ablaze. No, I am not one of yours, I
> am the outside and the deterritorialized, "I am of an inferior race from
> all eternity... I am an animal, a nigger"... Oedipus explodes, because
> his conditions of possibility themselves have exploded. The *nomadic
> and polyvocal function* of conjunctive syntheses is opposed to the
> *segregative and bi-univocal* [that is, dialectical/univocal] *function*. Desire
> has as if two poles, racist and racial, paranoiac-segregative and
> schizoid-nomadic.
>
> [L'investissement révolutionnaire inconscient est tel que le désir...
> recoupe l'intérêt des classes dominées, exploitées, et fait couler des
> fluxs capables de rompre à la fois toutes les ségrégations et leurs
> applications oedipiennes, capables d'halluciner l'histoire, de délirer
> les races et d'embraser les continents. Non, je ne suis pas des vôtres, je
> suis le dehors et le déterritorialisé, "je suis de race inférieure de toute
> éternité... je suis bête, un nègre"... Oedipe saute, parce que ses

conditions elles-mêmes ont sauté. *L'usage nomadique et polyvoque* des synthèses conjonctives s'oppose à *l'usage ségrégatif et bi-univoque*. Le délire a comme deux pôles, raciste et racial, paranoïaque-ségrégatif et schizo-nomadique.][28]

Though the aptness of the medical terminology used by Deleuze and Guattari to characterize postcolonial differential discourse and the discourses of power in European and Islamic countries may be questionable, the nature of the discourses in opposition are formidably characterized, for the magisterial discourses have, in several instances, operated as discourses of servitude, imprisonment, and repression, posited on closure, continuity, assimilation, and reduction to a unitary, univocal principle – that of the Master. Whereas postcolonial discourses such as we shall consider are nomadic in the sense Deleuze and Guattari give to the term, they are characterized by an opening up, polyvalence, divergence, disjunctiveness, and differentiality.

If the discursive tactics of postcolonial authors often make it impossible to reconstitute a unified "world," it is because a truly unified "world" exists only as an imaginary construct. It often means, among postcolonial authors, the impossibility as well of constituting being in terms of a stable and coherent subject. Even for Djebar, whose narrative, *L'Amour, la fantasia*, misleadingly appears on the surface to adhere to a more stable formulation of subject, we see that the figure of a woman is emphatically not a single subject but a compound subject, that she is the sum of her present being as well as of the beings of her sisters and women ancestors. She is by no means reducible to a unified notion of being.

I have used the term "univocal" in referring to certain underlying principles of master discourses. In treating the concept of being, however, Deleuze and Foucault propose quite a different formulation of the term. The concept of the univocity of being as originally put forth by Duns Scotus and Spinoza eliminates categories by reasoning that being is expressed in the same way for all things. This concept is reformulated by Deleuze, and Foucault posits that in this reformulation "Differences would evolve of their own accord, being would be expressed in the same fashion for all these differences, and being would no longer be a unity that guides and distributes them, but their repetition as difference" ("Theatrum Philosophicum," p. 187). In this way, "the univocity of being, its singleness of expression, is paradoxically the principal condition which permits difference to escape the domination of identity, which frees it from the law of the Same as a simple opposition within conceptual elements" (*Ibid.*, p. 192). This reformulation applies to most postcolonial discourses, which are freed from the philosophy of representation and from Hegelian dialectics – discourses in which categories are suppressed and replaced by the free play of recurring difference in a non-referential, non-figurative context.

My own point of contention with Foucault, who presents in the writings I cite a nearly exclusive view of domination and opposition, would be to stress the other side of the equation that he scants. Difference among oppressed segments of society usually works, as Foucault says, to elude what he calls the "domination of identity" or, put more concretely in the case of the authors I treat, to elude assimilation into Islamic-derived or Western logocentric systems in which the assimilee would lose her or his individual identity by being subsumed totally into an absolutistic (theocratic or philosophic) frame of reference. The postcolonial authors I study, however, give ample evidence of a willingness to "identify" with Islamic and European traditions and their variegated systems in their non-hegemonistic forms. I need only refer again to their predilection for European languages and their lack of reticence in drawing upon Islamic beliefs and customs. While attempting to skirt the threat of assimilation, they manifest, on the other hand, a desire to appropriate what is positive in Islamic and Western thought and turn it to their own use. As I mentioned earlier, the relation between most postcolonial writers and the dominant structures that confront them is one of give and take. To speak exclusively of opposition would be to skew the argument.

Homi K. Bhabha, in his essay on cultural difference, which treats of the peoples – migrants, refugees, nomads, displaced persons – inhabiting the liminal, disjunctive space of national society, speaks of a structure of indeterminateness inherent in forms of cultural hybridity[29] that allows for the development of an alternative discourse. Cultural difference should be understood, he insists, not as a free play of polar opposites or pluralities in the homogeneous empty time of the community,[30] but as a means to address the clash of variety and diversity generated by cultural plenitude. Its strategies rest on "a form of juxtaposition or contradiction that resists the teleology of dialectical sublation." In recognizing parallel practices existing side by side, cultural difference is the site where divergence between representations of social forms is articulated "without surmounting the space of incommensurable meanings and judgements that are produced within the process of transcultural negotiation" (312).

The assertion of cultural difference is not simply "to invert the axis of political discrimination by installing the excluded term at the centre," but to transform discursive relations by shifting "the position of enunciation and the relations of address within it; not only what is said but from where it is said; not simply the logic of articulation but the *topos* of enunciation." It seeks

> to re-articulate the sum of knowledge from the perspective of the signifying *singularity* of the "other" that resists totalization – the repetition that will not return as the same, the minus-in-origin that results in political and discursive strategies where adding-*to* does not add-up but serves to disturb the calculation of power and knowledge, producing other spaces of subaltern signification.[31]   (*Ibid.*)

The assertion of identity in cultural difference "is dialogical or transferential in the style of psychoanalysis... It is constituted through the *locus* of the Other which suggests both that the object of identification is ambivalent, and, more significantly, that the agency of identification is never pure or holistic but always constituted in a process of substitution, displacement or projection" (312–13).

The term "substitution" used by Homi Bhabha should not be construed as the mere replacement of one term or discourse by another but rather, as he indicates, a supplement or adding-to that opens up by generating alternative discursive spaces. "The very possibility of cultural contestation," Homi Bhabha adds, "the ability to shift the ground of knowledges, or to engage in the 'war of position,' depends not only on the refutation or substitution of concepts... [but] attempts to engage with the 'anterior' space of the [arbitrary] sign that structures the symbolic language of alternative, antagonistic cultural practices" (313).

As Homi Bhabha accordingly demonstrates, new forms of meaning are created "through processes of negotiation where no discursive authority can be established without revealing the difference of itself" (313). We cannot contextualize cultural difference "by explaining it in terms of some pre-given discursive causality or origin. We must always keep open a supplementary space for the articulation of cultural knowledges that are adjacent and adjunct but not necessarily accumulative, teleological, or dialectical" (313). This process works against the homogenization or totalization of cultural/human experience.

In regard to the freeing of difference and the articulation of the diversity resulting from the clash of hybrid forms of cultural plenitude, the writers I discuss, along with others who warrant the appellation "post-colonial," practice the dispersion of voices through enabling discourses that reject all claim to privileged knowledge, that are premised on the view that all discourses exist on equal footing. Postcolonial discourses volitionally assume the status of marginal discourses (though marginality is a highly relative concept) and speak in the person of the *metoikos*.

> **Métèque.** *n.m.* (1743, *mestèque* au sens 1; empr. du gr. *metoikos*, de *meta*, et *oikos*, "maison", propremt. "qui change de maison").
> **1.** *Antiq. gr.* Etranger domicilé en Grèce, qui n'avait pas droit de cité. (*Le Grand Robert* Dictionary)

> **Metic.** *n.*-s (1743, *mestic* first meaning, borrowed from Gk *metoikos*, fr. *meta* + *oikos*, "house," *lit* "he who changes houses").
> **1.** *Ancient Gr.* Foreigner domiciled in Greece, who was without civil rights.[32]

Jean-François Lyotard has discussed the marginal discourse of the *metoikos* in various of his writings. With reference to the famous adversarial discourses of those rhetoricians who opposed the master logicians in Hellenistic times (and with reference to alterity, outsidedness, in the particular context of the Greek word *politika*, which relates to a Hellenic notion of civil authority), Lyotard speaks of how there is no "inside" position, only the position of outside inhabited by the other:[33]

> Now the eccentricities of these mad Cynics, of these wild Megarites, of these Sophist clowns, will constitute no school and thus do not enter into this place [the university]: they are exteriorized like slaves, like women, like barbarians, like children who are excluded from the citizenry, from Hellenity, from virile homosexuality. But for them this outside is not an outside, because the last place, the last word, the ultimate referent, the absolute – have, to be sure, no positional value. For them, there is no outside, because there is no inside, no *en-soi*: the *en-soi* as pretended interiority immediately falls into exteriority. There is only exteriority. Or better, there is exteriority.

> [Or les excentricités de ces fous de Cyniques, de ces Mégariques incultes, de ces clowns les sophistes, ne feront pas école, et donc n'entrent pas dans ce lieu [l'université]: ils sont tenus enfermés au-dehors commes les esclaves, comme les femmes, comme les barbares, comme les enfants le sont au-dehors de la citoyenneté, de l'hellénité, de l'homosexualité virile. Mais pour eux ce dehors n'est pas un dehors, parce que le dernier lieu, le dernier mot, le référentiel ultime, l'absolu – justement n'ont nulle valeur positionnelle. Pour eux pas de

dehors, parce que pas de dedans, pas d'*en-soi*: l'en-soi comme
prétendue intériorité tombe immédiatement dans l'extériorité. Il n'y
a que de l'extériorité. Ou mieux: il y a de l'extériorité.][34]

No outsider discourse exists for the simple reason that, for a discourse to
be outside, it must be so positioned in relation to an other discourse that
claims "inside" positional value. Such a claim of "insideness" is
unjustified, however, because positional interiority is posited on arbitrary principles. The stratagem of the postcolonial writers I discuss is precisely to refuse all positional value to the statist discourse of the
metropole, to dominant European discourse, as well as to the discourse of
the patriarch in the case of Djebar and Ben Jelloun; to reveal dominant
discourses for what they are – not interior/insider discourses privileged
by absolute, universal truths, but discourses premised on arbitrary precepts, that, like any other discourses, are outside to the other. Non-hege-
monic Greek writers like the sophists, like those writers I call
postcolonial, like many writers the world over who seek to articulate
women's discourse, hold in common an effort to bring about a discursive
leveling process, to put all discourses on the same level – the logocentric
and the eccentric, the Eurocentric, Afrocentric and Muslimocentric, the
patriarchal and the feminine. If there is one descriptive concept important to my study of some forms of postcolonial narrative among Muslim
writers writing in European languages, it is the concept of what I shall
call *leveling*, around which postcolonial discourse constructs its tactics of
contestation and affirmation. The phenomenon of *leveling* emphasizes
not only the effect – displacement or, more accurately, dislodgment, relo-
cation or repositioning of the master discourse – but also the means by
which that effect is brought about.

In speaking of the discourse of science in *The Postmodern Condition*,
Lyotard avers that in categorizing reason on the one hand as cognitive or
theoretical and on the other as pragmatic or practical is indirectly to
attack the very legitimacy of scientific discourse by revealing it as a language game that contains its own set of rules and has no unique role in
controlling either the game of praxis (customary practice) or the game of
aesthetics. He thus sees the game of science as on equal footing with all
other games (40). This process of delegitimation is analogous to the postcolonial narrative tactics of leveling.

Literary and cultural intertextuality

The question of intertextuality – the traces left in the author's work of other languages and cultures that have preceded her or him – is of singular importance in postcolonial narrative with its transcultural crossings. Khatibi speaks of the beginnings (openings) of a book as not originating in the book itself but as having begun before the first pages have been opened: "Before these pages open, *that [everything] has already begun*. Opening of the book: beginning without beginning, time of writing of which the book – open or not – is only a crossing, a sort of waystop, marked, demarcated and carried away by the writing that works on its behalf" ["Avant que ne s'ouvrent ces feuillets, *ça a déjà commencé*. Début du livre: commencement sans commencement, temps de l'écriture et dont le livre – ouvert ou pas – n'est qu'une traversée, une sorte de halte, marquée, démarquée et emportée par l'écriture qui travaille pour son compte"].

As Lyotard has said in *Instructions païennes*, "we are always spoken by another's narrative, somebody has always already spoken us" ["nous sommes toujours sous le coup de quelque récit, on nous a toujours déjà dit"].[35] Every beginning has its roots in an elsewhere. "The author, the reader as well, are confronted by this: daring to begin there where the beginning has taken place in an elsewhere ceaselessly withdrawing towards the unheard of, there where the effacement of the subject plays itself out in manifold ways" ["L'auteur, le lecteur aussi, sont confrontés à ceci: oser commencer là où le commencement a eu lieu dans un ailleurs sans cesse reculant vers l'inouï, là où l'effacement du sujet se joue de toutes les manières"] (Khatibi, *Maghreb pluriel*, p. 180).

McNeece views this process, which is a form of intertexuality, as holding the potential of subverting authoritarian institutions and as serving as an implicit critique of any pretense to ideological integrity or purity. Intertextuality in this sense prepares the ground for the dismantling of cultural imperialism, whatever form it may take ("Decolonizing the Sign," p. 15).

Several Maghrebian writers, stirred by political and social events in the 1950s and 1960s (the Algerian Revolution, the 1965 uprising in Casablanca), gave voice to concerns for developing a literature that would contest authoritarian dogma and express the specificity of their culture as well as their aspirations to achieve a true measure of independence to replace neocolonial strictures. In Morocco, the radical review *Souffles* was founded by Abdellatif Laâbi in 1966, an unprecedented alternative publishing event in North Africa, and was to last through 22 issues in French and 8 in Arabic until it was banned in 1972. Laâbi and Abraham Serfaty, the latter of whom brought to *Souffles* an ideological program from 1968 on, were sentenced to ten years and life imprisonment respectively. During its brief life, the review rallied several French-language Moroccan writers to its cause, including Muhammad Khaïr-Eddine, Tahar Ben Jelloun and Abdelkebir Khatibi.

Laâbi and Serfaty, in putting forth the program of the Association de recherche culturelle (Association of Cultural Research), underscored the need for a reinterpretation of national culture. Aside from Arabic and Islamic culture, they wrote, "Moroccan culture has also been nourished, since its origins, by other sources: Berber, Judaic, Saharan, African and Mediterranean. It is the sum of these sources and of these additions that ought to be called upon in the elaboration of our national culture" ["La culture marocaine a été nourrie aussi, depuis les origines, par d'autres sources, berbères, judaïques, sahariennes, africaines et méditerranéennes. C'est la totalité de ces sources et de ces appartenances qui devraient être sollicitées lors de l'élaboration de notre culture nationale"].[36] Notably, Laâbi and Serfaty brought to the study of their national culture recognition that the rich tributaries of several cultures other than Arabic and Islamic also flowed into the main stream of Moroccan life.

The editors spoke about Moroccan culture being manipulated even after the so-called period of decolonization:

> the manipulation of our culture continues along the same lines laid down by political decolonisation. It arises this time from other motives, but it doesn't any the less adhere to a logic of approach, to ideological and cultural foundations that violate every radical and objective interpretation.
>
> In any case, it is high time that knowledge of and action on behalf of our culture cease being knowledge and action premised on an imposed culture and methodology.
>
> [la manipulation de notre culture continue dans le cadre même de la décolonisation politique. Elle relève cette fois-ci d'autres motivations, mais elle n'en garde pas moins une logique d'approche, des soubassements idéologiques et culturels qui faussent tout interprétation radicale et objective.
>
> En tout état de cause, il est grand temps que la connaissance et l'action sur notre culture cessent d'être connaissance et action par culture et méthodologie interposées.]   (*Souffles*, pp. 12, 153)

In a society dominated by the brutal oppression of Hassan II's neo-colonial government, such writers as these heroically protested against the hegemonic imposition of foreign-inspired ideology that failed to answer the needs of the Moroccan people. The editors emphasized their aim of taking in hand their own future action and approach:

> Colonialization has subtly imposed a strategy of depersonalization and alienation that has even filtered into the mental and psychic structures of the colonized people. And we find the effects of this insidious inner disintegration even in intellectual formulations and scientific approaches to pragmatic life.
>
> The decision to take matters in hand is therefore only a preliminary ethical step. What is further needed is that it be carried out by putting into question the entire colonial and Western fund of knowledge and experience, and that to be done at the level of intellectual possessions and scientific procedures.
>
> [La colonisation a secrété une stratégie de dépersonnalisation et d'aliénation qui a investi jusqu'aux structures mentales et psychiques du colonisé. Et l'on retrouve les effets de ce lent travail de minage intérieur jusqu'aux démarches intellectuelles et aux méthodologies scientifiques d'approche des réalités.
>
> La décision de reprise en charge n'est donc qu'un préalable moral. Encore faut-il qu'elle soit structurée par une exigence de remise en cause de tout l'acquis colonial et occidental, et ceci au niveau des outils mentaux et de la démarche scientifique.]   *(Ibid., p. 154)*

The *Souffles* group proposed to take back, to repossess, the past in a face-to-face encounter with not only Western hegemonic pressures, but also those of Arabic and Islamic cultures equally: "The same work of critical reevaluation must be undertaken for our cultural heritage, which is multidimensional. Arabic and Islamic culture has imposed its past and recent configurations on our society and on our culture, which have participated moreover for centuries in its evolution" ["Le même travail de revalorisation critique doit être effectué pour notre héritage culturel, qui est multidimensionnel. La culture arabe et islamique a donné sa configuration historique et actuelle à notre société et à notre culture qui participent d'ailleurs depuis des siècles à son évolution"] *(Ibid., p. 156)*. And,

> Islam, for its part, is a phenomenon springing forth from Arabic culture, which it has profoundly transformed and enriched by virtue of its expansion and its development, and by the new things it brought to it. These various contributions, as well as the movements that have grown up at the very heart of Islam in opposition to strict

traditionalism, putting emphasis on the creative Ijtihad, the freedom of man and the sovereignty of the community, are to be reevaluated.

[L'Islam, quant à lui, est un phénomène jailli de la culture arabe, qu'il a profondément transformée et qu'il a enrichie, de par son extension et son développement, de nouveaux apports. Ces différents apports, ainsi que les mouvements qui se sont développés au sein même de l'Islam en opposition au traditionnalisme étroit, mettant l'accent sur l'Ijtihad créateur, la liberté de l'homme et la souveraineté de la communauté, sont à révaloriser.]   *(Ibid., p. 156)*

Like Khatibi, the *Souffles* editors, in speaking of the "intertextual" character of Moroccan culture – its grounding in diverse cultures and ethic origins – laid the foundation for a critique of ideological purity and, eventually, for the subversion and dismantling of "cultural imperialism" – whether Western or Islamic. They challenged the hegemonistic supremacy of Western culture and Islam that has resulted in an exclusivist, totalizing form of cultural control.

Through bringing to light the bastardization of Moroccan culture, its *métissage* or interweaving of forms and influences, the editors of *Souffles*, as well as the authors I have chosen to study, have sought to reconfigure cultural hierarchies through the process of cultural leveling. *Métissage* is an apt term to give to this process of cultural leveling, for, while referring to the mixture of ethnic groups, its primary meaning signifies a mixture of materials, for example, cotton and linen, in the warp and woof of woven cloth. The French term *toile métis* refers to mixed fabric or cloth; the verb *tisser* means to weave and derives from the Latin *texere*, from which the word "text" also derives. The prefix of *métissage* (*mé-*) suggests undoing or misdoing, so that the word connotes simultaneously a mixture of different materials or a misweaving, reweaving or unweaving. The act of *métissage* thus implies an undoing and a redoing or an unraveling and a reweaving, which is precisely the aim of the act of cultural leveling.[37]

Of course, all writing, of Western or non-Western derivation, is marked, demarcated, and riven by the "already said," by the traces of other languages, literatures, and cultures. The particular importance of this phenomenon to the writers I study, however, is that they have undertaken, each in his or her own way, a concerted effort to uncover these disparate traces and introduce them into their writing as integral components of their mixed, alternative discourses and of their contestatory answer to magisterial discourse(s). By emphasizing that no originary source exists, they call into question the supposed universals out of which the dominant discourses claim to have sprung and upon which they base their supposed legitimacy as dominant discourses. The other side of the coin is that, far from such a contestatory mode representing a one-way street, the same phenomenon of intertextuality argues for positive contributions made to postcolonial discourses by the language and culture of the European colonizer and the discourse of Islam. We must not lose this fact from view when we talk about oppositionality, for the adversarial language and culture of European colonialism are indeed among those disparate sources that were to be opposed in terms of their authoritarian oppression but not to be denied in terms of the positive contributions they made. The inference that postcolonial writers are struggling to free themselves from the yoke of an alien culture or an imposed discourse (Balzac has said "We cannot shake the yoke of language" ["on ne secoue pas le joug de la langue" – *La Comédie humaine*]) is only a partial truth. By their efforts, they seek not simply to free themselves, but rather to engage this discourse on their own terms, to renegotiate its sinuous rhetorical pathways, and to place their own signposts along them. Their active participation in the discourse of a Western cultural sphere – alien to them in the sense that it has superimposed itself on their native cultures and languages – looms as importantly in their intellectual and writerly formation as their resistance to its oppressive character.

As I have pointed out in discussing intertextuality, and as Khatibi so perceptively lays forth, far from rejecting received ideas and structures of these superimposed languages and cultures, most postcolonial writers engage themselves in modifying its forms and reworking already existing discursive and political–social traditions brilliantly and to their own differing ends. Those cultures and languages are integral features of the translation of a European language Khatibi speaks of into an "other" discourse. As a matter of fact, the writers studied in this book have invested heavily in the culture of the European other. Ben Jelloun holds a doctorate in social psychology from the University of Paris and has written regularly for the Paris paper, *Le Monde*. Khatibi received his doctorate in sociology in Paris and, presently a Professor at the University of Morocco (Rabat), has served as a program director at the Collège International de Philosophie in Paris. Djebar studied at the Ecole Normale Supérieure in Sèvres and taught history at the University of Algiers, but now lives in Paris when she is not teaching and lecturing abroad. Both Khatibi and Djebar regularly contribute to symposia and Western cultural events.

And Rushdie, who had been active in London intellectual life before the
fatwa, even now actively participates in European and American literary
forums. My point is that, far from rejecting Western culture and language, these authors have integrated them, along with Islamic beliefs
and influences, into their life's work. We do well to recall Rushdie's words
put into the mouth of one of his narrators in his collection of short stories,
East, West:

> I, too, have ropes around my neck, I have them to this day, pulling me
> this way and that, East and West, the nooses tightening,
> commanding, *choose, choose*.
>   I buck, I snort, I whinny, I rear, I kick. Ropes, I do not choose
> between you. Lassoes, lariats, I choose neither of you, and both. Do
> you hear? I refuse to choose.[38]

With these words he tells us of his middle position between two cultures,
being called upon to choose one, but refusing, accepting both and mixing both. Again, a question of *métissage*.

The "métissage" of genres

Symptomatic of the consciousness of a plurality of origins and influences
and of the proclivity for literary and cultural *métissage*, the mixture of
genres distinctly marks the narratives of the writers I am interested in.
These writers draw on a remarkable variety of literary and cultural
sources and integrate them into their works in a singular mix of literary
and popular forms. Khatibi, speaking of the Moroccan novel written in
French, reminds us that "The novel is an imported literary genre, with its
structure and its models, its way of organizing time and space. As such, it
constitutes a certain world vision and presents itself for the psychologist
or the sociologist as a totality of perceptions and attitudes" ["Le roman
est un genre littéraire importé, avec sa structure et ses modèles, sa
manière d'organiser le temps et l'espace. Tel quel, il constitue une cer-
taine vision du monde et se présente pour le psychologue ou le sociologue
comme un ensemble de perceptions et d'attitudes"].[39] Early forms of the
North African or Maghrebian novel adhered closely to the pattern of the
traditional Western realist novel without meddling with the form or
structure of that genre. But, as Khatibi observes in his critical survey, the
Western novel form in the hands of several Maghrebian writers under-
went multiple permutations that profoundly affected its structure and

treatment of subject-matter so as to make it correspond more closely to perceptions and beliefs of Maghrebian peoples.

With such novelists as the Algerian, Kateb Yacine, and the authors I shall study, the novel form was turned to the purposes of a cultural affirmation of the Maghreb from a Maghrebian perspective (or the affirmation of the view of the migrant from the perspective of an Anglo-Indian author).

Such postcolonial authors, highly experimentalist in their writing, encapsulated into the narrative a mixture of genres, such that the narratives of Ben Jelloun, Assia Djebar, and others have often been described as being as much poetic fiction as prose, as much autobiography as fiction. Within the narratives I shall look at, a remarkable proliferation of generic forms appears – a medley of proverbs, songs, religious texts, poetry, popular and folk elements, oral speech patterns, traditional Arabic rhetorical forms, and dialogic writing, to name a few – a proliferation that results in the erosion of the traditional narrative, a bastardization of the novel that undercuts its pristine generic character.

"That confusion of literary genres is to be sure in [Kateb Yacine] a terrorist technique that shatters the structure proper to the novel and creates a dazzling language melding everything and endlessly going beyond itself" ["Cette confusion des genres littéraires est bien sûr chez lui une technique terroriste qui brise la structure propre au roman et qui crée un langage éblouissant fusant de toutes parts et se surpassant indéfiniment"] (Khatibi, Le Roman maghrébin, p. 103). Khatibi speaks of the same generic métissage and its contestatory qualities that Bernard Aresu refers to when he speaks of the symbiotic interplay of lyrical and satirical modes in Kateb's work that led to a cultural and political subversion of genres. Aresu sees Kateb's fiction as founding a postcolonial tradition that rewrote the formal rules of a foreign genre through the introduction of Arabic–Islamic esthetics.[40]

The boundaries between fictional and non-fictional discourse, moreover, between autobiographical and non-autobiographical writing, between expository, descriptive, and philosophical prose, become blurred.[41] At the same time that this intermixture of genres mimics the Qur'ān by blending historical and mythic narrative, poetry, and dramatic discourse, it disavows elements of the underlying religious dogma.

Postcolonialism and postmodernism

The characteristics of postcolonial narratives to which I have briefly alluded may very well suggest to the reader their close affinity with the phenomenon of postmodernism in its myriad apparitions. Postmodern narratives, like postcolonial narratives, are marked by spatial and temporal disjunction. Authors of both narrative modes have devised local tactics to counter prevailing hegemonies, whatever their source, so as to ward off totalizing fields of force. The narratives I study evince efforts in this direction that have led me to give to this process the name of leveling. Just as important, however, through a variety of ways, the authors have widened the scope of the narrative and improvised extensive changes that mark their discourses as true pluralistic, multicultural discourses.[42]

Among the traits the postcolonial and postmodern modes share is a questioning of absolute systems that lay claim to universality and affirm legitimization tautologically through referral to a set of principles that they themselves have arbitrarily implemented. Both modes reject the binaries and dualisms of dominant discourse (subject–object, fiction–reality, self–other, literature–criticism, to mention a mere handful), as we observe in their alternative process of *métissage* at work in the pluralist dynamics of their narratives. Some particular characteristics they share are the following:

1. Both modes challenge the sharp distinction between the work of art and empirical reality as drawn by Kantian esthetics and modernist theory. They reject formalism that creates of the work of art a closed, stratified world. As opposed to the notion of art as universal and exclusively concerned with esthetic representation of morally elevated (high) art, they view art rather as a local response to particular situations – the situation of women in the patriarchal societies of the Maghreb or that of non-Western immigrants in London examined in the postcolonial narratives of Djebar, Ben Jelloun, and Rushdie; and in postmodern narratives that of the erotic obsession with the automobile and violence in J. G. Ballard's *Crash* or the jumbled puzzles of everyday existence in Georges Perec's extraordinary French boardinghouse in *La Vie mode d'emploi*.

The two modes also challenge the regulation of literary subject-matter in terms of an exclusive, limited concept of what is proper to art, and expand the horizons of art by a mixture of genres such as I have discussed, and the introduction of popular or "low" art into literature. One of the specific ways the non-Western authors I study modify the traditional narrative is by the insertion into the subject–matter of magical realist elements that blur the traditional distinction in literary realist texts between fantasy and reality.[43] Such a differential mode of literary expression valorizes a discourse whose perceptual field is essentially non-Western and indicates affinities not only with the postmodern tendency to expand the subject–matter of narrative, but also with postcolonial discourses from other non-Western cultures in Africa and other parts of the world, notably, Latin America. We see these elements in particular in the three male authors we treat, but less so in Djebar, whose depiction of Maghrebian women's space often engages her in a much more material and domestic side of daily social existence.

These authors have also opened up the narrative by intertextuality in the narrower sense of the term, that is, by abundant recourse to works of other authors. Though postcolonial writing casts speech act as event, as I proposed earlier, it is not pure event in a vacuum in the sense that it exists without models. The writers I consider draw on models as diverse as Eastern folktales, oral stories transmitted matrilineally, eighteenth-century writers such as Sterne and Diderot, contemporary Latin American and Eastern European writers. Ben Jelloun makes of the historical Borges a fictional character and lifts characters from Borges' work to put into his own. He similarly exploits *The Thousand and One Nights*. Postcolonial writers of narrative such as those I consider often take as their models other writers of narrative as event. Their intertextual foraging assumes less the form of an attempt to organize and unify a mass of disparate events, moreover, than that of a type of bricolage we also find in postmodernism, by which they "make do" with fragments and disordered parts to forge something pragmatically (a text, a thought process) that responds to a local situation, need, or desire.[44]

2. Irony is of unquestionable importance as a perceptual mode for postcolonial as well as postmodern writers. It lies, according to Ross Chambers, in the "production of difference" between narrative function and textual function.[45]

Let us recall here that the notion of irony derives from the figure of the Eiron who, for Aristotle, denoted a personage who was always more or less than what he seemed to be.[46] The use of irony comes out most dramatically in the revisiting of the past and a reworking of history filtered through a divergent, distanced perspective, rather than the (his)story imposed by authoritarian narratives, whether (in the case of our authors) Islamic, European, or patriarchal.

Both Albert Memmi, the Tunisian Jewish author, and Frantz Fanon, the Martinican psychologist–philosopher who devoted his efforts to the Algerian Revolution and the cause of oppressed peoples in Africa and elsewhere – both of these writers have spoken of the forgetfulness of the colonized peoples, who are intent on wiping from their memory the history of their oppression.[47]

The writers I study are for the most part intent on combatting this amnesia, by instituting a process of recovery through the memory or re-membering of the past. Through this re-membering or *anamnesis*,[48] the writers rewrite the official histories of dominant cultures. This rewriting may take the form of historically verifiable past events such as those surrounding the French occupation of Algeria following the fall of Algiers in 1830 to the Algerian War of Independence (1954–1962), culled by Assia Djebar, who was formally trained as a historian, from fragmentary accounts of historians, diarists, and travelers or from the remnants of oral accounts passed down in a timeless chorus by Algerian women.[49] Or this re-membering may be largely imagined, as in the "pre-history" of love contemplated by Djebar. In the case of Djebar, the writer becomes the amanuensis for the silent and silenced voices of her Algerian sisters of past and present. For Salman Rushdie, that rewriting involves the confronting of the Qur'ānic account of the visit of the Archangel Gabriel to Muhammad as related in Surah LVIII with the alternate version of the apocryphal "satanic" verses condemned as heretical by Islamic authorities. These authors, particularly Rushdie, along with Khatibi and Ben Jelloun, have also written an alternate history of the traditional Western narrative through the destructuration of temporal and spatial elements.

Irony is directed as often towards self as towards other, such that the texts of postcolonial and postmodern authors are both marked by authorial self-reflexivity and self-referentiality – an acutely conscious attitude towards the act of artistic creation that results in the author focusing on the writing process rather than the narrative elements of character, plot, and setting. This is one reason why the worlds of postcolonialism and postmodernism tend to be chaotic and disorderly. There is, if not a celebration of disorder, a lack of concern about the nicely laid-out plot lines and stylistic coherence of traditional art. We witness considerable fragmentation. The disorderliness of narrative comes out in the type of "pure" event I spoke of, where narrative is born from enunciation, grows out of its own procedures so that it may be said to be self-generating. This disorderliness has to do with an "ironic" belief in the discontinuity of experience and the undecidability of things, their relationships, and meaning. The irony here lies in the distance between the effort to fix meaning and the inherent futility of that effort.

3. Rhetorical positioning characterizes both postcolonialism and postmodernism: a sophistic tendency to persuade by bridging the divide between diction (what must be said) and contra-diction (what must not be said). The aim of such positioning is, I believe, partly derivative from the desire to avoid appropriation by master discourses, but also partly derivative, in the case of the authors I treat, from the love of rhetoric and persuasive speech found in Arabic that feeds into the rhetorical emphasis extant in the European tongues they elaborate.

I once found myself in the city of Hama, halfway between Damascus and Aleppo, at a gathering of poets, politicians, and scholars in a café garden on the banks of the Orontes. Shaded by a grape-laden arbor, after a sumptuous meal, the guests – above the creaking of the gigantic wooden waterwheels (*norias*) that have been timelessly turning since medieval times – vied to outdo each other with the cleverness and beauty of their poetic declamations. Anyone experiencing the Arabs' love of language and persuasion in such a setting is left with one of those rare unforgettable moments found in life. As did I, as did Maurice Barrès writing down his memory of "A Garden on the Orontes" during a visit to Syria in 1921.

Persuasion also appears as ploy to a desire to build community, but, in the case of postcolonial and postmodern authors, usually a particularized community: the community of misfits or outcasts we see in the postmodern *Vineland* of Thomas Pynchon or the community of migrants (and that of the lunatic asylum) in *The Satanic Verses*; the community of female historical figures in Christa Wolf's *Cassandra*, of the sisterhood of Algerian women in *L'Amour, la fantasia*, or of the celebrated and often forgotten women of the past described in Djebar's *Loin de Médine*; the community of postmodern eccentrics of Roger Ackroyd's *Chatterton* or *The Trial of Elizabeth Cree: A Novel of the Limehouse Murders*, or of the marginal outcasts of Khatibi and Ben Jelloun. I cited Laâbi earlier in terms of nation building, but, whether we call it that or community building, we find implicit traces of that collective tendency in both postmodern writing and postcolonial writing. The communities may be that of the mad Cynics, the wild Megarites, the sophist clowns, the slaves, women, barbarians, and gays described by Lyotard; of the nomads, the deterritorialized, the inferior races, the animals and "niggers" described by Deleuze and Guattari; of the Hogarthian nether world, the *Lumpenproletariat* so despised by

Marx, or the anarchist outcasts of the 1890s – but they are still communities and, like all communities, in solidarity against the encroachments of the outside.

Inasmuch as media are a tool for persuasion, it should not surprise us that Khatibi expresses fascination with the potential of computers and translation machines ("my body plugged into the four corners of the world, disconnecting computer programs and replacing them with another program, that of the *bi-langue* – the uncommunicable" [*Amour bilingue*, p. 43]), nor that Rushdie introduces us to the film world of Bombay, or the worlds of talk shows, television commercials, and radio programs of London.

In characterizing postcolonial narratives, I could hardly do better than to cite Khatibi's words to describe the authors of these narratives as seeking "A rediscovered country [which] offers itself as what it is, without closure or totality" (*Amour bilingue*, p. 114). Postmodern narratives and postcolonial narratives cannot be categorized; their edges blur and their purposes are often crossed; they are marked by the disparate, incommensurable, unclassifiable, and indeterminate, as are their authors, narrators, characters ("she rendered herself unclassifiable," *Amour bilingue*, p. 120). The philosophy of postmodernism has taught us to look with suspicion on readymade, all-inclusive definitions, as Allan Megill and others have rightly stated (see Megill, "What Does the Term 'Postmodern' Mean?", p. 129). We would do well to remember these characteristics in the case of postcolonial narratives.

What the western outsider can learn

My education in institutions of higher learning, beginning with Sophia University (Jochi-Daigaku) in Tokyo, where I found myself immersed in Scholasticism, along with training elsewhere in American and French universities and extensive reading in and reflection on Western literature, philosophy, social and cultural thought, have irrevocably fashioned my personal frames of reference. As the reader has seen, in thinking about postcolonialism, I have found it useful (and valid, I believe) to speak of parallels with Western postmodern thought on which I have expended considerable reflection. I owe many of my ideas concerning oppositionality and difference, moreover, to Jean-François Lyotard and poststructuralist theorists such as Barthes, Derrida, and Foucault.

The postcolonial writer has learned from Western ideas and examples, and the Westerner can equally learn things of signal importance from the example of postcolonial writers. He must, however, learn to listen. I will take only one example. In a postface to Abdelkebir Khatibi's *La Mémoire tatouée*, Roland Barthes speaks of what he owes to the Moroccan philosopher and novelist, and how Khatibi has contributed to making him aware of how much the semiological enterprise he has participated in has remained "prisoner of the universal categories that, since Aristotle, have ruled Western methods" ["prisonnière des catégories de l'Universel, qui règlent, en Occident, depuis Aristote, toute méthode"] – how, in inquiring into the structure of signs, he, Barthes, perceived what he thought was a demonstration of generality but came to realize that the identity suggested to him as a Westerner was not a universal one so much as "that of the man of culture of my own country" ["celle de l'homme culturel de mon propre pays"].[50]

Barthes relates how he came to an awareness of the need for Westerners

> to invent for ourselves a "heterological" language, a "pile" of differences, whose mixing will shake up a little the terrible compactness (because it is historically very ancient) of the Western Ego. That is why we try to be "Mixers," borrowing here and there some scraps of "otherness"... to throw into confusion that Western identity that often weighs upon us like a cape... but we can open ourselves to other "populaces," we can "decenter" ourselves, as they now say. And it is in that way that the books of Khatibi provide us with a subtle and strong series of signs at the same time irreducible and explained: which permits us to seize the *other* through our *self*.

> [à inventer pour nous une langue "hétérologique", un "ramassis" de différences, dont le brassage ébranlera un peu la compacité terrible (parce qu'historiquement très ancienne) de l'*ego* occidental. C'est pourquoi nous essayons d'être des "Mélangeurs", empruntant ici et là des bribes d' "ailleurs"... brouiller cette identité occidentale qui pèse souvent sur nous comme une chape... mais nous pouvons nous ouvrir à d'autre "populaires," nous pouvons nous "décentrer," comme on dit maintenant. Et c'est là que les livres de Khatibi nous donnent une suite subtile et forte de signes tout à la fois irréductibles et expliqués: de quoi nous permettre de saisir l'*autre* à partir de notre *même*.]

The benefit of such an encounter with writings from worlds beyond ours (as Westerners) would indeed be great should it enable us, formed wholly or in large part by Western culture, to develop a heterological language. We also have to be aware of how, through our language, we speak of and to the other.

To counter the possible impression that the several Western theorists upon whose ideas I draw may constitute yet another hegemonic chorus, it is important to foreground the fact that the writings of most of these theorists have been significantly inflected by their firsthand experience with non-Western cultures and offer specific cultural connections/relevance that mitigate the seemingly distanced (and potentially colonizing) nature of their theory.

Barthes taught in North Africa, at the Université Muhammad V in Rabat, where he met Khatibi and affiliated himself closely with Maghrebian culture. As a young graduate of the Sorbonne, Lyotard taught at a lycée in Constantine where he perceived with horror a people possessing an advanced civilization who were demeaned, humiliated, and denied their very sense of self. Lyotard witnessed firsthand the effort of the French colonial regime to "annihilate even the possibility of an Algerian political or cultural identity."[51] The work of Derrida has been marked by his North African Jewish origin. It is important to note that deconstruction and poststructuralist thought have affinities with the tactical positioning of postcolonial discourse, sometimes quite directly as in the case of Khatibi, who is a protégé of Derridean thinking.

My point is this: that my references to such Western theorists as I have mentioned, far from serving simply to amplify my own theoretical positioning, draw upon thought and conceptualization that have grown in part out of the same conditions as those of the postcolonial writers I refer to. I thus feel justified in reading through and occasionally against the works of certain Western theorists. No single theoretical system can sufficiently deal with postcolonial writing and the pluralistic and critical mixing that characterizes the works of the writers I study. The striking intertextual and transcultural nature of their narratives, as well as their relation to a multiplicity of sources grounded in linguistics, literature, sociology, history, and ethnology result in a complexity that can be most profitably approached heterogeneously, for no essentialist conceptualizing of identity is possible or desirable. The social, racial, and economic circumstances and origins of these writers are so varied that no study can claim to hear in them a single voice.

Moreover, we must not fail to overlook the important exchange that has occurred in *both* directions between major Western critics and writers, on the one hand, and postcolonial writers and the postcolonial situation, on the other.

Oppositionality

Michel de Certeau speaks of the invisibility necessary for oppositionality, the disguise necessary to hide its motives.[52] In the works of the authors I consider, following the model of oppositionality proposed by Ross Chambers, one might debate whether the "narrative function" always serves a disguised purpose by foregrounding the external structure of power so as to bring about an identification of the reader with the narratee ("the position of power"), while hiding a "textual function" that subverts that structure of power and ends by turning the reader towards the position of "interpretive subject" whose reading gives rise to a consciousness of the presence of oppositionality (citations from Chambers, *Room for Maneuver*, p. 17).

The postcolonial narratives that I shall examine are rather more overtly oppositional in "textual function" than the model proposed by Chambers. In their self-conscious oppositionality, they tend towards resistance, while maintaining the barest vestiges of "narrative function" – the "acknowledgement of power that constitutes the oppositional act *as* oppositional (by contrast, for example, with actual resistance)." For the most part, however, the "narrative function" is eclipsed.

Perhaps this fact exemplifies Chambers' suggestion that, in systems that are more repressive, opposition tends to be more covert than in less restrictive systems, for the adopted societies within which three of the authors I write of live are relatively without restriction for them – France (Djebar, Ben Jelloun) and England (Rushdie).

Their work within these non-Islamic societies has not been viewed as a serious threat to the structures of power. On the other hand, their work has been variously castigated and condemned in their countries of origin. Rushdie's narrative, *The Satanic Verses*, provides the most notable example, in incurring the wrath of fundamentalist forces in Islam and drawing down upon the head of its author a death sentence. To that extent it represents in certain Islamic countries (in Chambers' terms) "a failed form of 'opposition'" (*Room for Maneuver*, p. 9). The narratives of Ben Jelloun, by inference critical of Islamic thought on some counts, have also been criticized, though they have not fallen into disfavor with repressive civil authorities. Rushdie has discussed the critical attacks on Naguib Mahfouz and Tahar Ben Jelloun for their supposed religious views. And, in an interview, Ben Jelloun himself has described the sermons preached against him in the mosques and the attacks against him by integrationists and political and religious fundamentalists who have not even bothered to read his books.[53]

Assia Djebar, on the contrary, has been highly respectful of the Islamic faith as she has sought, in one of her recent works, *Loin de Médine*, to stress the tangible presence and importance of women in Islam, who have received only secondary acknowledgement from religious historians such as Ibn Hicham, Ibn Saad, and Tabari.[54] She has nonetheless not escaped criticism for her political orientation in the past. Her first novels, *La Soif* (1957) and *Les Impatients* (1958) were severely attacked by some supporters of the revolution as being reactionary bourgeois novels that did nothing to advance the Algerian War of Liberation. In following works, like *Les Enfants du nouveau monde* (1962), she took up the cause she was unjustly accused of ignoring. Presently, despite her firm faith in Islam, with the assassination of literary, political, and religious figures by fundamentalist fanatics, like other Algerians writers abroad she has with good reason felt threatened. The "proof" of these texts as being oppositional rather than revolutionary, however, lies in the fact that they seek not to overthrow the prevailing power structure (Islamic or Western) but to modify, democratize, and humanize the system from within.

The exception to my comments on the authors above is Abdelkebir Khatibi who still teaches and lives in Morocco, but whose work may be said to be less overtly oppositional. Though, in works such as *Amour bilingue*, he has indirectly questioned the exclusivity of the teachings of the Qur'ān (and the Book itself), he has not met with notable opposition.

Ultimately, the various tactical devices and narrative positionings we see in these writers, as I have discussed above, aim at a freeing of difference. Once achieving that, they have sought to forestall reappropriation through various means. Several critics have commented on their efforts as pursuing a relentless quest to name the unnameable.[55] To the contrary, however, the unfolding of their narratives is most often governed less by a desire to name the unnameable than to devise tactics to *ward off* the effort of Western critics and readers to name that ineffable space out of which postcolonial writers write – that space lying between the adversary's language and her/his mother tongue/culture; that same space likened by Assia Djebar to the *rebato* of the Spanish occupiers of Algeria in earlier times – a term referring to an "isolated spot," a no-man's-land lying between the aggressor and the aggressed, from which the former sallied forth to attack, and to which he withdrew in search of refuge or to replenish provisions.[56] To name is to render accessible, to transform the other into the same, to categorize, neutralize, and assimilate. The narratives I consider offer, as we shall see, numerous examples of this tactic.

By exploring and assessing the properties of a specific mode of writing by non-Western, Muslim authors utilizing European languages to frame their own discourse, which modifies and makes more supple the dominant discourses of European and Islamic cultures, it is my hope that this study will throw light however much it is possible on the varied means and aims of these discourses I have called postcolonial. I hope thus to push further the limited understanding we presently hold (we of the West) of the non-Western world in terms of its own heterogeneous dynamics, perceptions, needs, and desires. As we move closer to the twenty-first century, we approach a time that will demand greater parity with and understanding of the non-Western world by the Western world. We have much to learn from the confrontation of the non-Western writers with the language/discourse of the Western *other*. Their struggle with linguistic and cultural constraints makes of that encounter a privileged metaphor for the struggle of all writers – Western or non-Western – in face of language, who in similar ways seek to inscribe themselves, consciously or not, in the interval between identity and difference and so lessen the hold of the state over their minds and verbal expression. And the metaphor projects even further – onto human individuals in general.

2

Women's voices and woman's space in Assia Djebar's *L'Amour, la fantasia*

I have entitled this account: "A Fugitive without knowing it." Or not yet knowing it. At least up to that precise moment when I recounted these comings and goings of women of distant or recent times in flight... Up to the moment when, in Madrid, I grew aware of it: from then on I became conscious of my permanent state of fugitive – I would even add: of being rooted in flight – for the very reason that I write and in order that I might write. [Assia Djebar, in speaking of one of her recently published essays]

[J'ai intitulé cette suite de remarques: "fugitive et ne le sachant pas". Ou ne le sachant pas encore. Du moins jusqu'à cet instant précis où je relate ces allers et venues de femmes fuyantes du passé lointain ou récent... A l'instant où, à Madrid, je le constate: désormais je prends conscience de ma condition permanente de fugitive – j'ajouterais même: d'enracinée dans la fuite – justement parce que j'écris et pour que j'écrive.]   ASSIA DJEBAR, "Fugitive, et ne le sachant pas"[1]

Voices, from past and present, speaking "a flayed language," as Assia Djebar calls it, voices of Algerian women, "so many accents still suspended in the silences of yesterday's seraglio" ["Langue desquamée... tant d'accents encore suspendus dans les silences du sérail d'hier"]. Voices veiled and censored like their faces. Djebar has listened to these voices from work to work, and out of them has crafted a dialogue of empowerment.[2] The role of woman in Islam, Djebar points out, has been explored up and down, in historical and sociological studies, but the fact of her growing awareness of self remains the most salient fact of her existence and cannot be explained away by detractors or religious fundamentalists. As she has affirmed, "Every effort to explain woman in Islam historically or sociologically has not prevented her from henceforth thinking of herself in the first person" ["Tout effort d'explication historique ou sociologique n'empêche pas la femme d'Islam de se penser désormais à la première personne"].[3] *Being woman*, not in isolation, but as an integral part of the collective sisterhood that from ancient times has endured silence but has handed down its heritage to the present-day Muslim woman, lies at the heart of Assia Djebar's splendid 1985 narrative, *L'Amour, la fantasia*.

That narrative comprises three parts, entitled respectively "The Capture of the City, or Love-letters," "The Cries of the *Fantasia*," and "Voices from the Past."[4] The titles of these parts suggest the main lines of the story: the clash of aggressor and aggressed during the colonial period, from the fall of Algiers to the French in 1830 through the Algerian War of Liberation; and a concomitant story: the shrouding of voices in opposition (the French title of Part III is "Les voix ensevelies," literally, "buried voices"). The military–political struggle between French and Algerians allegorizes the struggle of Algerian women to inscribe themselves in a space they can identify as their own: for the women whose story the narrator tells, social–sexual–historical space in a society gendered for men; for the narrator, as for Djebar herself, a space of writing inscribed in the written language of the French and patriarchal adversaries – a language Djebar calls *la langue adverse* (the adversarial language).[5]

From the juxtaposition of nineteenth-century written commentaries of French military officers and soldiers, writers, and artists, who described the taking of Algiers and the action of colonization that followed, and from oral commentaries of Algerian women who participated in the Algerian Revolution of the 1950s and 60s,[6] arises a tension between the word of the oppressor and that of the oppressed, between the written (French) and verbal (Arabic, Berber) speech, between the masculine and the feminine ways of seeing, thinking, and being.

The narrator, an Algerian woman of the post-war Liberation generation, recounts how her experience in learning to speak and write French leads her to become the amanuensis for the collective voice of her Algerian sisters of today as well as of her women ancestors. She is especially mindful of the rebels (the *révoltées*) among her veiled Algerian sisters, those who cried out: "The only one who put herself straight away beyond the pale was the [one who cried out]" (203) ["La seule qui se marginalisait d'emblée était celle qui 'criait' "] (228). For a woman to refuse to "veil" her voice as well as her physical aspect, and to cry out, brought down upon her the accusation of indecency and dissidence. Her cry, in fact, revealed the lie of other women's existences: "For the silence of all the others suddenly lost its charm and revealed itself for what it was: a prison without reprieve" (204) ["Car le silence de toutes les autres perdait brusquement son charme pour révéler sa vérité: celle d'être une prison irrémédiable"] (229). The subtitle of Part I in the original French, *L'Amour s'écrit* (love writes itself or love is written), alludes both to the act of writing love and the act of love crying out (as reflected in the French homophone *s'écrie*, to cry out). The use of the reflexive in French suggests autobiographical writing with its self-referentiality, which is strictly allied to the agony of the speaker who painfully seeks her identity. Djebar has described to us how, in *Les Alouettes naïves* (1967), she realized for the first time that at the core of the novel "I was writing on the edge of autobiography" ["j'avais une écriture à la limite de l'autobiographie"], and consequently why she ceased writing for a decade. She gives as her reason that she refused to let the French language enter her life, her secret being ["dans ma vie, dans mon secret"] – she felt the French language to be her enemy. "To write in that language, but to write very near oneself, not to say *about* oneself, with an uprooting, that became for me a treacherous undertaking" ["Ecrire dans cette langue, mais écrire très près de soi, pour ne pas dire *de* soi-même, avec un arrachement, cela devenait pour moi une entreprise dangereuse"] ("La langue adverse," p. 238). We see in this admission that, as she continued to write in French, she felt it to encroach on her and to threaten to reveal her inner self to the world at large.

She who cries out thus breaks the silence of all Arab and Berber women buried in anonymity. The narrator likens her act of writing in French, "not in either of the tongues of my native country" (mountain Berber and Arabic), to that cry. But the positive aspect of writing in her assumed language is that, as she says, "writing has brought me to the cries of the women silently rebelling in my youth, to my own true origins." And she adds, "Writing does not silence the voice, but awakens it, above all to resurrect so many vanished sisters" (204) ["hors de l'oralité des deux langues de ma région natale… écrire m'a ramenée aux cris des femmes sourdement révoltées de mon enfance, à ma seule origine… Ecrire ne tue pas la voix, mais la réveille, surtout pour ressusciter tant de soeurs disparues"] (229).

Here, in crux, lies the generating principle of Djebar's narrative. Writing, vocalization, holds the power to counter the aphasia that for so long has rendered Algerian women silent. The space of writing so painfully sketched out by the narrator offers to these women the social–sexual–historical space that they seek as their own.

Women in Algerian society

How is the state of women in Algerian society represented by Djebar? After listening to stories of the brutal French occupation of Algeria, handed down by the ancestors of the old women who recount them to her, the narrator concludes: "Chains of memories: is it not indeed a 'chain,' for do not memories fetter us as well as forming our roots?" (178) ["Chaîne de souvenirs: n'est-elle pas justement 'chaîne' qui entrave autant qu'elle enracine?"] (201). The past shackles as well as secures the women to their past. The stories whispered, while preserving a collective memory of the past, relate another side of the women's heritage, a collective state of subjection and submission in a society dominated by the male. The remark that follows in the text illustrates this negative side: "For every passer-by, the story-teller stands hidden in the doorway. *It is not seemly* to raise the curtain and stand exposed in the sunlight" (178, my italics) ["Pour chaque passant, la parleuse stationne debout, dissimulée derrière le seuil. Il n'est pas séant de soulever le rideau et de s'exposer au soleil"] (201). The adverb "seemly" thrusts over the narrative the shadow of another's judgmental discourse. "And in fact," as Jean-François Lyotard observes, and as I cite once again, "we are always spoken by another's narrative, somebody has always already spoken something to us, and we have always been already said" ["Et de fait nous sommes toujours sous le coup de quelque récit, on nous a toujours déjà dit quelque chose, et nous avons toujours été déjà dits"].[7] The adverb "seemly" marks the umbrage-omnipresence of the male metadiscourse that demarcates and lays down the word for what is acceptable conduct for women.

Traditionally, in the harems, women were shackled to their past, incarcerated, out of sight of the male world, immured in their own private and invisible suffering. Harems were abolished in Turkey in 1909. The practice continued for several years in other Muslim countries. Though they do not exist as such in present-day Algeria, the social and psychological attitudes they expressed persist. In its sacred usage, the word *haram* in Arabic refers to something that is unlawful and forbidden in regard to the non-Faithful, that is protected from non-Muslims. One such example is the consecrated area surrounding Mecca and Medina, which is closed to all but the people of the Faith. *Haram,* in its secular usage, denotes that part of the living quarters in which women, children, and servants are kept in seclusion.[8] In the traditional setting, which is still to be found, Algerian women spoke out only when they attained an advanced age. They never referred to themselves in the singular, "since that would be to scorn the blanket-formulae which ensure that each individual [woman] journeys through life in collective resignation" (156) ["puisque ce serait dédaigner les formules-couvertures qui maintiennent le trajet individuel dans la résignation collective"] (177). The women to whom the narrator listens do not, moreover, speak aloud, but whisper their stories. "Words that are too explicit become such boastings as the braggard uses." The reverse side of the coin may lie in the fact that "elected silence [*l'aphonie*] implies resistance still intact" (178) ["Toute parole, trop éclairée, devient voix de forfanterie, et l'aphonie, résistance inentamée"] (201). But elected silence is still silence. Absence or loss of voice marks their existence, reduces them to whispers, broken only by the occasional cry of a *révoltée*.

In her Postface to *Femmes d''Alger*, entitled "Forbidden Gaze, Severed Sound," Djebar speaks of the artist Eugène Delacroix's visit in 1832 to a private harem in Algiers, where he sketched a scene whose exoticism intoxicated him. Djebar describes the paintings resulting from his feverish sketches, particularly the second version painted for the 1849 Paris Salon. In that version the women appear as enigmatic figures in a distant drama, "absent to themselves, to their body, to their sensuality, and to their happiness" during this instant of unveiling ["absentes à elles-même, à leur corps, à leur sensualité, à leur bonheur"] (173).

The Algerian woman is generally without voice. Her acquiescence to marriage is through a male intermediary "who speaks in 'her place.'" Her word, as later her person, is "deflowered" and violated. During her wedding night, "a living wound is opened in the woman's body through the taking of a virginity that the man furiously deflowers and through the martyrdom of marriage consecrated in the most trivial manner" ["Une plaie vive s'inscrit sur le corps de la femme par le biais de l'assomption d'une virginité qu'on déflore rageusement et dont le mariage consacre trivialement le martyre"] (*Femmes d'Alger*, pp. 177–78).[9]

After this sexual martyrdom, the woman henceforth becomes a mother, a desexualized woman without body and individual voice. She is able, however, to replace the binding chain of physical and psychological imprisonment by the long "chain" that connects her, not only to the "immense nourishing womb" of mothers and grandmothers confined like her to their separate quarters, but also to Arab women in other places, scattered abroad since the 1920s among immigrants to Europe, and to Arabic speakers and Muslim women who have come into contact with new ideas from the Arab East where they were trained – many with the PPA (Parti Progressiste Algérien) and the Ulema movements (*Femmes d'Alger*, pp. 183–84 and n7).

The woman in traditional Maghrebian society as Djebar portrays her is silenced and silent. The veil, or *haïk*, folds her into a space of feminine enclosure, described by Fatima Mernissi in *Beyond the Veil*.[10] The custom of veiling does not originate in the Islamic religion but is secular (and pre-Islamic) in origin. The closest thing to a direct injunction against veiling in the Qur'ān is Surah xxiv, v. 31: "Enjoin believing women to turn their eyes away from temptation and to preserve their chastity; to cover their adornments (except such as are normally displayed); to draw their veils over their bosoms and not to reveal their finery except to their husbands, their fathers, their husbands' fathers, their sons, their step-sons, their brothers, their brothers' sons, their sisters' sons, their women-servants, and their slave-girls; male attendants lacking in natural vigour, and children who have no carnal knowledge of women."[11] As Germaine Tillion notes, both the harem and the veil are infinitely older than the verses of the Qur'ān.[12] Abdelwahab Bouhdiba remarks that "To be a female Muslim is to live incognito" ["Etre musulmane c'est vivre incognito"].[13] The injunction levied against her is that she pass unnoticed. The sole gaze permissible emanates from the male, while the woman's gaze is strictly legislated by religious belief. The Prophet said of woman that the gaze is the capital sin of the eye [*zîna ul-aynî*]. Since *zîna* means sexual intercourse, a fairly accurate translation might be "love-making of the eye." Hence, despite the absence of a direct injunction against veiling in the Qur'ān, the existence of a moral imperative for veiling – of gaze as well as word – is strongly implied, for, in the Muslim idea of reality, the woman's eye is without doubt considered an erogenous zone.[14] Even more than the torso in traditional Islamic societies, in regard to which the prospect of standing naked in the market-place would be less disgraceful, according to Croutier, than to unveil the face. For these women, the face remains the most inviolate part of the female body (Croutier, *Harem*, p. 77). Finally, Mernissi maintains that veiling the gaze is as much to protect men from themselves as from women, for the Qur'ān bears out the notion that sequestration of the woman in Islam serves the function of protecting the unsuspecting male who is unable to control his sexual impulses in the presence of the woman who spurs him on to lust (83).

The position of women is entangled in oppositions that transcend their particular state, *vis-à-vis* the Arabo-Berber male, in Algerian society. Djebar's juxtaposition of the written accounts of the European colonizers with the oral accounts of the Algerian women projects these oppositions onto a larger screen: that of the relations of power obtaining, past and present, between France and the Maghreb. The former has historically served as the Sartrean "conscience néante" (annihilating consciousness) of the latter, that constitutes it as object and itself as subject through the former's negation. Such a process evinced itself in the phenomenon of colonial rule.

In their historical encounter with Maghrebian society, Western societies have often, in fact, inflected and controlled the particular constitution of gender difference, of male/female being and relation among the peoples of the Maghreb. Mernissi asserts, with reason, that the political and sexual are inextricably linked. Since time out of memory the ruling classes have manipulated the images people hold of their body and of their self for purposes of exploitation. Seen historically, the class struggle has appropriated and expressed itself through sexual relations.[15] In his study of North African male immigrant workers in France, Tahar Ben Jelloun, who received a doctorate in social psychiatry from the University of Paris and worked with North African immigrant patients for three years at the Dejerine Center for Psychosomatic Medecine, examines the sexual neuroses resulting from their displacement to French soil.[16] First, they are deprived of the figure of the mother, who plays a special role in Muslim society: "Her body censored, her desire repressed, her word forbidden, her image veiled, her reality denied under the mask and by tradition: woman in the Maghreb generally ceases to undergo oppression by male society only when she becomes a mother" ["Corps censuré, désir étouffé, parole interdite, image voilée, réalité niée sous le masque et la tradition: la femme au Maghreb ne cesse généralement de subir l'oppression de la société masculine que quand elle devient mère"] (*Solitudes*, p. 92).

The North African male immigrant also confronts the same subordinate position that prevailed under the French colonial occupation of the Maghreb – the same "perpetual phallic aggression" of the French male who ruled as the figure of male authority: "It is the repressive and foreign father who imposes himself on his 'imaginaire' in the form of the police, the boss, the foreman, the unreadable technical manuals" ["c'est le père répressif et étranger qui s'impose à son imaginaire sous la forme du flic, du patron, du contremaître, de la technique illisible"] (*Ibid.*, pp. 64–65).

In the power relations existing between France and the Maghreb, the North African male may be said to resemble a boy child, if not a eunuch, emasculated and shamed in the face of the supreme male figure of gallic authority. The campaign by French colonial authorities to unveil the Arab woman rested on the breaking down of traditional indigenous mores. In writing of the Algerian revolution, Frantz Fanon asserted, "To convert the woman, to win her over to foreign values, to tear her from her [traditional] status, is at the same time to obtain a real power over the man and to possess practical and efficient means to destructure Algerian culture" ["Convertir la femme, la gagner aux valeurs étrangères, l'arracher à son statut, c'est à la fois conquérir un pouvoir réel sur l'homme et posséder les moyens pratiques, efficaces, de destructurer la culture algérienne"].[17] The attempt by colonial authorities to unveil the Algerian woman and to destructure Algerian society by obtaining power over the Algerian man and driving a wedge between genders, as Fanon asserts – whether it was conscious or unconscious policy – miscarried, for, ironically, the unveiling of women facilitated their assimilation into the War of Liberation to work beside men. And, eventually, the greatest force for the eroding of role differentiation between sexes in Algeria was not the French but the War of Liberation itself.

What is more, wearing traditional dress became a means of aiding guerrilla resistance. "The veil removed and then put on again, the instrumentalized veil, was transformed into a technique of camouflage, into a means of battle" ["Voile enlevé, puis remis, voile instrumentalisé, transformé en technique de camouflage, en moyen de lutte"].[18] The veil, or its absence, became a revolutionary weapon. Wearing of the veil, or the extension of the veiling to dress itself, to the *haïk* or robe, offered a means of concealing weapons and ammunition carried to the fighters.

Women of the Maghreb confront obstacles to self-affirmation infinitely more pronounced than that of their male counterparts. They exist in a double-bind, not only oppressed by Western aggression against the Maghreb that has used them as a weapon against the Algerian male, but also oppressed by the male in Islam and by Islamic tradition. That same double-bind confronts the Algerian woman writer seeking an alternate language in French, for her discourse meets with repression as postcolonialist discourse by the Western magisterial discourses of power as well as repression by the patriarchal discourse of the male and by Islamic strictures. Djebar refers to the double-bind the Arab woman writing in French faces as a double exile ("La langue adverse," p. 232).

Bouhdiba remarks that "The great taboo of Islam is not so much the failure to respect a parental relationship as to violate the order of the world, the sexual division and the distinction between the feminine and the masculine" ["le grand tabou sexuel de l'islam n'est pas tant de ne pas respecter un rapport de parenté que de violer l'ordre du monde, la bipartition sexuelle et la distinction du féminin et du masculin"] (*La Sexualité*, pp. 45–46).[19] In Islamic society, "The primacy of man over woman is in effect total and absolute. The woman proceeds from the man. [As the Qur'ān asserts, Surah XLIX, v. 13] God 'has created us out of a single person (*nafs*) from whom he has drawn his female counterpart.' The woman is chronologically second. It is in the man that she finds her finality" ["La primauté de l'homme sur la femme en effet est totale et absolue. La femme procède de l'homme. [Comme le Coran nous dit, Surah XLIX, v. 13] Dieu nous a créés (à partir) d'une personne (*nafs*) unique dont il a tiré son épouse.' La femme est chronologiquement seconde. C'est en l'homme qu'elle trouve sa finalité"] (Bouhdiba, *La Sexualité*, p. 20). Even more preemptorily, while the Qur'ān speaks of a difference in degree between the sexes, the *fiqh* (the repertoire of Islamic jurisprudence) speaks of a difference in nature, such that "Groups of facts institutionalize the repression of the woman, her derealization, her negation" ["les groupements de faits institutionnalisent l'écrasement de la femme, sa déréalisation, sa négation"] (*Ibid.*, p. 260).

In a real sense, woman in traditional Arabo-Berber society occupies a non-state. Nor does the concept of the couple exist, for the woman is invisible, without name, without identity other than as chattel. The narrator of *L'Amour, la fantasia* describes her Algerian sisters as "white walking wraiths, shrouded figures buried upright... to prevent them uttering such a constant howl: such a wild, barbaric cry, macabre residue of a former century!" (115) ["fantômes blancs, formes ensevelies à la verticale... pour ne pas hurler continûment: son de barbare, son de sauvage, résidu macabre d'un autre siècle!"] (131–32). Customarily Algerian women addressed their spouses in the third person – a royal manner of address that blended the men "in the anonymity of the masculine gender" ["confondus dans l'anonymat du genre masculin"] (47, my translation). The narrator describes how she marveled at a postcard sent to her mother from her father, who addressed her mother by name – "Thus my father had actually written to my mother," she says ["Ainsi mon père avait 'écrit' à ma mère"] (48, my translation) – and the reader realizes what special power and significance the act of writing holds. Normally the father would address letters to the son, no matter how young he might be!

A linguistic (non-orientalist) abduction from the seraglio

In *L'Amour, la fantasia*, the first chapter of Part I begins with an introductory section opening with a scene that will become a primal scene in the narrative: the narrator as a young Arab girl setting off for school for the first time, her hand in that of her father, who is a teacher at the French school in a village of the Algerian Sahel. The neighbors observe, thinking of the unhappiness (*malheur*) that will befall the family. "For her the time will come when there will be more danger in love that is committed to paper than love that languishes behind enclosing walls" (3) ["Viendra l'heure pour elle où l'amour qui s'écrit est plus dangereux que l'amour séquestré"] (11). This scene fixes the two poles of the narrative: setting forth into the outer world (learning to write) versus sequestration. The voice of the anonymous masculine gender of Algerian society speaks: "So wrap the nubile girl in veils. Make her invisible. Make her more unseeing than the sightless, destroy in her every memory of the world without" (3) ["Voilez le corps de la fille nubile. Rendez-la invisible. Transformez-la en être plus aveugle que l'aveugle, tuez en elle tout souvenir du dehors"] (11). The space traditionally designated for the female child is that of the inside: to go to the French school, to learn to write, as outside-directed activities constitute an act of liberation from the inside. In point of fact, the female in that case is transgressing on the space of the male, for a sexual division of space exists. In an interview with Marie-Françoise Lévy, Djebar has said that the unveiling of an Algerian woman does not necessarily liberate her. A truly liberated woman is a woman who can move about freely.[20]

Near the end of her narrative, the narrator returns to the scene of her father leading her by the hand. She speaks of the "veil-shroud" [*voile-suaire*] which she, unlike her cousins, escaped. When she had the occasion later to don a veil at a wedding, it became for her, contrary to what it meant for the other Arab women, a mode of disguise (cf. the original French, p. 239). For the other women, the veil signifies loss of identity. For her, it merely hides from view an identity already affirmed by her exit from the enclosed space of sequestration, the harem. She becomes a subject-

voyeuse instead of an object of the male *voyeur*. This function of veiling finds an analogue in Djebar's conception of the adversary's language: "The French I used from the beginning is for me, in fact, a veil. A way of dissimulating oneself because I constantly had the feeling, in my relations with the outer world, that people did not perceive my image" ["le français que j'utilisais, en fait, dès le départ, pour moi est un voile. Une façon de se dissimuler parce que j'avais le sentiment constamment, dans mes rapports à l'extérieur, qu'on ne percevait pas mon image"] ("La langue adverse," p. 236).

When the mother was asked why her daughter, in her early teens, remained unveiled, she replied: "She reads!" (179–80) ["Elle lit!"] (202–03) – which meant in Arabic, "she studies." The narrator understands by the verb to read, used by Gabriel in the Qur'ān, that "writing to be read" is a source of revelation and liberation. Young girls of her generation, she says, used four languages: French for secret writing, Arabic for their "stifled aspirations" directed towards Allah, Libyco-Berber to revert to the mother-gods of pre-Islam, and that of the body whose language society attempted to silence. The first feminine reality [*réalité-femme*] for the Algerian woman is the voice; but writing in Arabic, likened because of its sinuous tracings to an act of sexuality, suggests woman to Djebar even more than the voice.

The potential for liberation the narrator will discover in the act of writing, however, does not mean that writing in Djebar's narrative always conveys the prospect of liberation. Part I, which describes her childhood summers spent with three young female Arab cousins, cloistered in a small village in the Sahel, compares the extensive correspondence of the young women with Arab males, contacted through the columns of a women's magazine, to the numerous writings of the French conquerors. The narrator speculates on the motives of the French chroniclers, who perhaps savored "the seducer's triumph, the rapist's intoxication" (45) ["la gloire du séducteur, le vertige du violeur"] (56). The narrator speaks of "this alien world, which they [the invaders] penetrated as they would a woman... Penetrated and deflowered, Africa is taken, in spite of the protesting cries that she cannot stifle" (57) ["Ce monde étranger, qu'ils pénétraient quasiment sur le mode sexuel... Y pénétrent comme en une défloration. L'Afrique est prise malgré le refus qu'elle ne peut étouffer"] (70). Winifred Woodhull and others point out how the colonist's fantasy equates the possession of Algerian women with the possession of Algeria itself.[21] Several examples of the possession of women and of the country through war exist in *L'Amour, la fantasia*: the description of Algiers as an oriental woman immobilized in mystery before the invader (6/14); the women of the town whom the narrator imagines as dreaming romance "as if the invaders were coming as lovers!" (8/16); the question of the narrator as to why "this first Algerian campaign reverberate[s] with the sounds of an obscene copulation" (16/26), to mention but a few examples.

For the girlfriends of the narrator, the written word was regarded as a means to escape from their confinement, just as writing for the colonists seemed another weapon of sexual and bellicose domination. Djebar observes:

> The girls who were my friends and accomplices during my village holidays wrote in the same futile, cryptic language because they were confined, because they were prisoners; they mark their marasmus with their own identity in an attempt to rise above their pathetic plight. The accounts of this past invasion reveal *a contrario* an identical nature: invaders who imagine they are taking the Impregnable City, but who wander aimlessly in the undergrowth of their own disquiet.
>
> (45)

> [Mes jeunes amies, mes complices du hameau de vacances, écrivaient même langage inutile et opaque parce que cernées, parce que prisonnières; elles estampillaient leur marasme, pour en surmonter plus ou moins le tragique. Les comptes rendus de cette intrusion d'hier décèlent *a contrario* une nature identique: envahisseurs qui croient prendre la Ville Imprenable, mais qui tournoient dans le buissonnement de leur mal d'être.]
>
> (56–57)

The comparison exemplifies the failures of writing that establishes no praxis, effects no escape, does not allow one to enter into meaningful contact with the "other." The language of sequestration and confinement, the language of the prisoner written by both the girl cousins and the French occupiers, is a "futile, cryptic language" because it opens no real relation, establishes no dialogue that results in a reciprocal exchange of understanding by each on the part of the other. Rather, each remains a prisoner of language, confined by words that stand between the writer and the unpossessable object. Djebar's original French word to describe that language of incarceration (that incarceral language) is "opaque," suggesting a language that is not just cryptic but closed and impenetrable. What can the written language become on the other hand for someone who emerges from confinement?

Writing in the language of the adversary

The narrator concedes that the love letters of the young cousins, though providing no escape from confinement, are a means of affirming their self-identity ("Is not writing a way of telling what 'I' am?" (58) ["Ecrire, n'est-ce pas 'me' dire?"] (72)). Writing is, moreover, the equivalent of unveiling. "Such incidental unveiling is tantamount to stripping oneself naked, as the demotic Arabic dialect emphasizes" (156–57) ["Le dévoilement, aussi contingent, devient, comme le souligne mon arabe dialectal du quotidien, vraiment 'se mettre à nu'"] (178). In a somewhat cryptic passage, the narrator compares the act of unveiling/stripping-bare of the Algerian woman writing in the language of the former conqueror (who, she says, for more than a century possessed everything he desired except the bodies of Algerian women) to the sacking of Algeria in the previous century (178). We are left to surmise that through the writing–unveiling of women the magisterial discourse will be plundered and the Impregnable City of male-dominated society will fall as women come to repossess their own spiritual and physical being. ("Writing in the face of love. To illuminate the body in order to help raise the interdiction, to unrobe... Unrobe and simultaneously keep secret what must remain secret, so long as the flash of revelation doesn't intervene" ["Ecrire *devant* l'amour. Eclairer le corps pour aider à lever l'interdit, pour dévoiler... Dévoiler et simultanément tenir secret ce qui doit le rester, tant que n'intervient pas la fulgurance de la révélation"] (75; my translation).

When the narrator receives her first letter from her classmate, written in French, she observes that French places her under a double and contradictory sign. She feels herself cut off from the words of her mother by a "mutilation of memory" (4). The danger of using the language of the oppressor is revealed in an anecdote concerning the French Commander De Bourmont who gives letters to an old Algerian to carry to the Arab army. The old man is assumed by the Arabs to be a spy, however, and is put to death. "So, the first written words, even while promising a fallacious peace, condemn their bearer to death. Any document written by 'The Other' proves fatal, since it is a sign of compromise" (33) ["Ainsi les premiers mots écrits, même s'ils permettent une fallacieuse paix, font, de leur porteur, un condamné à mort. Toute écriture de l'Autre, transportée, devient fatale, puisque signe de compromission"] (44). For Djebar, as for another writer born in an overseas French community, Marguerite Duras, writing is touched with death: "To write, I believe, is actually an activity that puts us in the presence of death each day" ["Ecrire, je pense que c'est, effectivement, l'activité qui fait que la pensée de la mort est là chaque jour"].[22]

The narrator's apprenticeship in French and Arabic in her youth, before her father chose for her the former over the latter ("light rather than darkness" [184]; "la lumière plutôt que l'ombre" [208]), placed her, she says, in a "dichotomy of location" (184) ["dichotomie de l'espace"] (208), between two spaces – the closed space of the harem and the open space of writing –, in which she did not comprehend the consequence of her father's option: "the outdoors and the risk, instead of the prison of my peers" (184) ["le dehors et le risque, au lieu de la prison de mes semblables"] (208). French, whose lexicon refers to objects unexperienced by the narrator, objects existing in a country across the sea, offers her a vocabulary of absence and exoticism without mystery. Referentiality would be lost to her until she crossed the sea, she says. What she does not say, the incommensurability of external being and "reality" will be exposed – the chasm between her cultural and sexual specificity *vis-à-vis* the European, traversible only through dialogic exchange. The incommensurability, moreover, has both a negative side, which puts up obstacles to communication, and a positive side, which shields one from appropriation by the other while also providing the necessary distance for understanding (empathizing) with other.

She calls French her stepmother language (214), as contrasted to her mother tongue which, even including the Arabic love-songs of her childhood, she has lost. She alludes to Spanish occupiers who, even before the French in the nineteenth century, established posts [*presidios*] and fought following the tactic of the "rebato" – a term that refers to a space, a no man's land, between the indigenous peoples and the aggressors, from which the latter launched their attacks and to which they retreated during breaks in the fighting, either to seek refuge or to replenish their supplies. For the narrator a similar no man's land exists between the French and Arabo-Berber languages. French has become for her a *presidio*, while the indigenous languages resist and attack. "In time to the rhythm of the *rebato*, I am alternately the besieged and the native swaggering off to die, so there is seemingly endless strife between the spoken and written word" (215) ["Le rythme du 'rebato' en moi s'éperonnant, je suis à la fois l'assiégé étrangère et l'autochtone partant à la mort par bravade, illusoire effervescence du dire et de l'écrit"] (241). She describes the space to which writing in French relegates her:

On the deserted beaches of the present, washed up by the inevitable ceasefire of all wars, my writing continues to seek its place of exchange, of fountains, of commerce.

That language was formerly the sarcophagus of my people; I bear it today like a messenger bearing a sealed letter ordering his condemnation to death ["au silence"], or to the dungeon.

To strip myself bare in that language makes me chance a permanent danger of being consumed by fire. As a penalty for undertaking to write an autobiography in the language of yesterday's adversary.   (215; my translation)

[Sur les plages désertées du présent, amené par tout cessez-le-feu inévitable, mon écrit cherche encore son lieu d'échange et de fontaines, son commerce.

Cette langue était autrefois sarcophage des miens; je la porte aujourd'hui comme un messager transporterait le pli fermé ordonnant sa condamnation au silence, ou au cachot.

Me mettre à nu dans cette langue me fait entretenir un danger permanent de déflagration. De l'exercice de l'autobiographie dans la langue de l'adversaire d'hier.]   (241)

A polylogue of sisters

At one point, the narrator compares her situation with that of Saint Augustine writing in Latin, the language of the conquerors, or Ibn Khaldun writing in Arabic, the language of those warriors who conquered the Maghrebian Berbers. Both languages imposed themselves as much by rape as by love, she remarks (242). Though, in *L'Amour, la fantasia*, she likens writing to unveiling, to being stripped bare, she also acknowledges that her writing rests on self-deception, for, in believing that she was writing of herself, in choosing the language of the enemy, she was simply choosing another veil. "While I intended every step forward to make me more clearly identifiable, I find myself progressively sucked down into the anonymity of those women of old – my ancestors!" (217) ["Voulant, à chaque pas, parvenir à la transparence, je m'engloutis davantage dans l'anonymat des aïeules!"] (243). Elsewhere, however, language as veil, in conferring on her a measure of anonymity, holds for her, as she implies in her interview with Le Clézio, the virtue of passing unseen, of dissimulation that enables her to escape being co-opted, that allows her the privileged view accorded to the distant observer.

In speaking of her childhood, the narrator switches from third to first person as she describes the penetration of her enclosed space by a letter written to her by a male classmate: "I blew the space within me to pieces, a space filled with voiceless cries, frozen long ago in a prehistory of love" (4) ["J'ai fait éclater l'espace en moi, un espace éperdu de cris sans voix, figés depuis longtemps dans une préhistoire de l'amour"] (13).

The mention of "voiceless cries" calls to mind the distinction Blanchot makes between what he defines as the narrative voice and the narratorial voice, as well as Derrida's gloss on Blanchot. Each voice of the woman, as narrator or virtual narrator, speaks through "a neutral voice that narrates the work from this place without place, this placeless place, where the work is silent (Blanchot): a silent voice, therefore [Derrida glosses], withdrawn into its own 'aphonia' [voicelessness]" ["une voix neutre qui dit l'oeuvre à partir de ce lieu sans lieu où l'oeuvre se tait (Blanchot): voix silencieuse, donc, retirée en son 'aphonie'"]. This voiceless voice – the "narrative voice," as Blanchot calls it – must be distinguished from the "narratorial voice," the voice that the literary critic contrives to locate in the system of the narrative, as the source of the narration. "The narratorial voice can be traced to a subject who recounts something, recalls an event or a historical sequence, knowing who he is, where he is and what he speaks of" ["La voix narratorial revient à un sujet qui raconte quelque chose, se souvenant d'un événement ou d'une séquence historique, sachant qui il est, où il est et de quoi il parle"].[23] The narrative voice, using Blanchot's term, is the unvoiced (unrepresentable) voice of the repressed cultural/sexual other.

The narrator's words not only allude to the woman as excluded third in the dialogue of society (Michel Serres, whom I will cite at greater length in my chapter on Khatibi, asserts that, when we open a dialogue we suppose the existence of a third man whom we try to prevent from entering in[24]), buried within and by language and speech, but prefigure the role that writing will play in exploding the inner space of the Arab women who shriek voicelessly in a "prehistory of love," that is, love never or not yet realized. Her narrative will externalize, give voice to those silent voices of her claustrated sisters, changing them from a cacophony of disparate cries into a polylogue of exchange and inclusion.

The narrator recounts the events of 1842–43 when the French occupiers, under their commandant Saint-Arnaud, burn the *zaouia* (the center for Islamic brotherhood) of the Berkani, the tribe from which she descends. They drive out the women and children who are forced to wander the mountains in the winter. When the Berkani return the next year,

Saint-Arnaud decides to take as hostages members of the caliph's family. He writes to his brother that he has seized eight leaders and their families. The women elders of the tribe (the *aïeules*) pass their version of the story down to their children, who pass it down to their own children – there follows a description of the oral history transmitted from mouth to mouth (by what Djebar calls *chuchotements*, whispers). "The legacy will otherwise be lost – night after night, wave upon wave, the whispers take up the tale, even before the child can understand, even before she finds her words of life, before she speaks in her turn and so that she will not speak alone" (177) ["L'héritage va chavirer – vague après vague, nuit après nuit, les murmures reprennent avant même que l'enfant comprenne, avant même qu'il trouve ses mots de lumière, avant de parler à son tour et pour ne point parler seul"] (200). It is these women elders [*aïeules*] who are the guardians of past times. They appear in several of Djebar's works. In *Les Alouettes naïves*, she describes the young girls as finding each other in the deep bed of the woman elder (the *aïeule*). In her film *La Nouba des femmes du mont Chenoua* (1978), Leïla heeds the voices of the past, of the *aïeules*, in which legend and history surrounding the 1871 revolt of the Beni Menacer Tribe are entangled. A collective identity is passed from the women ancestors to the young female generations that follow.[25] The collective voices of the past are described by Djebar as "the voice of the unknown woman ancester, timeless chorus where history is retold" ["voix d'aïeule indéfinie, choeur intemporel où se redit l'histoire"] (184). Djebar's affinity with postmodern thought reveals itself in this rewriting of history from a woman's perspective that we find in *L'Amour, la fantasia*, as well as in her recent work such as *Loin de Médine* (1992), in which she resurrects the buried women of the Algerian and Islamic past and reinscribes them in their rightful place, or *Vaste est la prison* (1995), which recounts events concerning women of the Algerian past as well as past events in the life of her own family. She speaks of the scandal of the voice of the Arab woman being silenced: "my training as a historian motivates me to seek in texts how, by what process, that writing of the Arab woman has been stifled" ["ma formation d'historienne me pousse maintenant à rechercher dans les textes comment, par quel processus, cette écriture de femme arabe a été étouffée"] ("La langue adverse," p. 232). She consequently questions the historical context underlying the suppression of the voice of the Arab woman that has become an accepted fact of public life.

Djebar's postmodern turn to history recalls Christa Wolf's retelling of the story of the fall of Troy through the voice of Cassandra, in Wolf's novel by that name. The stories of the women elders of *L'Amour, la fantasia* and the legendary and real-life heroines of the birthing days of Islam, long forgotten, speak again, just as the prophetess Cassandra, who was disbelieved by those about her, speaks to the present day. In so speaking, such postmodern interlocutors enlarge the frontiers of discourse, extend them to comprise a multiplicity of equally valid narratives that includes that of women, and consequently waters down the totalistic preeminence of the dominant discourses of Eurocentric and patriarchal provenance.

Djebar replaces the traditional Western narrative, marked by the logos of cause and effect continuity, spatial consistency, and chronological coherence, with a discontinous narrative that superimposes and mixes discourses from widely disparate times and places in a discursive *métissage* (mixing) made cohesive by a collective identity, a narrative whose structure utilizes, as its principal discursive tactic, fragmentation and displacement.[26] The univocal nature of the traditional narrative is broken up, displaced by the plurivocality of women's voices from the distant and recent past, as well as the present. The identity of the narrator herself, moreover, becomes diffuse as the narrative shifts between first and third persons.

Yet another narrative device is the use of epigraphic material. Anne Donadey analyses how epigraphs in Djebar's narratives function (following Gérard Genette's categories) to legitimize the text by grounding it in tradition (the women's voices of oral tradition) and to link it to a particular intellectual and cultural tradition. To characterize Djebar's method, Donadey refers to Luce Irigaray's strategy of mimicry, which repeats hegemonic discourse and subverts it through parody. She gives the example of how Djebar undermines the hegemonic texts of the French invaders of the previous century by repeating them and decentering them through a dislocation of their meaning that reveals their unreliability.[27] Djebar thus makes use of colonial texts, through whose parodic subversion she rewrites the history of Algeria. In brief, a not unfamiliar postcolonial and postmodern strategy. The very use of the epigraph, a text marked by marginality, makes it a conveyance *par excellence* of the marginal perspective of postcolonial authors.

The women who whisper correct the details of the French version. Among these women is one who told the narrator of another story, from another war (the Algerian War of Liberation), of how she gave her 14-year-old son a silver jam-spoon handed down to her from her father (173ff.). When the French soldiers raided their house, her son fled with the maquisards, the resistance fighters, carrying away with him the spoon. Several years later, he returned safe and sound. For the narrator, the silver spoon, symbol of the heritage passed down, appears as a "heraldic object" (177) ["emblème héraldique"] (200).

> The fires in the orchards gutted by Saint-Arnaud are finally extinguished, because the old lady talks today and I am preparing to transcribe her tale. To draw up the inventory of the tiny objects passed on thus, from febrile hand to fugitive hand!   (177)

> [Les vergers brûlés par Saint-Arnaud voient enfin leur feu s'éteindre, parce que la vieille aujourd'hui parle et que je m'apprête à transcrire son récit. Faire le décompte des menus objets passés ainsi, de main fiévreuse à main de fugueur!]   (200–01)[28]

The narrator surmises that she was born in 1842, the year Saint-Arnaud put fire to the *zaouïa* of her tribe. That same fire lights her emergence from the harem (claustration) a century later, (en)lightens her and gives her the strength to speak. The magical property that accounts for the apparent longevity of the narrator comes, not from the integration of fantasized elements in the narrative, but from the transubstantiation she undergoes as she is infused with the histories of her women ancestors brought to life in her growing consciousness of their past lives. Her chant, born of this state, is accompanied by the sounds of all her Algerian sisters who suffered in the past.

> The language of the Others, in which I was enveloped from childhood, the gift my father lovingly bestowed on me, that language has adhered to me ever since like the tunic of Nessus, that gift from my father who, every morning, took me by the hand to accompany me to school.   (217)

> [La langue encore coagulée des Autres m'a enveloppée, dès l'enfance, en tunique de Nessus, don d'amour de mon père qui, chaque matin, me tenait la main sur le chemin de l'école.]   (243)

The story of Nessus tells of how Hercules slew the centaur, Nessus, who attempted to rape his wife, Deianira. The dying Nessus gives her a potion mixed with his blood under guise of it being a love potion. Later, Deianira, attempting to reclaim Hercules' affection, bestows on him a cloak soaked with the potion containing Nessus' blood. The cloak burns him horribly, giving him such agony that he causes himself to be immolated. The story of Nessus' cloak invokes the myth of the fire-ritual, associated with fertility. On one level we can analogize the narrator's own situation, in which writing French (whose words she calls "torch-words" – see below) at once produces agony and gives birth to her potential as amanuensis for her sisters. It is, for the narrator, simultaneously a gift of love from her father and the cause of her painful exile. I might further note, however, that the male–female relationship alluded to in the classical myth is reversed. This reversal strikes me as most important, for it is paradigmatic of the reversal of the male–female role through women's writing, which is central to Djebar's narrative. Such a reversal, however, does not involve a mere inversion of binary opposites whereby the woman assumes the male role, but results in a reversal rather of emphasis that throws light (by "torch-words"), necessary for the creation of an enabling discourse, onto the autonomous existence of the Algerian woman.

As the narrator describes the hostages of Saint-Arnaud being put aboard a ship for transport to France in 1843, she addresses a *narrataire* in the second person singular. The story of the "unknown woman," the "invisible woman," as she calls her, has been passed down among the women from story-teller to story-teller. She is one of the nameless hostages, the "ancestress of ancestresses," who holds special significance for the narrator, for she is, on the one hand, the prototype of the silent and invisible Algerian woman and, on the other, "the first expatriate" in whose footsteps she (the narrator) follows (189) ["aïeule d'aïeule," "la première expatriée"] (214).[29]

Paradox lies at the center of the narrator's destined task to serve as amanuensis for her silent sisters. To draw near to them in telling their story, she must exile herself in a foreign tongue. When she describes Chérifa, one of the Algerian women whose story of the War of Liberation she recounts, she relates how the very words in French – "torch-words" (*mots torches*; cf. *Femmes d'Alger* where she speaks of "words like torches," 46) that bring light to the lives of the women whose story she tells – definitively separate her from her Algerian sisters: by the stigmata of foreign words she finds herself, like the nameless *narrataire*, expatriated from them (142).

Part III closes with a soliloquy where the narrator speaks of how she is called an exile, but "It is more than that: I have been banished from my homeland to listen and bring back some traces of liberty to the women of my family." In attempting to execute this task, she flounders, as she says, "in a murky bog" (218) ["La différence est plus lourde: je suis expulsée de là-bas pour entendre et ramener à mes parentes les traces de la liberté";

"dans un marécage qui s'éclaire à peine"] (244). In writing, she creates a fiction, for the story of her past is unwritten in the mother tongue, and her imagination, like a beggar woman in the streets, crouches in absences and silences (218–19).

In speaking of veiling, the narrator says that, during her childhood, the women would don their veils whenever a male approached, unless he was a foreigner, a non-Arab, because, if a non-Arab looked at them, he did not really see them – he only imagined he saw them. And, at a distance, behind a hedge, his glance failed to touch them (126). The narrator cites a Westerner enslaved by the Algerians in the seventeenth century who spoke of how the women were indiscreet in the presence of a Western captive because they considered him blind, themselves "invisible," in contrast to the vilest of Arab males of the "dominant society," who felt himself to be their master (128). To this relation between the Algerian woman and the foreign captive, the narrator compares her reaction to the French language, which served her as a recess from which she could spy upon the world and into which she could withdraw from the unwanted attentions of Western males. But she discovered that in so doing she became a veiled woman, "not so much disguised as anonymous" ["moins déguisée qu'anonyme"] (143), that her imagined invisibility was an illusion. With the French language, she found herself unable to control her body-presence – it signified more than she intended to signify (126).[30] Moreover, with French she experienced an "aphasia of love" ["aphasie amoureuse"], an inability to express intimacy, which she could do only in her mother-tongue (128–29). She had described herself earlier as seeking her mother-tongue's "rich vocabulary of love," of which she had been deprived (62). (She also compares it to her mother's milk: "like a milk from which they had once weaned me, the rich plethora of my mother's tongue" (my translation); "comme un lait dont on m'aurait autrefois écartée, la pléthore amoureuse de la langue de ma mère" (76).) In her interview with Le Clézio, she speaks of how, during her decade of silence, she contemplated writing in classical Arabic, but came to understand that classical (written) Arabic was not the language of her Arab ancestresses either: that it had served as the dominant official language for centuries, just as French had served as the dominant language during 130 years of colonization ("La langue adverse," p. 242).

Such antimonies at the center of writing, reflective of its force to destroy as much as to create, are paradigmatic of the intimate union of love and war signified in the title in the original French of Djebar's narrative:

L'Amour, la fantasia. For the word "fantasia," the Oxford English Dictionary cites the Italian origin, meaning "fancy," hence "an instrumental composition having the appearance of being extemporaneous" [Tommaseo] – a word used today to denote a musical composition in which form subserves fancy. Its secondary meaning approaches that of the Arabic *fantaziya* (derived from Spanish), denoting both ostentatiousness and pomp, as well as a kind of Arab dance, and also the equestrian maneuver in which Arab or Berber horsemen gallop full tilt and at a given moment rein up in unison and discharge their rifles in the midst of fearsome cries – a custom that has been recorded in another Delacroix painting, "Fantasia," dating from 1833.

In regard to the musical connotation of the term "fantasia," Winifred Woodhull, in speaking of Part III of *L'Amour, la fantasia* (which is divided into five movements followed by a coda), suggests that the term calls attention to the musical sonority of Djebar's narrative and its intermixture of the vocal and the written that carry into her French prose the rhythm and intonations of the Arab language. She notes that Djebar's French is itself a writing over of the texts of the French conquerors of Algeria as well as of the texts read by students (including the author and narrator) in schools in the former French colonies (*Transfigurations*, pp. 79, 80).[31]

The combination of love and "fantasia" in the title brings together the love of the languages the narrator has at her disposal and of her ancestors, as well as the intimate relation between fantasy and the violence of military engagement (*fantasia*). Djebar somewhat disingenuously writes: "Love, if I managed to write it down, would approach a critical point: there where lies the risk of exhuming buried cries, those of yesterday as well as those of a hundred years ago. But my sole ambition in writing is constantly to travel to fresh pastures and replenish my water skins with an inexhaustible silence" (63) ["L'amour, si je parvenais à l'écrire, s'approcherait d'un point nodale: là gît le risque d'exhumer des cris, ceux d'hier comme ceux du siècle dernier. Mais je n'aspire qu'à une écriture de transhumance, tandis que, voyageuse, je remplis mes outres d'un silence inépuisable"] (76).

The allusion to "buried cries" relates to a macabre historical event related by Djebar in her narrative. In June 1845, some 1500 Berber tribespeople – men, women and children – sought refuge with their animals from the invading French forces in a cave beneath the plateau of el-Kantara. The commanding officer, Colonel Pélissier, ordered his men to set fires at the mouth of the cave to smoke out the resisters. Nearly everyone died of asphyxiation. The motives of "buried cries" and asphyxiation contained in the accounts of the aggressors are, as Woodhull puts it, resignified to give to Algerian women the possibility of reclaiming their buried past and to give sound to voices of the asphyxiated (*Transfigurations,* 82). The shepherd metaphor Djebar employs, in saying she aspires to writing that is "transhumance" (in French meaning to move flocks from one pasture to another), and replenishing her water skins "with an inexhaustible silence," is ambiguous. "Transhumance" etymologically signifies movement beyond the earth (from the latin *trans-,* "beyond," and *humus,* "earth") and would seem to imply that she would indeed exhume the cries of her buried sisters of the recent as well as the distant past, and the "inexhaustible silence" with which she would replenish her water skins suggests that, as a "voyageuse," she would carry them with her (through her writing) – from which one might conclude that she alludes to the act of giving voice to those buried ones.

She thus, out of the historical narrative of the aggressor, creates a metaphor that changes the terms of that narrative, creates a counter-movement that reconstrues it to express a "libertory" dimension for the silent, asphyxiated women without voice, as Woodhull holds (*Transfigurations,* 82). But, even while she sees Djebar as writing the story of those others, the silent women, Woodhull concludes that Djebar reinscribes a pessimistic view of Algerian women by emphasizing their mutilation and dispossession, as symbolized in the closing part of the narrative by the description of the severed hand found by another nineteenth-century artist-visitor to Algeria, Eugène Fromentin, alongside a path in Laghouat (*Ibid.,* p. 84).

Let us look more closely at the closing part, entitled "Tzarl-Rit (Finale)." Two epigraphs give conflicting definitions of the term "tzarl-rit," the women's cry that accompanies the *fantasia*: one denoting a cry of joy, the other denoting a cry elicited by the arrival of misfortune. To be sure, the act of breaking the silence, of crying out, betrays the mixed emotions attending liberation, writing, unveiling. It is in the last of three sections of this finale, entitled "Air de Nay" (a musical air played on a flute), that the narrator brings together the time of Fromentin's visit to Algeria in 1852–53 and the period twenty years earlier than the present moment of the narrative, at the end of the Algerian War of Liberation, when Djebar visited the Algerian *diseuses* who recounted stories of the war. Fromentin, in his travel journal *Un été dans le Sahara,* had described how, alongside a

path, he found the severed hand of an unknown Algerian woman. Djebar's narrator remarks that she writes with that mutilated hand. She concludes her story by evoking the death of another young woman, Haoua,
witnessed by Fromentin in 1852, as she was struck down by the hooves of
a horse ridden in the *Fantasia* by an angry lover she had spurned. The narrator envisages the threat against any woman who, like Haoua, dares to
demand freedom. "Yes, in spite of the tumult of my people all around, I
already hear, even before it arises and pierces the harsh sky, I hear the
death cry in the *Fantasia*" (227) ["Oui, malgré le tumulte des miens alen-
tour, j'entends déjà, avant même qu'il s'élève et transperce la ciel dur, le
cri de la mort dans la fantasia"] (256). One can agree with Woodhull that
the severed-hand metaphor conveys a pessimistic view of the Algerian
woman's fate, for the severed hand is not solely the multilated trace of the
narrator's sisters, but the writing hand that severs her from them. Such a
conclusion seems to me one-sided, however, for it glosses over the antinomical quality of Djebar's narrative that is implicit in the coexistence of
the apparent contradictory states of joy and suffering, freedom and
repression, love and war.

Early in her narrative, the narrator remarked how the women prison-
ers of the French rendered the latter's victory hollow by refusing to look at
their enemy, refusing to "recognize" him, to "name" him. "What is a victory if it is not named," she asks (56) ["Qu'est-ce qu'une victoire si elle
n'est pas nommée"] (69). If a victory that is not named is an empty victory,
can we not say that a defeat that is named might be considered not to be a
total defeat by the very fact of its being named? Inherent in naming
(bringing it into consciousness) is a coming to terms with it, the possibility of future change. Djebar's narrative world reveals the operation of an
antilogical narrative that holds the potential of moving from one predicate to an opposing, if not contradictory, predicate. Her narrative moves
between negative and positive poles, plays off one logos against another
in such a fashion as to dissolve absolutes. Its incommensurable character
serves as an allegory for the incommensurable character of the Algerian
woman who, in spite of the oppression of a patriarchal society that has
buried her or hidden her from view, remains alive in her very invisibility
and vocal in her very aphonia.

In describing letters sent by the French soldiers from a bivouac in the
nineteenth century, the narrator speaks of how they wrote home of an
"Algérie femme" that is impossible to tame. And she interjects: "A tamed
Algeria is a pipe-dream; every battle drives further and further away the

time when the insurgency will burn itself out" (57) ["Fantasme d'une Algérie domptée: chaque combat éloigne encore plus l'épuisement de la révolte"] (69). The terms of the narrator's discourse lie in these remarks: the French invaders are to Algeria what the man is to the woman in Algerian society – an *Algérie-femme* ostensibly mastered in accord with the male phantasm but ultimately untamable.

Conclusion

The two perceptions of woman's space come together: the collective–social–historical space in which the Algerian women struggle to inscribe themselves and the personal-written space in the adversary's language in which the author struggles to inscribe herself – the plural chronicle and the singular autobiography. The tension between oppresser and oppressed, written and oral, is resolved through the narrator's assumption of the role of amanuensis in her writing, which renders written what was oral, vocal what was silent.

In traditional Algerian society, as we see in Djebar's narrative, women possess no public enabling dialogue. Their speechlessness, their aphasia, present an otherness that is characterized by a hermeneutical aporia that inclines one to doubt the possibility of interpreting that otherness. To be without speech in its broadest sense (including body language) is to be without the possibility of dialogue. In effect, writing permits the narrator to create an enabling dialogue between women, between present and past, between singular and collective, allowing the women to recuperate their historical consciousness, giving them a sense of common purpose. In *Femmes d'Algers*, as the European woman Anne listens to her Algerian friend Sarah, she wonders:

> In this strange city [Algiers], drunk with sun but hemmed in with prisons high up on every street, does every woman live first for herself, or for the succession of women of other times imprisoned generation after generation, while the sky poured down the same light, an unchangeable blue that rarely faded?

> [dans cette ville étrange, ivre de soleil mais des prisons cernant haut chaque rue, chaque femme vit-elle pour son propre compte, ou d'abord pour la chaîne des femmes autrefois enfermées génération après génération, tandis que se déversait la même lumière, un bleu immuable, rarement terni?]   (66)

The imperfect past tense describing the light that poured forth while past generations of women were incarcerated within their chambers suggests that, while the same light continues to pour forth, the modern Algerian woman is no longer always locked in, but is often free to move about outside, and has the choice of engagement or non-engagement with the women of her past. As Djebar said in the interview cited earlier, an unveiled woman is not necessarily liberated, while a liberated woman is "a woman free to circulate." Thus, the "liberated" woman (or the woman in the process of liberating herself or being liberated) confronts a choice that is opened to her in the company of other women. The narrator's initiation into writing and realization of its potential for this "opening" is tantamount to discovering the other in oneself as well as oneself in the other.

It is nonetheless true that, by using the Euro-logo-phallocentric language of the adversary to recount the history of the Algerian women, the chronicle of their otherness, there is no unmediated access to the past such as the narrator finds in the stories passed down orally. Her telling manages, nevertheless, to transcend the ideological limitations of the adversary's language through an allegorical process that operates as a distancing factor. Distancing or disengagement (from language and its ideological underpinnings) is seen by most critics of dialogical encounter, as a necessary precondition for dialogue to take place.[32] But a cost is also exacted on the narrator, for she becomes alienated, exiled through her use of that very language.

Speaking of her personal experience of writing in the language of the adversary, in her essay in *L'Esprit Créateur* entitled "Fugitive, et ne le sachant pas" ("A Fugitive without knowing it"), Djebar indicates that she writes in order to make her "secret way," and tells of how she becomes more and more a fugitive. She compares herself to the Captive, Zoraidé (a historical personage described by Cervantes in *Don Quixote*, who was the first Algerian woman to write), stripped of her maternal heritage, but finding freedom:

> I write to make my secret way [or: "to make my way in secret"]; and it's in the language of the French corsairs who, in the story of the Captive, stripped Zoraidé of her diamond-studded robe, yes, in the language of the other that I become more and more the fugitive. Like Zoraidé, the unveiled. Having, like her, lost the riches I started out with, in my case the maternal heritage and having gained what, if not the simple mobility of a denuded body, if not freedom.

[J'écris pour me frayer mon chemin secret; et c'est dans la langue des corsaires français qui, dans le récit du Captif, dépouillèrent Zoraidé de sa robe endiamantée, oui, c'est dans la langue dite 'étrangère' que je deviens de plus en plus transfuge. Telle Zoraidé, la dévoilée. Ayant perdu comme elle ma richesse du départ, dans mon cas, celle de l'héritage maternel et ayant gagné quoi, sinon la simple mobilité du corps dénudé, sinon la liberté.][33]

Djebar alludes thus to her "permanent state of fugitive"; she speaks paradoxically of being "rooted in flight – precisely because I write and *in order that I might write*" ["condition permanent de fugitive... d'enracinée dans la fuite – justement parce que j'écris et pour que j'écrive"] (133; my italics). The state of a fugitive, of estrangement, is, in fact, an enabling state that allows her to write.

We have seen how Djebar has valorized the anonymity that writing in French conferred on her, the possibility of passing unseen and assuming the privileged space of a distant observer. In so doing, however, she bore out what Simone Rezzoug observed with regard to the Maghrebian woman: her difficulty in emerging from group anonymity. Rezzoug argues that narrative devices like quotations, doubling, and polyphony, serve as masks for her, to hide her individual presence.[34] What serves, consequently, as positive narrative devices in speaking for her Arab sisters, in speaking out of the "anonymity of the elders" (217) ["l'anonymat des aïeules"] (243), also glides over the painful difficulty Djebar experienced in exposing the individual self and putting it up against the institutionalized sources of repression bearing against the Maghrebian woman, in putting forward her naked personal presence. As we have seen, when Djebar, by her own admission, discovered for the first time in *Les Alouettes naïves*, that she was unconsciously writing "on the edge of autobiography," she gave up writing for nearly a decade. With her return, we still see in the three works that have appeared of her projected literary quartet, *Quatuor algérien* (*L'Amour, la fantasia*, *Ombre sultane*, and *Vaste est la prison*), her tendency to blend into the anonymity of collective sisterhood. We also witness, however, that Djebar has taken a revolutionary step forward in acknowledging – haltingly but forthrightly – her individual struggle for self-expression. We see in her interview "La langue adverse" and in her essay on Zoraidé, that she no longer shrinks from autobiographical reference in written form.

In sum, for a woman of the Maghreb to break out of the interdiction laid upon her by institutionalized social forces, takes a woman of singular strength. And that, indeed, characterizes Assia Djebar in all her endeavors.

Irigaray, who speaks of how woman has been viewed negatively as a "place," space that has been colonized, occupied by the aggressor, man, holds out the possiblity of a third possible space, which woman and man may commonly share: "A world to be created or re-created so that man and woman may again or finally cohabit, meet each other and live sometimes in the same *place.*" "Everyone must be a place," she adds. ["Un monde à créer ou recréer pour que l'homme et la femme puissent à nouveau ou enfin cohabiter, se rencontrer et parfois demeurer dans le même *lieu*"; "Il faut que chacun soit un lieu"].[35] Even in its utopian guise (and owing to it), this position seems to offer certain dangers, for, in diminishing the distance and difference between Self and Other, it tends to devalorize their incommensurability. The diminishment of difference involved in the notion of "egalitarianism" (*Egalité*), implied by the "third possible space" of Irigaray, has, as I have said elsewhere, been touted as representing the highest good in relations between oppressor and oppressed but, on the other hand, has long served the hegemonistic purposes of Empire.[36] Egalitarianism as a desired end of well-meaning reformist colonizers repeats the ethnocentric tendency of ethnography that functions as an intertextual practice operating by means of an allegorizing identity, which, as Stephen Tyler puts it, anesthetizes us to the other's difference.[37] The egalitarianism posited by colonial authorities differs from the type of egalitarianism proposed by Edouard Glissant through the optic of what he calls *métissage*: "This practice of *métissage* doesn't involve us in some vague humanism, which would allow us to become fused with the other. It forms a cross-cultural relationship [*Relation*] on an egalitarian basis previously unknown, Caribbean histories that today we realize converge" ["Cette pratique de métissage ne se ramène pas à un vague humanisme, où il serait loisible de se fondre dans l'autre. Elle met en Relation, sur un mode égalitaire et pour une des premières fois connues, des histoires dont nous savons aujourd'hui dans la Caraïbe qu'elles sont convergentes"].[38] Françoise Lionnet glosses Glissant's idea of egalitarian space expressed by the term *métissage* in the following way:

Within the conceptual apparatuses that have governed our labeling of ourselves and others, a space is thus opened where multiplicity and diversity are affirmed. This space is not a territory staked out by exclusionary practices. Rather, it functions as a sheltering site, one that can nurture our differences without encouraging us to withdraw into new dead ends, without enclosing us within facile oppositional practices or sterile denunciations and disavowals.[39]

This space resembles woman's space opened up by Assia Djebar's writings, which will derive not from mere reversal or displacement of man's space, or from fusion into a space of sameness, but rather from the creation of a unique and separate space that will express what Tzvetan Todorov calls "difference in equality," or Theodor Adorno calls "distinctiveness without domination."[40]

3

Tahar Ben Jelloun's *"Sandchild"*: voiceless narratives, placeless places

And thus a book, at least as I conceive of it, is a labyrinth consciously devised in order to confound readers with the intention of losing them and bringing them back to the narrow confines of their ambitions.

[Et puis un livre, du moins tel que je le conçois, est un labyrinthe fait a dessein pour confondre les hommes avec l'intention de les perdre et de les ramener aux dimensions étroites de leurs ambitions.]

The Blind Troubadour in The Sandchild[1]

Not for nothing am I the great grandson of that Ts'ui Pen who was governor of Yunnan and who renounced worldly power in order to write a novel that might be even more populous than the *Hung Lu Meng* and to construct a labyrinth in which all men would become lost.

STEPHEN ALBERT IN JORGE LUIS BORGES'
"The Garden of Forking Paths," Labyrinths[2]

The Sandchild (1985) opens with an absence. The reader reading Ben Jelloun's tale for the first time is apt to be unaware of a pair of missing quotation marks failing to enframe the words of the speaker that begin it. The speaker describes in considerable detail an enigmatic personage-subject whose features have been ravaged by time, who is shut up in voluntary seclusion, afflicted by the incursions – the sights, sounds, smells – of the outer world. The speaker goes on to tell us how the subject sets about to order the details of his impending death and alludes to "the outline of a story to which he alone [the subject] held the keys" ["l'ébauche d'un récit dont lui seul avait les clés"] (9).

After five pages of opening narrative, a two-line blank space appears in the text, marking the conclusion of the introduction and the beginning of what turns out to be the "real" narrative or narrative proper, which opens with the question: "And who was he?" ["Et qui fut-il"] (12). The words that immediately follow introduce a shift for which we are unprepared, because a voice we discover to be that of another speaker intervenes to inform us that the interlocutor who asks the question is not a first-level (extradiegetic) narrator after all, but a second-level (intradiegetic) narrator, called the *conteur* (story-teller), who all along has been speaking without benefit of quotation marks. The *conteur* purportedly possesses a "great notebook" carrying the secret of the now-dead subject's identity. "The secret is there, in these pages, woven out of syllables and images" ["Le secret est là, dans ces pages, tissé par des syllabes et des images"] (12), the *conteur* assures us, and immediately takes up the narrative again – still without benefit of quotation marks.

Of quotation marks, Jacques Derrida says, "Once [they] demand to appear, they don't know where to stop... not content merely to *surround* the performance [speech act]... they divide it, rework its body and its insides, until it is distended, diverted, out of joint, then reset member by member, word by word, realigned in the most diverse configurations."[3] Their absence at the outset of Ben Jelloun's narrative marks the narrative to follow as a free-floating "event," in constant struggle to liberate itself from historical, social, and cultural restrictions, from determinations that would rework, reconfigure, and realign it in accord with others' preformulated ideas.

This chapter will examine the various forms of this agonistic encounter, while taking into account the mode of popular story-telling suggested by the missing quotation marks, for the narrative is composed almost wholly of a series of tales related by a succession of story-tellers. Most of the narrative, with the exception of intercalated dialogue, lacks quotational marking. This oral character of Ben Jelloun's narrative attests to his contestation (transformation) of Western narrative and his intertextual borrowings from Arab and Middle Eastern folk culture.

In the present chapter, I will consider how Ben Jelloun sets out to free his narrative from cultural and literary constraints and to extend it through intertexual borrowings. I will look at two of the many stories being told. The first section of this chapter will center on the principal story – that of Ahmed/Zahra – which deals with the question of the Arab woman, her voice, her sexuality; section two will analyze the tale of the Troubadour, occurring late in the narrative, with regard to how Ben Jelloun creates an interval for writing that becomes the scene of the text.

First, to the principal or frame story. The tale commences before the birth of Ahmed, the protagonist. His father felt a malediction weighing over him, for all his offspring had turned out to be girls, whom he rejected. His shame grew as each successive birth elicited jeers from his younger brothers who, with the lack of a male child, stood to inherit two-thirds of the wealth of their brother. Obsessed by the need for a male inheritor, he consulted doctors, quacks, healers, and sorcerers. He put his wife through a frightful regime of spells and cures until she was worn out. But each new birth brought another girl. "Daughter by daughter their hatred of the body grew, they were carried into the darknesses of life" ["Fille par fille jusqu'à la haine du corps, jusqu'aux ténèbres de la vie"] (19). The father decided finally to make an end to "fatality" ("d'en finir avec la fatalité") and rejected all those who exploited him. He had a dream in which death visited him in the guise of a youth who seemed one moment a young man, the next a young woman. Inspired by this dream, with his wife's complicity he arranged for an old midwife to deliver the newborn as a male, whatever its sex. At the birth of his eighth child, the midwife announces a boy. The father, though observing a girl, is so taken with the force of make-believe that he "sees" a boy, rejoices, and throws a feast remembered to this day.

Ahmed is raised as a boy, doted upon, with great ceremony passed from one stage of masculine development to another – even circumcision (with the connivance of a barber and blood provided by the father's slashed finger). Growing up "according to the law of the father" ["selon la loi du père"] (32), Ahmed enters fully into the deception, and strives to emulate a male in speech and bearing; (s)he asserts her authority over her sisters; to her parents' consternation (s)he even insists on marrying. Upon the death of her father (s)he becomes master of the house and takes to wife her cousin Fatima, a lame epileptic, who lives with her in seclusion from both families. Fatima willingly accepts a life without sexuality, sensing, and finally learning, Ahmed's secret. Ahmed comes to hate Fatima, while the latter renounces life and, through self-neglect, lets herself die. Ahmed withdraws into reclusion. Succeeding events are tenuous, but the story-tellers affirm that Ahmed eventually decides to leave her life of deception and to rediscover the woman within her. By one account, (s)he wanders through the country and finally joins a circus. When a male dancer who masquerades as a woman quits, the circus head, Abbas, proposes that Ahmed replace him. (S)he appears on stage dressed first as a man but leaves to reappear as a *femme fatale*, Lalla Zahra. (S)he becomes the star of the circus.

At this point (we are more than three-fifths of the way through the narrative), the *conteur* disappears and his tale is taken up by three aged personages among his listeners: Salem, Amar, and Fatouma, each of whom offers his or her version of the end of the story of Ahmed/Zahra. They are finally joined by the Blind Troubadour, who in turn tells his story.

I
Veiled woman and veiled narrative

A great deal has been written about the privileges accruing to males and the exploitation of women in the Islamic societies of the Maghreb and the Middle East. This situation comprises part of a much broader system of exploitation, coming not solely from forces within these societies, but from their interaction with forces outside – most specifically, from the so-called First World of the West.[4]

Since the appearance of Kateb Yacine's *Nedjma* in 1956 and Rachid Boudjedra's *La Répudiation* in 1969, as well as in the more recent work of women authors such as Assia Djebar (Algeria), Evelyne Accad (Lebanon), and Nawal el Saadawi (Egypt), the sexual exploitation of Muslim women has provided a recurrent theme in North African and Middle Eastern narratives in French and Arabic. In few Maghrebian narratives, excepting the work of certain women authors including those mentioned, is the problem of sexuality more graphically explored, however, with all its ties to extended social and political problems, and linked more indissolubly with literary revolt, than in Tahar Ben Jelloun's *The Sandchild*.[5]

The main character of Ben Jelloun's narrative writes to her anonymous correspondent, "To be a woman is a natural infirmity to which everyone accommodates. To be a man is an illusion and a violence that everything justifies and privileges. To be, in a word, is an act of defiance" ["Etre femme est une infirmité naturelle dont tout le monde s'accommode. Etre homme est une illusion et une violence que tout justifie et privilège. Etre tout simplement est un défi"] (94). The oppositions here are reflected in the larger context of the relations of power obtaining between Western societies and the so-called emergent societies of the "Third World." The West has historically served as the source of definition that has posited the non-West as object and constituted itself as subject through the non-West's negation.[6] Such a process evinced itself in the phenomenon of colonial rule.

In my study of Djebar's *L'Amour, la fantasia*, we have amply seen the nature of the historical encounter of Maghrebian society and Western society (most particularly French) and how that encounter has had an impact on the constitution of gender difference. We have also considered the implications of the attempt of the French authorities to unveil the woman, as a means of destructuring Algerian society. Finally, we have looked in some detail at the practice of veiling and the question of the gaze. Ben Jelloun's depiction of woman emphasizes the indigenous situation of women of the Maghreb under Islam.

The process of unmaking and remaking the female subject (or the fact of her never having been constituted as subject in the first place, except by being manipulated to serve the purposes of the male, indigenous and foreign) and her emergence from a void of absence provide the principal motif of Ben Jelloun's narrative. It is closely related to the motif of hermaphroditism, with which it simultaneously unfolds. These two motifs allegorize the unmaking/remaking by the feminine and postcolonial marginals of traditional, magisterial narratives of legitimation and most particularly of the infrastructures supporting the male, Eurocentric discourse of power.

The female persona of Ben Jelloun's principal character, Ahmed/Zahra, inhabits precisely that placeless place of which Derrida speaks in his discussion of Blanchot (see p. 52 above). She relates her story in the "voiceless narrative" of the Arab woman. Ahmed, her male persona, answers to the demands of external authority, the exigencies of the conventional forces of literary/cultural law and order, while Zahra, the veiled woman, "replies" in the etymological (and modern French) sense of folding back into herself and remaining silent and hidden, inaccessible: "I am myself the shadow and the light that gives it birth, the master of the house... and the guest... the look that seeks itself and the mirror, I am and I am not that voice that adapts itself and accustoms itself to my body, my face wrapped in the veil of that voice" ["Je suis moi-même l'ombre et la lumière qui la fait naître, le maître de la maison... et l'invité,... le regard qui se cherche et le miroir, je suis et ne suis pas cette voix qui s'accommode et prend le pli de mon corps, mon visage enroulé dans le voile de cette voix"] (44–45). The voice, which is the speaking voice of the subject, detaches itself from the speaker, such that the words have no source, no origin, giving rise to a series of oppositions of which the subject is (and is not) composed: "I am the architect and the place of habitation; the tree and the sap; I and a male other; I and a female other" ["Je suis l'architecte et la demeure; l'arbre et la sève; moi et un autre; moi et une autre"] (46).

The story of Ahmed/Zahra is recounted by the multiple voices of a series of story-tellers who often refer to his/her alleged diaries. These "narratorial voices," to use Blanchot's term, convey to the extradiegetic world of readers and critics an arbitrary, agreed-upon knowledge of something – event, historical sequence, identity, place, and time. These voices, along with the male persona of Ahmed, articulate things that respond to pre-existent ideas, concepts, and systems, things as they "ought to be": for example, the birth of a male heir and his assumption of the law of the father that "affirms" the system of the male "right" to succession in Islamic society. In similar fashion, the voices of the story-tellers and the omniscient narrator *appear* to tell things in a telling way, to order and organize things as they are or are conventionally expected to be in regard to the telling: that is, the revelation of truths, of the identity of the subject, of the adherence of things and events within the novel to the system of things and events as they "ought to be" outside the novel – Islamic custom and law, in the first instance; the Western law of the narrative and the discourse of power, in the second.

This surface stability soon dissolves, however, for nothing abides by the law in this lawless novel. The narrative refuses to be told in a coherent, definitive way, and the silence of the voiceless narrative of Zahra comes to reverberate louder than the voiced narrative (narratorial voices) of Ahmed and the story-tellers. Hence, the reader, given entry into "the placeless place where the work is silent" (Derrida), is doubly privileged by being introduced to the voiceless narratives, placeless places in Ben Jelloun's work that are redolent of the repressed significations of postcolonial society.

The voiceless narrative of Zahra evokes the state of aphonia in which woman exists in traditional Arab society. Zahra's story, while evolving around the unmaking and remaking of the female subject, as I proposed earlier, also evolves around the unmaking/remaking of the traditional narrative of legitimation, as well as the relentless deconstruction of a coherent (male) subject/narrative. In an extended sense, Zahra becomes for Ben Jelloun a privileged metaphor for the postcolonial author striving to reconstruct an idiom expressive of her/his own perceptions and cultural specificity out of the discourse inherited from the French colonial antagonists.

The woman in traditional Arab societies like that of Morocco, as we have noted in the previous chapter, is in many ways silenced and silent.[7] She is traditionally veiled and draped, in the eternal posture of avertment, a state tellingly represented in the photograph on the dust-jacket of the first edition of *L'Enfant de sable*, which shows two women covered from head to foot in black djellabas, flitting like shadows from one darkened doorway into another. It is only the male who moves openly in the external world, whose gaze is permitted. Malek Alloula's *The Colonial Harem*, which reproduces postcards of the colonial era sent, during the first three decades of this century, by French voyagers/voyeurs to their families and friends in France, deals principally with the gaze. He characterizes such postcards, which take as their subject prostitutes, entertainers, or dancers in harem-like settings, as resulting from an act of compensation that seeks vengeance for the inaccessibility of the world of traditional Algerian women closed to foreigners. The gaze in such a case, however, is not that of the Algerian man but of the European. It derives from exoticism which, as Alloula says, is always a function of the other's gaze (*The Colonial Harem*, 129, n11), and from voyeurism, which is a gaze from afar (without presence), occurring in a setting of absence (*Ibid.*, 86).[8]

The male gaze, the dominant gaze, a trope for authoritarian discourse, as Nancy Miller phrases it, evokes vision that delimits.[9] Just as the Western discourse of the father circumscribes the North African male, and just as the male colonial gaze fixes the female, so traditional Arab discourse fixes and circumscribes the Arab woman. Stephen Heath describes the forbidden female gaze in a Western context in this way:

> What then of the look for the woman, of women subjects in seeing?
> The reply given by psychoanalysis is from the phallus. If the woman
> looks, the spectacle provokes, castration is in the air, the Medusa's
> head is not far off; thus, she must not look, is absorbed on the side of
> the seen, seeing herself seeing herself, Lacan's femininity.[10]

Heath, following the interpretation of several contemporary psychoanalysts, describes the woman's gaze as provocative, assertive to the point of being castrating. From a traditional male perspective, the woman is only to be seen. This view seems to apply equally well to traditional Arab society.

Zahra resists being fixed and situated by the male gaze, by the patronymic "dialectics of power" (Miller, *Subject to Change*, p. 164). The opening paragraph of *The Sandchild* describes how, in having renounced the male persona, Zahra has renounced "the place of the father" (10) and leads a solitary existence in a darkened room, avoiding the light of day, of lamps, even of the full moon, because it threatens her with exposure: "It stripped him [Ahmed/Zahra] bare, penetrated his skin and uncovered the shame and secret tears that lay beneath. He sensed it passing over his body like a flame that would consume his masks, a blade that would slowly strip off the veil of flesh that maintained between him and the others the necessary distance" ["Elle le [Ahmed/Zahra] dénudait, pénétrait sous sa peau et y décelait la honte et les larmes secrètes. Il la sentait passer sur son corps comme une flamme qui brûlerait ses masques, une lame qui lui retirerait lentement le voile de chair qui maintenait entre lui et les autres la distance nécessaire"] (7).

The placeless place Zahra inhabits distances her from others – those of the world about her who mistakenly identify her as Ahmed and who situate her as male, and those who would reinscribe her, should she be unveiled, in the defined "space" of an other – that of woman submissive to paternal edict. As an alternative to the veil, Zahra seeks distance. To preserve her self, distance from others is "necessary." Otherwise, s(he) "would be thrust nude and defenseless between the hands of those whose curiosity, suspicion and even tenacious hatred had ceaselessly pursued him; they refused to accept the silence and intelligence of this figure that disturbed them by its very authoritarian and enigmatic presence" ["il serait projeté nu et sans défenses entre les mains de ceux qui n'avaient cessé de le poursuivre de leur curiosité, de leur méfiance et même d'une haine tenace; ils s'accommodaient mal du silence et de l'intelligence d'une figure qui les dérangeait par sa seule présence autoritaire et énigmatique"] (7–8). The silence is of otherness; presence is absence. The blade of light metaphorizes the castrating knife that would unveil the flesh of the false male. Her sequestration behind the mask of the male parodies the veiled woman by countering the religious, socially imposed prohibition against the female gaze with an act bearing against the ideology of (male) desire.

The effect of distancing functions on several levels in the narrative of Ben Jelloun. The sole female in the succession of story-tellers, Fatouma, whom numerous details suggest as being an avatar of Zahra herself, speaks of her life, during which she had trod an endless road: "Countries and centuries have passed before my eyes" ["Des pays et des siècles sont passés devant mon regard"] (163). She admits, however, that she has invented all these travels – "All these travels, all these nights without dawns, without mornings, I fabricated them in a narrow, circular, high room. A room on the terrace. The terrace was on a hill and the hill was painted on a pale red silk cloth" ["Tous ces voyages, toutes ces nuits sans aurores, sans matins, je les ai fabriqués dans une chambre étroite, circulaire, haute. Une chambre sur la terrasse. La terrasse était sur une colline et la colline était peinte sur un tissu de soie rouge blafard"] (164). The narrative, like the character, becomes ever more distanced, elusive: first through revelation that these travels are invented and then that the place where they were invented was itself, like fiction, a product of artistic creation – a painted object.

Fatouma relates a pilgrimage to Mecca that resulted in an ocean voyage in which she felt suspended "in the immediate moment" ["dans l'instant immédiat"] (166). Upon her return she decided not to go back to her family house but to disguise herself as a man:

> And then everything came to a halt, everything froze: the instant became a room, the room became a sunlit day, the time an old carcass forgotten in this cardboard box, in this box there are old mismatched shoes; a handful of new nails, a Singer sewing machine that runs on its own power, an aviator's glove taken off a dead man, a spider that had taken up its permanent abode in the bottom of the box, a Minora razorblade, a glass eye, and also the inevitable dilapidated mirror that had rid itself of all its images, moreover all the objects in the box come from its own, unique imagination, since it extinguished itself, since it became a simple piece of glass, it gives no more objects, it emptied itself during a long absence... I know presently that the key to our story is among these old things... I don't dare forage for fear of having my hand torn off by some mechanical jaws that, in spite of their rustiness, still function... they don't come from the mirror but from its double... I forgot to tell you about it, in fact I didn't forget but it was owing to superstition... so much the worse... We will not leave this room without finding the key, and for that it will be necessary to evoke, if only by allusion, the double of the mirror... Don't look around for it; it is not in this room, at least it is not visible. It's a peaceful garden with rose laurels, smooth stones that capture and hold the light, this garden is also frozen, suspended, it is secret, its path is secret, its existence known only by rare persons, those who have familiarized themselves with eternity, seated over there on a flagstone that keeps the day intact, held by their look; they hold the threads of the beginning and the end; the flagstone closes the entry to the garden, the garden gives onto the sea, and the sea swallows and carries off all the stories that are born and die between the flowers and the roots of the plants... as for the day, it has taken into itself, into its

space, the summer and winter, they are there mixed with that same light.

[Et puis tout s'est arrêté, tout s'est figé: l'instant est devenu une chambre, la chambre est devenue une journée ensoleillée, le temps une vieille carcasse oubliée dans cette caisse en carton, dans cette caisse il y a de vieilles chaussures dépareillées; une poignée de clous neufs, une machine à coudre Singer qui tourne toute seule, un gant d'aviateur pris sur un mort, une araignée fixée dans le fond de la caisse, une lame de rasoir Minora, un oeil en verre, et puis l'inévitable miroir en mauvais état et qui s'est debarrassé de toutes ses images, d'ailleurs tous ces objets dans la caisse sont de sa propre et seule imagination, depuis qu'il s'est éteint, depuis qu'il est devenu un simple morceau de verre, il ne donne plus d'objets, il s'est vidé durant une longue absence... Je sais à présent que la clé de notre histoire est parmi ces vieilles choses... Je n'ose pas fouiller de peur de me faire arracher la main par des machoires mécaniques qui, malgré la rouille, fonctionnent encore... elles ne proviennent pas du miroir mais de son double... j'ai oublié de vous en parler, en fait je n'ai pas oublié mais c'est par superstition... tant pis... Nous ne sortirons pas de cette chambre sans trouver la clé, et pour cela il va falloir évoquer ne serait-ce que par allusion le double du miroir... Ne le cherchez pas des yeux; il n'est pas dans cette chambre, du moins il n'est pas visible. C'est un jardin paisible avec des lauriers-roses, des pierres lisses qui captent et gardent la lumière, ce jardin est figé lui aussi, suspendu, il est secret, son chemin est secret, son existence n'est connue que de très rares personnes, celles qui se sont familiarisées avec l'éternité, assises là-bas sur une dalle qui maintient le jour intact, retenu dans leur regard; elles détiennent les fils du commencement et de la fin; la dalle ferme l'entrée du jardin, le jardin donne sur la mer, et la mer avale et emporte toutes les histoires qui naissent et meurent entre les fleurs et les racines des plantes... quant au jour, il a retenu en lui, dans son espace, l'été et l'hiver, ils sont mêlés à la même lumière.]   (166–68)

The elements in this conceit elaborated by Fatouma figure her silent narrative and the placeless place she inhabits. It is a place where an instant in time becomes a moment frozen in space, likened to a box full of unrelated and useless objects – mismatched (shoes), bearing within them power/signification without relation to an external source (the Singer sewing machine), bereft of context and function (a dead aviator's glove, a glass eye). The objects are described as being formerly images in a mirror that has rid itself of them and is itself transformed into an object without reflection ("a simple piece of glass"). The box described by Fatouma is inexplicably modified by the deictic "this" (*cette*), suggesting a metaphor for the book the reader holds or the manuscript in which Fatouma (Zahra) kept her journal. The mirror, an object of specularity, reflection, and representation, evokes the conventional narrative that is now emptied out, exhausted of its store of images, an object that can be "seen through." On two occasions, narratives in the story (apparently the *grand cahier* that holds the story of Zahra) are described as being emptied of their word-images – first carried off by insects and washed away by rain (107–08), later effaced by the moonlight (201). The objects lying scrambled and unrelated in the box-narrative of the writer take on importance in and of themselves. Freed of their delimiting frame, they are metamorphosed into pure incorporeal event, liberated from history and representation. Thus, they figure the silent narrative of the North African woman as well as that of the postcolonial Maghrebian writer, in the process of liberating themselves from the ideological underpinnings of male Eurocentric narrative.

Michel Foucault speaks of a neutral "meaning-event" requiring a special grammar that emphasizes not the predicate but the verb, which distributes everything around two asymmetrical and unstable poles: the infinitive mode and the present tense. The present tense undergoes displacement in the operation of the "meaning-event," while the infinitive is endlessly repeated.[11] The "key" to the story (presumably the key to the "reading" of the silent narrative) lies in the box-narrative, protected by "mechanical jaws" that threaten anyone reaching into it. The "jaws" come, we are told, from the double of the mirror, described as a peaceful and enchanted garden, the *locus amoenus* of legend, from which neither light nor sound emerge. It is a secret place where stories are born and die, where the narrative of the Arab woman is uttered in silence.

If the mirror emptied of images (now plain glass) is conventional narrative shorn of its ideological and representational function, the double of the mirror may suggest a reverse or counternarrative that, according to Fatouma's description, sets a trap. The trap may lie in wait for a reader, seeking the coherence of traditional narrative and the "key" to the story, who suddenly finds her/himself seized by the mechanical jaws of disrupted discourse. But the trap also appears to be set for Zahra's avatar, the teller-character Fatouma. In the paragraph following the description of the garden, Fatouma says:

> I have learned thus *to be* in a dream and *to make* of my life a story of
> pure invention, a tale that recalls what really happened. Is it out of

boredom, out of lassitude that one takes on *another life*, thrown over the body like a marvelous djellaba, a magic garment, a mantle, celestial cloth worked with stars, color and light?

[J'ai appris ainsi *à être* dans le rêve et *à faire* de ma vie une histoire entièrement inventée, un conte qui se souvient de ce qui s'est réellement passé. Est-ce par ennui, est-ce par lassitude qu'on se donne *une autre vie* mise sur le corps comme une djellaba merveilleuse, un habit magique, un manteau, étoffe du ciel, paré d'étoiles, de couleurs et de lumière?]   (168; my emphasis)

The infinitive, through its suggestion of unending repetition of events, posits Fatouma's existence/life as pure meaning-event unconfined by borders, just as existence equated with dream evokes that other life with its marvelous, free-floating qualities.

With the conjunction "thus" (*ainsi*), Fatouma links her experience of the mirror's double to dream and story-telling, which, paradoxically, through non-empirical narrative (fiction), recount "what really happened." On the surface, such a description would fail to distinguish counternarrative from conventional narrative were it not for the particularity of Fatouma's invention, which entails a story of masquerade that reverses the traditional narrative of male domination in Islamic society by allowing a woman, through disguise as a man, to dominate in her turn.

Nonetheless, we have thus far come no closer to understanding the nature of the trap set for Fatouma by her own counternarrative. Seeking further, we encounter an abrupt allusion to the harshness of social reality that clashes with the tranquility and enchantment of the secret garden: "Since my seclusion, I witness, mute and immobile, the emptying out of my country: the men and History, plains and mountains, the prairies and even the sky. The women and children remain. One might say that they remain to watch over the country but they watch over nothing" ["Depuis ma réclusion, j'assiste, muette et immobile, au déménagement de mon pays: les hommes et l'Histoire, les plaines et les montagnes, les prairies et même le ciel. Restent les femmes et les gosses. On dirait qu'ils restent pour garder le pays, mais ils ne gardent rien"] (168). This observation, alluding to the problem in non-Western societies such as those of the North African littoral, where immigration to Europe has resulted in the flight of the male population, presents an ironic parallel between the Western narrative undermined (emptied out) by the postcolonial writer/story-teller and the process of social vitiation of the Maghreb resulting from Western encroachment. The Maghreb, like a reverse pendant of the mirror, has been emptied out, has become plain glass, whose silvering (*tain*, substance) has worn away and through which the gaze of the European other can pass unimpeded. The power of the European other over the Maghreb, like its power over narrative (by which it seeks to contextualize and delimit words and images within a determinant structure), works to dissolve the Maghreb's opacity, to naturalize its "foreignness," strangeness, and specificity.

Fatouma goes on to describe the poverty and plight of those left behind, particularly the female children: "To be born a boy is a lesser ill... To be born a girl is a calamity, a misfortune placed negligently on the path by which death passes at the end of the day" ["Naître garçon est un moindre mal... Naître fille est une calamité, un malheur qu'on dépose négligemment sur le chemin par lequel la mort passe en fin de journée"] (168). She then reveals the trap of her counternarrative:

> Oh! I am not teaching you anything. My story is ancient... it dates from before Islam... My word carries little weight... I am only a woman, I have no more tears. They taught me early that a woman who cries is a lost woman... I have acquired the will of never being that woman who cries. *I have lived in the illusion of another body, with the clothes and the emotions of someone other. I deceived everyone until the day when I perceived that I was deceiving myself. Then I began to look around me and what I saw profoundly shocked me, overwhelmed me.*

> [Oh! je ne vous apprends rien. Mon histoire est ancienne... elle date d'avant Islam... Ma parole n'a pas beaucoup de poids... Je ne suis qu'une femme, je n'ai plus de larmes. On m'a tôt appris qu'une femme qui pleure est une femme perdue... J'ai acquis la volonté de n'être jamais cette femme qui pleure. *J'ai vécu dans l'illusion d'un autre corps, avec les habits et les émotions de quelqu'un d'autre. J'ai trompé tout le monde jusqu'au jour où je me suis aperçue que je me trompais moi-même. Alors je me suis mise à regarder autour de moi et ce que j'ai vu m'a profondément choquée, bouleverseé.*]   (168–69; my emphasis)

Fatouma has passed her life disguised as a man, living "in a glass cage, in a lie, in scorn of others" ["dans une cage de verre, dans le mensonge, dans le mépris des autres" (169)]. She sheds her mask, quits the room, and encounters a demonstration by starving street urchins confronting "the forces of order" (169). In the ensuing mêlée, she is wounded. The women around her treat her with compassion. A shift occurs at this point – the counternarrative opens onto social praxis and rebellion. She turns to the world and to womanhood: "From that day on, I call myself Fatouma" ["Depuis ce jour, je m'appelle Fatouma"] (169–70).

As she realizes, in masquerading as a man Fatouma reverses the role of male domination by dominating in her turn. By this means, however, the trap set by the counternarrative and counteraction of the second-level narrator has sprung, for, while she has dominated, it has been *as a male*. Domination in these terms becomes nothing more than the extension of the male narrative. The woman has merely arrogated to herself the power that others (males) hold over her (as a woman). The error Fatouma perceives herself to have committed, in playing man, is to have denied the feminine – her inner otherness, as opposed to the outer otherness of disguise. By extension, the analogy suggests itself that the Western other is to the Maghrebian writer as Ahmed is to Zahra.

Being woman as self-in-difference

Ben Jelloun's narrative ostensibly takes as its project the undermining of structuring values in traditional Moroccan society. He puts into his character's mouth (the notebook of Ahmed/Zahra) a questioning of the nature of social being dictated by authoritarian rule: her statement – "To be, in a word, is an act of defiance" (94) – addresses the disparate expectations and acceptances regarding male–female roles while also suggesting the contestatory nature of an alternative discourse that privileges being in itself as distinguished from socially constituted being. Zahra sets out "to find the words of return" ["de trouver les mots de retour"] (98) that will lead her back to her female being. In asking the question "To resemble oneself, is it not to become different?" ["Ressembler à soi-même, n'est-ce pas devenir différent?"] (104), she posits the reconstitution of self as self-in-difference as opposed to the social construct of self as other-object.

The Sandchild questions what strategy might allow the Arab woman to escape the structuring values of male prohibitions and custom while avoiding the trap of a mere reversal of the male–female binary relation (the assumption of the male discourse by the female) that leaves the underlying ideological system undisturbed. Is it possible to develop an effective counterdiscourse, to constitute a self-in-difference?

Zahra seeks to will her exclusion from family, society, (masculine) body (99). By this willed exclusion from system ("My time has nothing to do with calendar time, completed or not" ["Mon temps n'a rien à voir avec celui du calendrier, achevé ou non"], she says [105]), she strives to escape appropriation by the authoritarian "other":

These days I am seeking to free myself. From what in fact? From the
fear that I have stored up? From that layer of mist that served me as
veil and covering. From that relation with the other in me [which is
the male other], the one who writes me and gives me the strange
impression of still being of this world? ... It is time to be born again. In
fact I am not going to change but simply to return to myself.

[Aujourd'hui je cherche à me délivrer. De quoi au juste? De la peur que
j'ai emmagasinée? De cette couche de brume qui me servait de voile et
de couverture? De cette relation avec l'autre en moi, celui qui m'écrit
et me donne l'étrange impression d'être encore de ce monde? ... Il est
temps de naître de nouveau. En fait je ne vais pas changer mais
simplement revenir à moi.]   (111)

The voiceless person in the text speaks – the narrative voice, using
Blanchot's distinction, of the silent woman. In refusing male authoritarian structures, Zahra excludes the arbitrary principles that empower
them, the truth functional operation that legitimates patriarchal metanarratives by legislating the conditions of truth, by defining the criteria
for judging what is true and what is false, what is acceptable and what is
unacceptable, for validating the sexual division and hierarchization laid
down by Islamic law. Zahra's act of exclusion, her "willed return to self,"
is tantamount to negating negation.

As noted earlier, Zahra's story revolves around the unmaking of the
female subject as defined by the male narrative of legitimation and the
remaking of the female subject in terms that respect its specificity and
difference. As I have suggested, in Ben Jelloun's narrative, Zahra, the
silent woman in Maghrebian society, becomes the privileged metaphor
for the postcolonial author writing in a European tongue, who also exists
under threat of being veiled and negated by another's discourse. Just as
Ahmed the male serves as mask/veil (that is, a veil donned out of volition)
for Zahra, however, so the succession of storytellers/narrators, who seemingly adapt to the demands of conventional narrative, serve as masks/
veils for the postcolonial author. Both Zahra and Ben Jelloun exist somewhere below or apart from the authorized discourse. We again recall Mallarmé's description, cited above, of alternative languages that flourish
below the surface of common discourse.

A dilemma faces the woman in traditional, Islamic society and the
postcolonial author seeking to create an alternative language. Fatouma,
one of Zahra's avatars, fears losing "the thread of the present" ["le fil du
présent"] and being shut up in the "famous luminous garden from which

not a single word must filter" ["ce fameux jardin lumineux d'où pas un mot ne doit filtrer"] (170). If the secret garden is the place where the death of narrative transpires, that is, the death of voiced – male, social – narrative, it is also the placeless place where voiceless narrative is born. One faces the choice of either living in the world and using another's narrative or existing out of the world in a placeless place where one falls silent, voiceless. Fatouma longs for involvement in the present, in the (voiced) narrative of her own womanhood. The postcolonial writer faces the same dilemma of voicing another's narrative or falling silent. The question again arises as to whether an alternative exists. Is there a possibility of manipulating the other's discourse so as to turn it to one's own purpose? of creating an effective counterdiscourse, an alternative language allowing one to narrate the feminine, one's otherworldness, one's difference?

In speaking of difference in postcolonial (feminist) discourse, I have cited in my introduction the words of Abdelkebir Khatibi to the effect that the Arab author writing in French must succeed in creating a new space for writing by inscribing herself in the "interval" between identity (sameness, assimilation) and difference (radical alterity to Western culture). The result is a discourse of "absolute outsidedness." Here, in *The Sandchild*, in the search for an alternative language, and for a discourse of "absolute outsidedness," Ahmed/Zahra's story comes together with the tale of the Blind Troubadour.

II

In creating such an interval as Khatibi speaks of, Ben Jelloun develops a discourse that takes as intertexts two non-Western works: the writings of Jorge Luis Borges and the Middle Eastern (Indo-Persian–Arabic) *Alf Layla wa Layla* or *The Thousand and One Nights*. Borges' fictional counterpart who appears in *The Sandchild* in the guise of the Blind Troubadour, a blind man who "sees," and *The Thousand and One Nights* with its teller who does not finish, exemplify respectively the voiceless voices that speak and the discourse or narrative without end. These intertexts will serve as touchstones for my discussion of how Ben Jelloun counters and reforms the system of traditional narrative, in the course of which he rejects the reductive ideology that underlies it.

The Blind Troubadour, who joins the story-tellers Amar and Salem (chapter 17) while they meditate on the tale just told by Fatouma, relates in his turn how he has set forth in search of a mysterious Arab woman who visited him in his library in Buenos Aires. His narration, starting out in a fairly straightforward manner, undergoes permutations, shifts in a way that often makes it difficult to comprehend who is speaking, and at times becomes so entangled that it is impossible to straighten out. Chapter 17 concludes, for example, with the Blind Troubadour describing gifts given him by the mysterious woman, including a dream narrative. The first words of the opening paragraph of chapter 18 tell us, "The dream was precise and very dense. I was setting forth in search of long and black tresses" ["Le rêve était précis et très dense. Je partais à la recherche d'une longue et noire chevelure"] (191). With these words we embark on a confusing, discontinuous narrative that appears to be a dream narrative (allusions to that effect occur and it has the undeniable stamp of dream-work), whose central character is a male (masculine agreements in French). But we confront a proliferation of possibilities in trying to identify the progenitor of the dream: the possibility that (1) the Blind Troubadour relates the dream of the mysterious woman in which he is dreamt by the character; that (2) the dream related is a direct retelling by the Blind Troubadour of his own dream; that (3) he and the mysterious woman are fused; that (4) more than one dream is being alluded to (perhaps both his and hers); that (5) the dream related is her dream of herself; that (6) everything is encompassed within a dream in which the Blind Troubadour dreams of her and her recitation of a dream (he calls her a "metaphor elaborated in a dream" ["métaphore élaborée dans un rêve"] 188); that (7) the dream is a dream of yet a third person: an unknown stranger (as the dream narrative breaks off, a new narrative – that comes to be attributable to the Blind Troubadour – begins: "Friends! You have heard the stranger with a show of patient hospitality" ["Amis! Vous avez écouté l'étranger avec la patience de votre hospitalité"] (194), and so forth.

The dream described in the narrative following the words "I was setting forth" *appears* to be the unknown woman's dream, the recitation of which she had left him (190), in which the allusions to the subject's library and a coin she has given to him seem to mark the Blind Troubadour as subject. Who, then, is the "stranger"? Does the Blind Troubadour address himself in the third person? To complicate matters, in the dream account the dreamer-subject has his sight and a "blind man" appears, who is one of the three characters who "participated in my story underway" ["(qui) faisaient partie de mon histoire en cours"] (192).

The reader can choose the likely hypothesis by remembering that the Blind Troubadour was formerly called a "stranger," etc. That hypothesis is, however, but one of several, and the narrative here as elsewhere conjoins, intricates, imbricates the threads of all these possibilities. Its structure resembles that of the medina described in the dream itself: "The medina presented itself to my eyes like an entanglement of places – streets and squares – where all miracles were possible" ["La médina se présentait à mes yeux comme un enchevêtrement de lieux – des rues et des places – où tous les miracles étaient possibles"] (192). Like the air space Rushdie describes as a "defining location" at the beginning of *The Satanic Verses*, where anything is possible, the medina serves Ben Jelloun as a metaphor for unconfined narrative space – more particularly space for the Arab woman and the postcolonial writer.

The Blind Troubadour's tale reflects two processes integral to the narrative of Ben Jelloun: (1) the interpenetration of characters, narrators, and authors, and (2) the folding into itself of a narrative, whereby the external becomes internal, the outside and inside become reversed. Let us look in turn at these two processes and their implications.

The interpenetration of characters, narrators, and authors

In the manuscript of Ahmed/Zahra read by Amar, the former speaks of his/her desire to escape – "To choose a discreet hour, a secret road, a soft light, a countryside where lovers, without past, without history, would be seated as in those Persian miniatures where everything appears marvelous, outside time" ["Choisir une heure discrète, une route secrète, une lumière douce, un paysage où des êtres aimants, sans passé, sans histoire, seraient assis comme dans ces miniatures persanes où tout paraît merveilleux, en dehors du temps] (157) – to make her way through the hedge to join the "old story-teller" (*vieux conteur*) on a precious carpet (158). Such an interpenetration of separate narrative realms marks one of the important structuring elements that engenders Ben Jelloun's doubling narrative.

Another instance occurs with the declaration of Fatouma that she lost the "great notebook," tried in vain to reconstitute it, and set out in search of the narrative of her former life, which she found being told by the *conteur* in the great square. The revelation of Fatouma's identity as Ahmed/Zahra introduces the anomaly of a second-level (intradiegetic) narrator simultaneously fulfilling the role of a third-level (metadiegetic) character.

The Blind Troubadour, whose intrusion in the tale takes up some twenty pages, provides the most curious examples of interpenetration of narrative levels in Ben Jelloun's text. From the outset, the text signals our initiation into a quixotic game with the words of the stranger who joins the story-tellers (second-level narrators) Ahmed and Salem: "The Secret is Sacred but is nonetheless somewhat ridiculous" ["Le Secret est sacré, mais il n'en est pas moins un peu ridicule" (171)], for the stranger draws this sentence word for word from Borges' short story, "The Sect of the Phoenix," and properly encloses it in quotation marks.[12] Several allusions in the succeeding pages link the Blind Troubadour to the historical Borges: the fact of his blindness and vocation as a writer, his life in Buenos Aires, knowledge of Spanish, livelihood as a librarian, his mention of Borges' character Stephen Albert in "The Garden of Forking Paths" as being one of his characters (he also cites an aphorism taken from the same story [181]), his allusion to an unnamed story from which he cites a passage (Borges' "The Circular Ruins"), the references to the "zahir," a coin that gives its name to one of Borges' stories, and his preponderant interest in esoterica ("I know... that the Zahir is the bottom of a well in Tetouan, as well as, according to Zotenberg, a vein running through the marble of one of the 1200 pillars in the mosque at Cordova" ["Je sais... que le Zahir est le fond d'un puits à Tetouan, comme il serait, selon Zotenberg, une veine dans le marbre de l'un des mille deux cents piliers à la mosquée de Cordoue"] 176). Yet, in Ben Jelloun's anomalistic manner, nothing is ever certain, for we concurrently encounter numerous allusions that problematize the Blind Troubadour's identity.

In addressing Amar and Salem, he speaks of being in their "tale" (*conte*), of coming from afar, "from another century, poured into one tale by another tale" ["d'un autre siècle, versé dans un conte par un autre conte"] (172), of having been "expulsed" from other tales (172). He declares that he is passing between dreams. Places, like dreams, become interchangeable, exist simultaneously and within each other just as tales within tales. He speaks of their frequenting a cafe in Marrakesh while at the same time finding themselves in the heart of Buenos Aires! During the visit of the unknown woman to his library in the latter city, he tells of having had the sensation of being a character in a book, even of being a book (177–78). The woman ("probably Arab") who visits him presents a letter of introduction from one of his (Borges') characters, Stephen Albert. Her voice recalls to him a voice he had previously heard in a book he had read – the voice of Tawaddud in *The Thousand and One Nights*.[13]

The Blind Troubadour operates on several levels: as a fictional replication of the historical author Jorge Luis Borges, he functions as one of the second-level (intradiegetic) narrators and is, in that function, a character in the tale of the first-level (extradiegetic) narrator; he functions also on various metadiegetic levels in his direct interaction with the character of the mysterious (Arab) woman visitor and participation as character in other stories (including his own and *The Thousand and One Nights*). When the Blind Troubadour enters the tale, it commences to fold back on itself. The pivotal figure of his unknown woman visitor, while on the same level as the Blind Troubadour, bears a strong resemblance to Ahmed/Zahra, for she speaks of like episodes in her life, like misfortunes and flight, and the Blind Troubadour has a vision of her tormented father. Moreover, he describes her as "a character or rather an enigma, two faces of a selfsame being" ["un personnage ou plutôt une énigme, deux visages d'un même être"] (178). He later refers to her as being from Morocco (184). We learn at the end of the narrative (taken up again and ended by the *conteur*), however, that Ahmed/Zahra is a fictional representation invented by the *conteur* and adapted to a Moroccan setting to tell the story of an Alexandrian woman's uncle, Bey Ahmed, who had undergone similar experiences (207–08).

Thus, the Blind Troubadour, who brings outside inside, is the device whereby levels of discourse are displaced and characters are put on the same level as their creators. His remark to the effect that he was the "prisoner of a character whom I would have been able to create if I had stayed a while longer in Morocco or in Egypt" ["prisonnier d'un personnage que j'aurais pu modeler si j'avais séjourné un peu plus longtemps au Maroc ou en Egypte"] (179) is an allusion to the two levels: fiction (first level) – the unknown woman/Bey Ahmed; and fiction of a fiction – Ahmed/Zahra (second level).

The most extreme instance of movement from one narrative level to another occurs when he speaks of himself as coming from, and having lived, a story whose concluding words he cites: it happens to be Borges' short story, "The Circular Ruins." Those words, which he says may help to unravel the enigma that unites him with the other narrators, describe a character, a magician awaiting death, who, desiring to dream into being a man, comes to understand that "he too was a mere appearance, that another was in the process of dreaming him" ["lui aussi était une apparence, qu'un autre était en train de le rêver"] (*Sandchild*, p. 173; Borges, *Labyrinth*, p. 50; my Englishing of Ben Jelloun's French translation).

What purpose does this interpenetration of narrative levels serve? The difficult demands exacted upon the reader push illogic and contradiction to the limit. We are refused the possibility of getting a fix on the narrators and characters, of making the story itself intelligible. The Blind Troubadour, referred to repeatedly as the "stranger," of foreign origin, whose tale turns on encounter, loss, and unending quest for a mysterious woman of Arabic origin, is homologous with the North African, at once subject of his proper narratives and object-Other (shadow without substance) of the narratives of Western society, recounting his "tale" in the language of another, menaced with the loss of his own culture and autonomous existence.

The description I have already cited of Ahmed/Zahra by the *conteur* in the opening paragraph of *The Sandchild* – "the veil of flesh that maintained between him and others the necessary distance" – adumbrates the movement of the narrative, motivates it in a Shklovskian sense, and articulates the development of narrators and characters, just as it valorizes the positive potential of alterity (serving the same purpose as Khatibi's interval or Serre's gap or *écart*) in regard to the North African writer himself, in his resistance to assimilation. The veil of flesh providing distance can also function as a protective covering that allows the North African writer to lead his own existence equidistant from sameness (assimilation) and otherness (alienation), to exist in the face of the power play of Western culture as well as of traditional Muslim culture.

Rather than action in *The Sandchild* becoming, in Jamesian terms, an illustration of character, Ben Jelloun's narrators/characters may be viewed as subserving the action, such that we encounter what Tzvetan Todorov has called an a-psychological narrative.[14] Considered grammatologically, by valorizing the predicate rather than the subject of the verb, by emphasizing intransitive action – even to the extent of threatening a loss of the psychological coherence of character – a-psychological narrative throws into relief the *event* itself. Historical process with its cause and effect relationship, in which events become subordinated to an overall narrative, is replaced by evenemential process, that is, a process consisting of discrete individual events. Character comes to represent thereby a story that is in the making or is potential – the story of the character's own life. Each new character we meet offers us a new story such that we find ourselves in a fictional world of "narrative-men," that is, characters that are inseparable from their story ["une histoire virtuelle qui est l'histoire de sa vie. Tout nouveau personnage signifie une nouvelle intrigue. Nous sommes dans le royaume des hommes-récits"] (Todorov, "Les hommes récit," p. 82). In *The Sandchild*, the story of a woman masquerading as a man, we confront narrative-(wo)men whose loss of psychological coherence is vital to the reversal of roles or rather the leveling of sexual differences. Also, as in *The Satanic Verses*, the tactic of leveling or equalization reflects what is occurring on the discursive level. The story of Ahmed/Zahra told by Ben Jelloun's succession of characters/narrators exhibits a variable relationship with preceding stories, which are always under revision, just as on the discursive level a process of revision goes unendingly on.

Folds of the narrative

What results from this process of a-psychological narrative, as in *The Thousand and One Nights*, is the enclosure of one story within another, or the phenomenon of embedding and embedded narrative, a consequence of which is, as Todorov reminds us, that characters can migrate from one story to another (*Ibid.*, 84). In *The Thousand and One Nights*, moreover, the narrative, passing through several degrees of embedding, ends, Borges tells us, by the story (of Scheherazade) embedding itself:

> None [no interpolation in *The Thousand and One Nights*] is more perturbing than that of the six hundred and second night, magical among all the nights. On that night, the king hears from the queen his own story. He hears the beginning of the story, which comprises all the others and also – monstrously – itself. Does the reader clearly grasp the vast possibility of this interpolation, the curious danger? That the queen may persist and the motionless king hear forever the truncated story of the *Thousand and One Nights*, now infinite and circular.
>
> [Ninguna (interpolación de *Las Mil y Una Noche* está) tan perturbadora como la de la noche DCII, mágica entre las noches. En esa noche, el rey oye de boca de la reina su propria historia. Oye el principio de la historia, que abarca a todas las demás, y también – de monstruoso modo –, a si misma. ¿Intuye claramente el lector la vasta posibilidad de esa interpolación, el curioso peligro? Que la reina persista y el immóvil rey oirá para siempre la trunca historia de *Las Mil y Una Noches*, ahora infinita y circular.][15]

Borges' recounting of the content of the 602nd tale calls for a striking aside that is, however, wonderfully relevant to Ben Jelloun's own writing techniques. Borges calls this interpolation "perturbing" in terms of its function, but it is perturbing as well to the reader who rushes off to the Burton translation that Borges consulted, for, instead of finding the 602nd tale as represented by Borges, she will find a completely unrelated tale. Why? Because the tale Borges speaks of does not exist – Borges has invented it! The word "interpolation" could not be more appropriate (*Webster's Dictionary* gives as the first meaning of the verb *interpolate* "to alter or corrupt… by inserting new or foreign matter").

That is precisely what Borges does, by creating his own non-existent version (a fictive fiction). To what end? So far as I see it, out of playfulness and a "perverse" sense of the world, he makes of *The Thousand and One Nights* a collection that, like many of his own tales, refuses closure. But he also does that which *The Thousand and One Nights* and Tahar Ben Jelloun do themselves: create tales that free themselves from boundaries (ironically, in this instance, by embedding) and hold the potential of serpentine movement, of gyrating in unforseen directions and even turning back on themselves.[16]

Ben Jelloun carries such a process of narrative embedding or enclosure – corresponding to the space of feminine enclosure – to its furthest reaches by embedding stories within stories to such a degree that levels meld; barriers separating characters and creators/tellers are breached and become traversible, fused, confused; and narrators/characters pass freely from one level to another, moving in and out of stories without impingement, just as we move in and out of dreams and in and out of the characters themselves. As the principal story-teller, the *conteur*, says, "It is useful to know that throughout the story there exist entryways and exits" ["c'est commode de savoir que dans toute histoire il existe des portes d'entrée ou de sortie"] (49). In fact, openings abound in *The Sandchild*: doors, gates, entryways, exits, windows, and shutters – openings that may also become closings. Many objects serve simultaneously to enclose and protect: walls, rooms, and hedges. On one level, these objects signify the disparity between the male and female condition: Ahmed/Zahra tells her father that her condition (of male) opens up doors for her (50), for in conservative Islamic societies the male can move freely, whereas the movement of women is sharply circumscribed by walls and closed doors. On the level of story-telling or discourse, a male narrator such as the *conteur* can move, male-like, in and out of stories, while Zahra, following the example of Scheherazade, must resort to stratagems to turn closure into a liberating discourse. Interestingly, the metaphor governing the structure of Ben Jelloun's narrative changes about a quarter of the way into it: the *conteur* remarks that, despite his intention to lead us through seven doors, he will make of the fourth door, the Bab El Had, the last, for the death of Ahmed's father changes her life. Henceforth the story will not pass through doors but "will turn in a circular street" ["Elle tournera dans une rue circulaire"] (62). The story will now pass through fissures and breaks: at the opening of chapter 6, entitled "The Forgotten Door" ["La porte oubliée"], the *conteur* remarks: "We must at present slip through breaches in the wall, forgotten openings" ["Nous devons à présent nous glisser par les brèches dans la muraille, les ouvertures oubliées"] (63).

The Sandchild is a discourse or narrative without end, that folds back on itself. The secret of the subject's identity at the beginning of the novel was said to be found in the "great notebook" possessed by the story-teller, "there, in these pages, woven out of syllables and images" ["là, dans ces pages, tissé par des syllabes et des images"] (12). We should indeed have been forewarned, for the secret was after all purely one of language: Ahmed at one point reveals his paper identity as he speaks of himself as being enclosed in an image (54); at another point the *conteur* speaks of the story as a blind man's dance in which one could fall at any moment, held up only by a few commas inserted by God (ostensibly the author [65]); finally, the *conteur* describes his story in theatrical terms – "Companions! The stage set is made out of paper! The story I recount to you is old wrapping paper" ["Compagnons! La scène est en papier! L'histoire que je vous raconte est un vieux papier d'emballage"] (126). The narrative is indeed susceptible to all of the vagaries of language under the pen of the author, whom his own character (The Blind Troubadour) calls "a contrebandist, a trafficker in words" ["un contrebandier, un trafiquant de mots"] (173); the Blind Troubadour designates himself as "the biographer of error and falsehood" ["le biographe de l'erreur et du mensonge"] (*Ibid.*). At its end, the instability of the narrative that has all along haunted us leaves its final mark: we are told that "the book was emptied of its writings by the full moon" ["le livre fut vidé de ses écritures par la pleine lune" (208–09)], washed clean, ready to be written over and over, endlessly. (A cluster of such metaphors of erasure or illegibility appears: the grand *cahier* [notebook] made undecipherable by tears that have dropped onto it [54]; letters whose signature is unreadable [59]; the "petits billets" [brief notes] of Ahmed that are unreadable or "strange" [89]; the crossed-out words in the anonymous correspondent's notes [96]; the insects carrying off words and images from the manuscript in disintegration, a process hastened by the stream that runs through its pages [107–09]; the mirror of Zahra that fogs over [115]; and so forth).

The structure of *The Sandchild* resembles the invaginated structure of which Derrida speaks in regard to Blanchot's *La Folie du jour* ("Living On," p. 97), another of whose avatars we find in *The Thousand and One Nights* – a structure I prefer to term *involuted*, which recalls its Latin root *involvere*, as well as its English derivatives *involvement* and *voluble*, implying not solely hidden involvement but being rolled inward at the edges, like a conch in which the whorls (volutes) are wound tightly around an axis that is concealed. The pauses between different narrations/story-tellers, that indicate a provisional end and provisionally a new beginning, may be seen as inner whorls or folds of this structure (see "Living on," p. 114). These pauses suggest a parallel with the phrase *qala al-rawi* ("the story-teller said") or *qala* (simply, "he said"), functioning as a marker in the Arabic of *The Thousand and One Nights*, as David Pinault points out, to indicate the termination of a tale-within-a-tale narrative recited by one of the characters or to signal a transition from poetry to prose or a shift from speech to straight narrative.[17]

Ben Jelloun does not counter the various dichotomies in the discourses of the Islamic faith system or of Western cultural systems by the simple act of reversal, for in such a case the binary oppositions that legitimize discourses of power – truth/falsity, male/female, for example – would merely be reaffirmed. The motif of hermaphroditism intricated in my preceding commentary, that operates as a rejection of the binary, is pervasive in *The Sandchild*. We encounter numerous allusions to men with women's breasts, bearded women, and the like; we recall the tenth-century poem describing a young girl hidden in the body of a man (190), also the description of Ahmed-Zahra as "two faces of a same being" ["deux visages d'un même être"] (178) – to enumerate just a few examples.

Hermaphroditism functions as a counter to the binary by the affirmation of that which is and is not, that is not either/or but both/neither. As a discursive tactic it corresponds to the seventh-century concept of *alieniloquium* – other speech, Ironia – the rhetorical category of *adoxos* in Hermagoras (the fifth category that stands outside the *doxos*), or the Sophist strategy of antilogic. G. B. Kerferd describes the latter as consisting "in causing the same thing to be seen by the same people now as possessing one predicate and now as possessing the opposite or contradictory predicate" – that which applied to sophistic rhetoric results in the articulation of the very same rhetorical proposition as being predicated simultaneously on mutually negating premises. Lyotard's concept of paralogism represents one of the most important reintroductions of sophistic rhetorical tactics into contemporary theories of oppositional discourse.[18] Of

Lyotardian *paralogism*, Fredric Jameson says that the object is not to find accommodation, but to sap the very foundations of previous science and knowledge from within. The rhetoric in which Lyotard communicates this struggle is contestatory, conflictual, and agonistic. It is the guerrilla action of the people on the margin, the non-Greek barbarians from without, against the repressive and ubiquitous order of the philosophically based thought of Aristotle and those who follow in his footsteps.[19]

Conclusion

The inside/outside, postcolonial text of *The Sandchild* resembles the deconstructionist text described by Derrida ("Living On," p. 84), constructed around a network of differential traces referring endlessly to something other than itself, scene of a spillover having no respect for margins, frames, or partitions, actively engaged in breaking down those infrastructures of resistance supporting ideological and literary systems that attempt to assign limits in accord with a male Eurocentric discourse of power. This discourse is reconfigured from a contiguous structure into a structure of substitution, in which a woman's space takes into its vortex, into itself (invaginates), the male linear narrative and plot. Ben Jelloun's tale points up the historical illusion of, the philosophical and epistemological insistence on, a fixed center, source or origin.[20] Zahra rejects that fixed center from which emanates the law of the father, the patriarchal law of Western narrative.

Female sexuality, without which there would be no story, is perhaps the primordial generative term in Ben Jelloun's *Sandchild*. The question necessarily arises as to what extent the author, by placing himself in the placeless place of the Arab woman, appropriates her place, her voiceless voice. No definitive answer is possible. He unavoidably appropriates the place of the woman in the way any male writing on/in the feminine does. To the extent that he is a postcolonial writer who has suffered under colonialism, however, his appropriation is qualified by empathy. He shares with the Arab woman the larger context of postcolonial awareness. In another sense, Ben Jelloun's very argument rests on the proposition that the suffix *-less*, qualifying woman's place and discourse, signifies that they are ultimately inappropriable ("*intraitable*," Lyotard would say[21]). Thus, the answer ultimately lies perhaps in his own narrative of impossibility, which speaks the secret languages of the Arab woman and the postcolonial writer, for which there are no adequations, no equivalents.

The inside/outside text of *The Sandchild* is indeed constructed around a network of differential traces. Each story or narrative segment contains traces of that which has preceded as well as of that to come, such that no story or segment is identical to itself but always somewhere else, present and absent simultaneously, never where or what it appears to be.

The *conteur* near the outset of his tale-journey describes the great square at Marrakesh as a "square where there occurs an exchange between the city and the country" ["place de l'échange entre la ville et la campagne"] (41);[22] it is the perfect site for story-telling, for it is a place of transition, center and not center, and its "exchanges" are woven out of the peripheral – a perfect Derridean place of *différance* and thus, by metonymy, the place of telling and the tale itself. The *conteur* calls this square a stage (*un étape*) on the journey (of the *conteur* and his listeners, of the tale itself), which corresponds to the "stage of adolescence" of Ahmed, which the *conteur* terms "a rather obscure period" of Ahmed's life that leaves in the book (the *grand cahier*) a "blank space, nude pages left thus in suspension, offered to the liberty of the reader" ["un espace blanc, des pages nues laissées ainsi en suspens, offertes à la liberté du lecteur"] (41–42). The ultimate differential text!

Another model for the narrative of Ben Jelloun is the fictional model proposed by Borges in "The Garden of Forking Paths." The character Stephen Albert describes to the narrator the solution of Ts'ui Pen, who has set out to write an infinite book. It must be circular in nature, like Borges' imaginary tale told by Scheherazade midway through *The Thousand and One Nights* when she embeds in it word for word the story of *The Thousand and One Nights*, in the middle of which she must recommence – infinitely. The novel Ts'ui Pen chose to write was a novel "forking in time, not in space" ("The Garden of Forking Paths," p. 26). As with traditional fictional narrative, when confronted with alternatives, one chooses one and omits the others, whereas Ts'ui Pen's narrative would choose all simultaneously: rather than one of the paths at a fork, all paths – the image of the universe in which there is no "uniform, absolute time" (*Ibid.*, p. 28).

One is struck by the similarity of Ben Jelloun's narrative, with its diverse twists and turns and varied endings, to that of Ts'ui Pen, which offers a choice of all possible paths. One is also reminded of how the Blind Troubadour, reading a narrative by Al Mo'atassim discovered in the fifteenth century, finds the meaning of seven keys left to him by Ahmed/Zahra to open the seven portals of the city: "I believe a *conteur* from the far

South tried to open these gates. Destiny or malevolence prevented this poor man from carrying out his task to the end" ["Je crois savoir qu'un conteur de l'extrême Sud a essayé de franchir ces portes. Le destin ou la malveillance empêcha ce pauvre homme d'accomplir jusqu'au bout sa tâche"] (189). This evident allusion to our *conteur* implies that either he lived simultaneously at the time of the medieval manuscript and in the twentieth century, or the manuscript speaks into the future, such that chronology shatters and the *conteur* wanders unimpeded through any and all times and places. The motif of "keys," moreover, that appears throughout the narrative (keys to the seven doors of the city, to the seven gardens of the soul [208], the key to the "secret" that lies within the box, the keys given to the Blind Troubadour by the unknown woman), by the close of the narrative leaves the reader thoroughly disbelieving of keys. This is indeed a significant accomplishment of Ben Jelloun's narrative, for it draws us in, spits us forth, and we are wiser for being no wiser, for realizing that "keys" do not exist and, if they do, are not to be trusted, for they either do not open doors or open doors onto illusion or nothingness.

Derrida also speaks of a person "committed to breaking down the various structures of resistance, his own resistance as such or as primarily the ramparts that bolster a system (be it theoretical, cultural, institutional, political or whatever)" ("Living On," pp. 84–85). In Ben Jelloun's text, we find a spillover that has no respect for margins, frames, or partitions, that breaks down those "structures of resistance" of ideological and literary systems that attempt to assign limits to it, and that renegotiates the form and content of narrative, partly through intertextual borrowings from Western as well as from Eastern texts.

By the reversible inside/outside maneuvers of his writing, Ben Jelloun literally and literarily turns inside out the conventional Western narrative form and, by extension, the relation of power between the West and the so-called Third World. Through just such devices as the interpenetration of narrative levels and the transformation of the tale into an event without end, the discrete elements of the conventional narrative disintegrate; it is reconfigured from a contiguous structure into a narrative of substitution, reconstituted out of the very flaws and imperfections that exist in the systems it counters. This tactic, to which I have given the name leveling, deprives the discourse of power of its positional value, exposes the arbitrary nature of the underlying philosophical precepts that legitimate it, and reveals it as just one discourse among many. Such a discursive operation–shared by the postcolonial authors I treat as well as by many others, such as the magical realist authors of Latin America and other regions of the world–has strong affinities with the work of experimental French novelists like Claude Simon, Alain Robbe-Grillet, and Georges Perec, and non-French writers like Italo Calvino, Thomas Pynchon, and Peter Ackroyd.

Earlier, I spoke of the discourses of Arab women, as well as of those of the male postcolonial authors, as narrating their difference, in however varied a manner. How different *is* difference if it responds to the difference already posited in a certain Western discourse on counternarration, running from Mallarmé to such contemporary writers as those I have just mentioned and critics such as Lyotard, Derrida, and Foucault – all of whom have used the convention of discourse against itself. The profound resemblance between this countertendency in Western thought and postcolonial writing suggests to me less that Western writing has recuperated postcolonial writing by bringing it in through the back door, so to speak, than that resistance against totalizing doctrine in whatever form it might take has resulted in homologous strategies of contestation. If we mistake homology for the reappropriation of postcolonial discourse by Western thought, as I have pointed out in my introduction, we also overlook the important exchange that has occurred in *both* directions between major Western oppositional critics, on the one hand, and postcolonial writers and the postcolonial situation, on the other; we forget that Lyotard's early writings grew out of his involvement with the Algerian opposition to French rule, that Derrida, Cixous, and many others have profound ties with non-Western cultures. As I have also indicated in my introduction, Roland Barthes has acknowledged his debt to Ben Jelloun's fellow Moroccan, Abdelkebir Khatibi, for making him aware of how much the Western semiotic enterprise has remained prisoner of the categories of Aristotelian totalism. He found Khatibi's originality to lie in the fact that Khatibi sets out to rediscover identity and difference as opposite sides of the same coin – identity of such purity, of such incandescence that we are obliged to read it as difference.[23]

Ben Jelloun's counterdiscourse calls into question the notions of author and authority, as well as the "truth functional" ground of hegemonic discourse. The restoration in it of the evenemential character of discourse undermines the sovereignty of the signifier (see Foucault, *L'Ordre du discours*, pp. 53–56, 59–61). Ben Jelloun's tale points up the historical illusion, as Derrida calls it, the philosophical and epistemological insistence on a fixed center, source or origin (*L'Ecriture*, p. 421). As Ahmed/

Zahra breaks with the "law of the father" so her creator breaks with the paternal law of conventional Western narrative.

Or, put differently, Ben Jelloun works from a poetics of resistance: to the conventional narrative with its ideological power base, posited on light and logic, elucidation and equilibrium, clarity and control, he opposes a narrative triggered by a dynamics of concealment and instability. The signification of his utterances shuns (pre)established contexts (signifieds) and pivots inward, as George Steiner says of Mallarmé's poetry, such that we are forced to follow as best we are able.[24] Ben Jelloun's narrative of impossibility, like language, like translation in its broadest sense (the transfer of meaning from one subjectivity to another), develops fissures, shatters, and falls apart, and no critical *bricolage* is capable of locating the "narratorial voice" in the system of the narrative, of putting the narrative back together, of repairing it, of recreating of it anything but ghostly simulacra, pale approximations that are no approximations at all.

The Sandchild calls into question a certain assumption of Western civilization that has imprisoned us since the creation of the printing press – namely, that life is made up of a space and time continuum that is forward flowing, dominated by sight and vision.[25] Ben Jelloun's narrative does so by breaking through the bounds of the visual universe and opening up another universe in which discontinuity and indeterminacy rule; where narratives are unending, circular, and turn back on themselves; where words cohabit with insects and give themselves up to natural processes; where writing cedes to a blank page or superimposes itself on previous writing in an endless palimpsest; where blindness turns us from vision to a world of auditory, tactile, olfactory sensations.

The Sandchild draws precisely on those powers of the human mind and senses that Steiner speaks of when he asserts that, "Beyond the present chaos lies the possibility of 'new configurations' of perception; man's dormant senses, his powers of integration, the chthonic, magic fiber of his being, will be liberated from the closed, passive system of Gutenberg literacy" (*Language and Silence*, p. 256). Ben Jelloun's counternarrative offers just such a liberation. While often drawing upon the resources of European and Islamic thought, it leaves behind the consequent, linear, closed worlds of Eurocentric and Islamic magisterial narratives and discourses as it fashions an alternative discourse expressive of postcolonial sensibilities and perceptions.

4

"At the Threshold of the Untranslatable": *Love in Two Languages* of Abdelkebir Khatibi

What has always awaited, what forgets itself and doesn't forget itself,
are the inaudible words... speech saying nothing, or saying too much,
always there, unpronounceable.

[Ce qui attend depuis toujours, ce qui s'oublie et ne s'oublie pas, ce
sont les mots inaudibles... parole ne disant rien, ou bien disant trop,
toujours là, imprononçable.]

ABDELKEBIR KHATIBI, *Amour bilingue*, p. 114[1]

At the outset of his 1983 book *Maghreb pluriel*, the Moroccan
philosopher and novelist Abdelkebir Khatibi asks of his readers from the
Maghreb, "who, among us – groups or individuals –, has undertaken the
work essentially decolonizing in its global and deconstitutive import,
with relation to the image that we hold of our exogeneous and endoge-
nous domination?" ["Mais qui, parmi nous – groupes et individus –, a
pris en charge le travail effectivement décolonisateur dans sa portée glob-
ale et déconstitutive de l'image que nous faisons de notre domination,
exogène et endogène?"] (16–17). He breaks the ground for this essential
work of decolonization in *Maghreb pluriel*, where he theorizes a literature,
written in the language of the adversary, that will answer in that same
language the aspirations and cultural specificity of the North African
writer of French.

Khatibi proposes the creation of what he calls a *pensée-autre*, an "other-
thought," that will revolutionize and renew Maghrebian culture. That
"other-thought," set apart from the political discourses of our time, will
seek to bring to light the misunderstanding existing between Europe
and the Arab world (16). Part of a strategy shunning closed, absolute systems, the other-thought must build on its marginality, its poverty, Khatibi

insists, because "a thought that does not draw its inspiration from its own poverty is always elaborated with the object of dominating and humiliating; a thought that is not *minority, marginal, fragmentary and incomplete* is always a thought of ethnocide" ["une pensée qui n'inspire pas de sa pauvreté est toujours élaborée pour dominer et humilier; une pensée qui ne soit pas *minoritaire, marginale, fragmentaire et inachevée,* est toujours une pensée de l'ethnocide"] (18). He does not call for and exalt a philosophy of the poor and economically deprived, but rather speaks for a thought characterized by egalitarian generosity, what he calls a "plural thought" ("pensée plurielle"), that does not seek to reduce "others (societies and individuals) to the sphere of its own self-sufficiency [*autosuffisance*]" (18).

> On the one hand, [Khatibi says] we must listen to the Maghreb resound in its linguistic, cultural, and political pluralism; on the other hand, only the outside rethought, decentered, subverted, diverted from its dominating determinations, can put us at a remove from unformulated identities and differences. Only the outside rethought – for our purposes – is able to rend our nostalgia for the Father and topple him from his metaphysical ground; or at least bend him towards such a toppling, [that works] towards an unyielding difference that takes itself in charge in its sufferings, its humiliations, and, I will add, in its insoluable problems.
>
> [D'une part, il faut écouter le Maghreb résonner dans sa pluralité (linguistique, culturelle, politique), et d'autre part, seul le dehors repensé, décentré, subverti, détourné de ses déterminations dominantes, peut nous éloigner des identités et des différences informulées. Seul le dehors repensé – pour notre compte – est à même de déchirer notre nostalgie du Père et l'arracher à son sol métaphysique; ou du moins l'infléchir vers un tel arrachement, vers une telle différence intraitable qui se prend en charge dans ses souffrances, ses humiliations, et dirai-je, dans ses problèmes insolubles.]   (39)

He asserts the right to difference, but one that questions itself and the bases of its own insurrection (12). The other-thought he posits builds on its difference at once from Western metaphysics and culture and Islamic theocracy. Khatibi's critique responds to the particular problem of the Maghreb: "the space of our word and of our discourse is a double space owing to our *bilingual situation*" ["le lieu de notre parole et de notre discours est un lieu duel par notre *situation bilingue*"] (57) – a space of confrontation with the totalizing metadiscourses of both Western and

Islamic society (57). He speaks of the risk of passing from one metaphysical system to the other "without bringing to light the translation and the passage that occur, imperceptibly, from one archaeology to the other and from one language to the other" ["sans mettre au jour la traduction et le transport qui s'y opèrent, imperceptiblement d'une archéologie à l'autre et d'une langue à l'autre"] (57). The place of the other-thought will be "a margin on alert" ["*Une marge en éveil*"] (17; author's italics).

What is needed, Khatibi says, are a decolonization of thought, that would affirm "a difference, a free and absolute subversion of the mind" ["l'affirmation d'une différence, une subversion absolue et libre de l'esprit"] (48), and the will to "oppose to every universalizing demonology a necessary differentiating thought" ["d'opposer à toute démonie universelle une nécessaire pensée de la différence"] (136). The project of "decolonizing" he mentions is twofold: (1) "a deconstruction of the logocentrism and the ethnocentrism" of Western thought; (2) a "critique of the knowledge and discourses elaborated by the different societies of the Arab world in regard to themselves" ["Une déconstruction du logocentrisme et de l'ethnocentrisme [de] l'Occident… [et] une critique du savoir et des discours élaborés par les différentes sociétés du monde arabe sur elles-mêmes"] (48–49).

More particularly, Khatibi urges the necessity of overturning the very notion of language, of defamiliarizing it by rendering it foreign to itself. Such an act would call upon a "Superhuman power, impossible power, madness of difference that is unyielding, irreducible, not shored up by its traditional foundations and its maternal tongue, [which is] almost rendered silent" ["Pouvoir surhumain, pouvoir impossible, folie de la différence que se veut intraitable, irréductible, sans appui stable sur ses fondements traditionnels et sa langue maternelle, ici presque rendue au silence"] (58).

Here Khatibi broaches his notion of bilingualism – what he calls "a *thought in tongues*, a translating, worldly rendering of the codes, systems and constellations of signs circulating in the world" ["*une pensée en langues*, une mondialisation traduisante des codes, des systèmes et des constellations de signes qui circulent dans le monde"] (60). Bilingualism operates a "double critique" that "consists in opposing to the Western epistemè its unthought-of outside while radicalizing the margin, not only in an *arabic thought*, but in an other-thought that speaks *in languages*, listening in to all language – from wherever it comes" ["La double critique consiste à opposer à l'épistemè occidentale son dehors impensé tout en radicalisant la marge, non seulement dans une *pensée arabe*, mais dans une pensée autre qui parle *en langues*, se mettant à l'écoute de toute parole – d'où qu'elle vienne"] (63).

In my introduction, I cited Khatibi who speaks of the process by which the *bilangue* is created (and creates itself) as being not solely a process of contestation, but one of complementarity as well. The foreign language utilized by the Maghrebian writer of French, in being actualized as writing ("word enacted"), transforms the mother tongue by structuring it and pushing it towards the "untranslatable." The result is not simply an overlay or layering of languages, nor mere juxtaposition. Rather, each language "makes a sign to the other," calls upon it to maintain itself as outside. Each language affirms its singularity, rigorous alterity, and irreducible nature.

The process Khatibi calls translation operates in terms of the mutual distancing and intractibility of the two languages that have been interiorized by the writer. The North African narrative in French is a narrative of translation, a narrative that Khatibi characterizes as "speaking in tongues" (*Maghreb pluriel*, p. 186).

With relation to the North African writers of French, in my Introduction I also cited Khatibi's discussion of their strongly felt urge to discover a new space for their writing by inscribing themselves in the gap or interval between identity (sameness), which leads towards assimilation, and difference, which marks their radical alterity to Western culture and thought. Khatibi calls that interval "the scene of the [French-language] text," the space in which writing, through its radical alterity, seeks its roots in the mother tongue (Berber or Arabic).

In narratives written in French by Maghrebian authors, the ever-present mother tongue (Arabic, Berber) is ever at work in the foreign language. "From one to the other there plays out a constant translation and a dialogue *en abyme*, extremely difficult to bring to light" ["De l'une à l'autre se déroulent une traduction permanente et un entretien en abyme, extrêmement difficile à mettre au jour"] (179). The violence of the text occurs precisely in this crossing, this chiasmus, this intersection between the two tongues, which marks their irreconciliable nature (179).

A number of Maghrebian authors writing in French have attempted to inscribe themselves in a new space on the order of that one described by Khatibi. In his essay on "Bilinguisme et littérature," to illustrate the operation of the maternal language within or on the margin of the narrative written in French, Khatibi presents a detailed analysis of the work of one of these writers: the Tunisian Abdelwahab Meddeb and his novel, *Talismano* (1979).[2]

But just as fascinating and even more curious is his own novel, *Amour bilingue*, published in 1983. The title of this novel, which I propose to look at through the reading lens of Khatibi's discussion of bilingualism and literary discourse in *Maghreb pluriel*, can be translated into English in more than one way. Though I, as Richard Howard, prefer to translate it as "love in two languages," it can be taken as well to mean "bilingual love" or "love of the bilingual." All the more so since the story of the Maghrebian narrator's love for a nameless, mysterious, and ineffable French woman, with only the slenderest of biographical specification, may be read as an allegory for the pursuit by the postcolonial writer of an idiom of "impossibility," as Khatibi calls it – written over by the colonizer/adversary's language – that will express his or her own cultural, aesthetic, and political aspirations: "I was a talking book," the narrator of *Amour bilingue* tells us,

> who tore itself out of its palimpsests, to succeed in making itself understood, to become accepted. I am therefore a text of that tearing out, and I am perhaps the first madman of my mother tongue: to mute one language in another is impossible. And I desire this impossibility.

> [J'étais un livre parlant, qui s'arrachait de ses palimpsestes, pour parvenir à se faire comprendre, se faire admettre. Je suis donc un texte de cet arrachement, et peut-être suis-je le premier fou de ma langue maternelle: faire muter une langue dans une autre est impossible. Et je désire cet impossible.]   (AB, p. 35)

The title, *Amour bilingue*, is so packed with meaning that, though the English translation, *Love in Two Languages*, preserves the inference that the author/narrator writes of a mysterious French woman as well as of the doubled language (*bi-langue*) itself, it unavoidably loses several resonances, including those conjured up by the Arabic equivalent: *ishq al-lisaanayn*, which suggests the translation "a passion of two tongues."[3] The postfix *lingue* in the French title word *bilingue* along with the Arabic "lisaan" add to the ambiguity of the title inasmuch as they are associated with both language and the physical appendage – the equivalents of the English "tongue" (Sellin, "Khatibi's Passion for Language(s)", p. 50).

"The story fell joyously that autumn: the leaves, the leaves of paper, all that very real enchantment of my summer" ["Le récit est tombé joyeuse-ment en cet automne: les feuilles, les feuilles de papier, toute cette féerie très réelle de mon été"] (*AB*, p. 127) – so begins Khatibi's Epilogue to *Amour bilingue* (115), which describes the interpenetration of the supernatural and the real in his story, as well as the metaphoric exchange, in a play on "leaves," between objects (the loved one, nature) and writing. This phrase is redolent of the metatextual character of the text, a characteristic I will discuss later.

Khatibi's *Amour bilingue*, whose title inscribes it under the sign of a double writing, begins appropriately with a brief section entitled "Epigraph" (from the Greek *epigraphe*, which derives from the suffix *epi-* plus the root verb to write, *graphein*). Curiously, the opening paragraph is enclosed between parentheses, as if to insist on closure of the speech act within a circumscribed space. Indeed, the first sentence seems to say as much: "He [the narrator] left, returned, then left again. He decided to leave for good" ["Il partit, revint, repartit. Il décida de partir définitivement"] (9). There is a beginning and an end, past definite verbs in French that convey the sense of a completed action, an action frozen in repetitiveness, and an allusion (in the original) to the *definitive* character of that action. The very next sentence, however, still within parentheses, spills over boundaries, undercuts the implied containment – "The story should stop here, the book should close on itself" ["Le récit devrait s'arrêter ici, le livre se fermer sur lui-même"] – by introducing the element of uncertainty with the verb "should" (*devrait*) that suggests deviation from the expected. Customarily, the use of an epigraph signals the theme or spirit of the work. Based on the title and first paragraph of *Amour bilingue*, the spirit is one of deviation in the frame of writing and language. That deviation will extend as well to story: for example, the narrator–protagonist describes the movement of the woman he loves as "an infinite digression, wrapped in landscapes, in signs and emblems" ["une digression infinie, enrobée de paysages, de signes et d'emblèmes"] (33).

Digression, deviation, difference – characterize Khatibi's narrative. In usage, the prefix *epi-* denotes several relationships: besides, near to, over, outer (as in "epidermis"), anterior, prior to, and even after. In all cases it imparts the sense of otherness, something apart from the text or extratextual. In specific relation to what occurs in Khatibi's narrative, it suggests thematically the act of writing-apart that characterizes not only the metatexts (Epigraph/Epilogue) but the author's entire discourse of the non-Western other and the introduction of the other-than-natural (supernatural) into the natural (conventional narrative) on equal footing, which allies the text with postcolonial writing that has been called magi-cal realist.

As the Epigraph indicates, the narrative does not stop; language car-ries on on its own ("A sentence that had formed itself all alone" ["Phrase qui s'était formée toute seule"] (9)) and the narrator–protagonist voices the sensation of being written by his surroundings (3). Allusions to the madness of language – reminiscent of Rimbaud's *dérèglement de tous les sens* ("derangement of all the senses") – will occur throughout the narrative. The supernatural that erupts in the middle of the ordinary arises, in fact, from language run riot.

The narrator, an Arab writing in French, reflects that the foreignness of a language makes it more beautiful, more terrible for a non-native. The latter can look at words more objectively, from afar, shorn of their cultur-al context, while the native speaker is apt to be unconscious of their forms and relations, unaccustomed to playing with them, to dissociate himself from his language, as the narrator tells us (5). The way he describes them, words from another language operate like Marcel Proust's *petite madeleine* or uneven paving-stones – objects that detach us from a specific day-to-day context and come to serve as catalysts for the foreign speaker or writer, who experiences them in contexts usually unperceived by the native speaker.

For the foreign speaker, words from his multiple tongues hold the potential of playing with each other. Through detachment from cultural contexts, word meanings become amplified, dispersed, diffuse, subject to endless transformation through interchange and fusion of forms and new semantic contexts. Everywhere in his speech the narrator engages in a cabalistic, glossophilic verbal play: the French noun *mot* ("word") calls forth *mort* ("death"), the French past definite *calma* ("he calmed down") establishes a cratylusian-like[4] *correspondance* with the Arabic word *kalma* ("word"), which then unleashes a chain of associated words. Words observe words within the narrator, "preceding the rapid emergence now of memories, word fragments, onomatopoeias, garlands of phrases, entwined to the death: undecipherable" ["précédant l'émergence main-tenant rapide de souvenirs, fragments de mots, onomatopées, phrases en guirlandes, enlacées à mort: indéchiffrables"] (AB, p. 10).

Reflecting on the words for sun and moon whose genders in French become reversed in Arabic, the narrator believes that in this inversion he has found the explanation for his obsession with androgyny. In inhabit-ing "a middleground between two languages" ["un milieu entre deux langues"] (10–11), the foreign language takes on limitless power, that enables it to "withdraw into itself, beyond any translation" ["se retirer en elle, au-delà de toute traduction"] (10). The closer he approaches the middle, he says, the further he finds himself from it ["plus je vais au milieu, plus je m'en éloigne"] (11). He comes to speak a *bi-langue* emerging from a linguistic space "at the threshold of the untranslatable" ["au seuil de l'intraduisible"] (11). His madness (the division of his being between two languages), "that denies itself in affirming itself in a double structure that is itself fleeting, keeps me," he says, "in good health: infinite truth and madness" ["qui nie en s'affirmant dans un double fondement lui-même évanescent, me maintient en santé: vérité, folie infinies"] (11). He equates not only well-being but truth with madness.

Having been brought up speaking his mother tongue and learning the language of the French colonizers, the two languages (colloquial Moroccan Arabic and French) coexist in his unconscious if not his consciousness. In fact, a plurality of tongues coexist: not solely French and his colloquial Arabic dialect, but classical Arabic and the Berber dialect as well. The manifold linguistic and cultural traces tracking through his "mother tongue" emphasize the fundamental impurity of the origin-less language he speaks and consequently problematize the notion of an authoritarian discourse based on unitary stabilized speech.[5] Each time he speaks, these languages play back and forth. When he speaks the language of the French woman he loves, he occasionally substitutes a word from Arabic for a word in French. At such times he has no feeling of grammatical error ("breaking a law," as he puts it) but rather of speaking two languages simultaneously – enunciating "one word that was intelligible to her... and another, that was there but distant, vagabond, turned in on itself" ["l'une qui parvenait à son écoute... et une autre, qui était là, et pourtant lointaine, vagabonde, retournée sur elle-même"] (*AB*, p. 35).

He asks her where his mother tongue lies forgotten when he speaks to her in hers.

> Where does it continue to speak in silence? Because, at such times it is never lost. When I speak to you, I sense my mother tongue moving in a double fluctuation: one silent (a so gutteral silence) and the other turning in the void, undoing itself in a collapsing into bilingual disorder. I don't know how to speak, even with the whole chain of names and sounds of my native speech – I who was born in the mouth of an invisible god – that entire chain, like a speech impediment, is destroyed and comes back reversed even to the extent of stammering.

> At that moment I lose my words, and I confuse the languages in which I utter them.

> [Lorsque je t'entretiens dans ta langue, où s'oublie la mienne? Où parle-t-elle encore en silence? Car, jamais, elle n'est abolie à ces instances. Quand je te parle, je sens ma langue maternelle glisser en deux flux: l'un, silencieux (silence si guttural), et l'autre, qui tourne à vide, se défaisant par implosion dans le désordre bilingue. Je ne sais comment dire, toute la chaîne nominale et phonétique de ma parole natale – je suis né dans la bouche d'un dieu invisible – toute cette chaîne, pareille à un trouble de langage, se détruit et revient à l'envers jusqu'au balbutiement. Je perds alors mes mots, je les confonds de langue en langue.]   (*AB*, pp. 48–49)

While this interplay of languages can result in linguistic impediment (or versatility and richness, depending upon the point of view), it is important to note that it is rendered possible by a space of difference which the narrator inhabits:

> Difference that exalted me. What I also sought was to maintain myself in that gap, putting it at a re-move in a place from which was banished all opposition between dead languages and living languages, where everything that unites through separation was affirmed, everything that separates by continually translating itself.

> [Différence qui m'exaltait. Ce que je visais aussi était de me maintenir en cet écart, le dé-portant dans une écoute où fut bannie toute opposition entre langue morte et langue vivante, où fut affirmé tout ce qui unit en séparant, sépare en se traduisant continuellement.]   (*AB*, p. 35)

This *écart* or gap or middleground, where mutually cancelling oppositions and the contradictory terms of the oxymoron coexist, constitutes that very same space of writing Khatibi referred to in *Maghreb pluriel*. In *La Mémoire tatouée*, Khatibi says, "In rereading myself, I discover that my most finished (French) sentence is a *calling to mind*. The calling to mind of an unpronounceable entity, neither Arab nor French, neither dead nor living, neither man nor woman: generation of the text. Wandering topology, schizoidal state, androgynous dream, loss of identity – on the threshold of madness" ["En me relisant, je découvre que ma phrase (française) la plus achevée est un *rappel*. Le rappel d'un corps imprononçable, ni arabe ni français, ni mort ni vivant, ni homme ni femme: génération du texte. Topologie errante, schize, rêve androgyne, perte de l'identité – au seuil de la folie"] (*La Mémoire tatouée*, p. 207).

Elsewhere, Khatibi has spoken of Moroccan literature as being inscribed in a *chiasme* (chiasmus, intersection). As being "worked" by the maternal tongue – a "working that reveals its effects everywhere: what appears sometimes as a perturbation or a subversion of the French language points to a process of translation (conscious or unconscious) from one language to another. It's that *écart* that decides the originality of such or such text. Where does the violence of the text play itself out if not in this chiasmus, this intersection, which is in point of truth, irreconcilable?" ["Travail qui a ses effets partout: ce qui paraît parfois comme une perturbation ou une subversion de la langue française indique un processus de traduction (conscient ou inconscient) d'une langue à l'autre. C'est cet écart qui décide de l'originalité de tel ou tel texte. Où se dessine la violence du texte, sinon dans ce chiasme, cette intersection, à vrai dire, irréconciliable?"].[6]

The word *écart* connotes gap or interval, but it means more than simply the space of separation. The first meaning glossed by the *Grand Robert* is the "distance that separates two things that one moves apart or that move apart from each other," while its second meaning is the "difference between two magnitudes or values (of which one in particular is a mean or a scale of reference)." Still another meaning is the act of "deviating from a moral rule, social etiquette," etc. *Ecart* connotes, then, the separation of two things, which may be magnitudes or values, or separation from an established frame of reference.

Michel Serre's use of the word/concept *écart* in *The Parasite* (*Le Parasite*) comes to mind. Offering the example of La Fontaine's poem "Le rat de ville et le rat des champs" ("The City Rat and the Country Rat"), Serre points to the flaws inherent in the phenomenon of system that allow the writer to counter it. No system functions to perfection, he states, "without loss, without leakage, without erosion, without slips, without irregularities, without opacity."[7] He consequently reconceptualizes system as integrally bound to its own *écarts* (lapses, slips, gaps). "The book of slips [*écarts*]," he says, "of [strange] noise and of disorder would be the book of distress only for those who would defend a God who has calculatedly authored an incorruptibly dependable world. It is not that way. The slip is part of the thing itself," he concludes, "and perhaps produces it" (*The Parasite*, pp. 22–23). Derrida's assertion that "Law implies a counter-law [...] lodged at the very heart of the law, a law of impurity or a principle of contamination,"[8] accords fully with Serre's idea of slippage in systems. The *bi-langue* operates as a disordering noise, entails a counterdiscourse, at the heart of the ruling linguistic/cultural systems/discourses of Europe, the Maghreb, and the Middle East, the corrosion within the engine of system that admits the exceptional, the unknown, as a coexistent entity alongside the ordinary or "known."

The bilingual person has supernatural powers, for he speaks the language of the other within. But he is and is not that other: while he speaks the language of that other, he effaces himself in the other's traces ["Te parlant dans ta langue, je suis toi-même sans l'être, m'effaçant dans tes traces"] (*AB*, p. 11). The bilingual speaker is freed from the bonds of a single language, divided in two, educated, as he says, in thoughts of emptiness, of the void. He describes himself in positive terms as living in a state of amnesia (*Ibid.*).

Bilingualism and an other narrative

Sitting in a rocking chair in the dazzling sunlight, the narrator thinks about a book whose pages he turned moments before. The impression he had of leafing through a book of blank pages brought to his mind an ancient tale that replaced the narrative of his reading by another. A fabulous substitution ["substitution fabuleuse"], he thought. He resumed reading, dizzied by the blackness of words. He had the feeling that, although intelligible and decipherable, his reading circled around an incomprehensible word that was not part of the text – a bothersome incomprehensibility that suddenly destroyed the pages, words, lines, and punctuation, through the interposition of a black spot floating between his eyes and the book ["Par instants simultanés, il lui semblait que sa lecture, bien qu'intelligible et déchiffrable, tournait autour d'un mot insaisissable qui n'appartenait pas au texte. Insaisissabilité harcelante qui dévasta, d'un coup, les pages, les mots, les lignes et la ponctuation, à travers une tache noire flottant entre ses yeux et le livre"] (46).

The incomprehensible word allowed the book to flow beyond its pages. Remindful of the narratives in Ben Jelloun's *Sandchild*, whose words are first carried away by insects and rain and later effaced by the moonlight, in *Amour bilingue* night entered and exited the book, effacing the white by black. The narrator remained fixed between the book and the outside ["Il resta cloué entre le livre et son dehors"] (47). Closing his eyes, again in his mind he saw "that imperative presence of the outside that attracted him and excluded him at the same time" ["cette présence impérative du dehors qui l'attirait et l'excluait à la fois"] (47).

The episode is a paradigm for the circumstances of his own cultural situation and for the *bi-langue*, which, bringing about a textual substitution for the narrative and its contents, represents a departure from the text of Islam. For the text he holds in his hands is none other than the Qur'ān, and the outside suggests the lay world, the secular world of his youth, overlaid by the culture and language of another people. The tension between outside and inside is instructive, particularly since the description of the outside is at the same time in the form of an imperative presence and an excluding force. The outside draws him, imposes itself upon him, but he is excluded from it. Carrying out the analogy, the inside would be his mother tongue, Arabic, and his Islamic heritage that remain readable and comprehensible but blank, replaced by a fable, a black spot such as that which imprints itself on one's eyes when gazing too long upon the sun.

The important thought here is that another story arises, another narrative, a space between inside and outside. The black spot substitutes itself for whiteness, the blankness of the (traditional) text from which meaning is effaced, just as the ancient tale substitutes itself for the words of the book. That it is a "fabulous" tale suggests secular tales of untrammeled imagination and inventiveness, unbound by the inner formality of the material book (the Qur'ān) or the imperative outerness of the dominant (French) language and culture. In such a tale, it is as though no inner or outer exist, only the unbounded, limitless, spontaneous.

In the section appearing just before the passages in which the narrator recounts this episode of the black spot, he speaks of the Qur'ān, recalls intoning its words which he did not understand, words of a prayer brought, he says, by an angel descended from heaven. He describes the angel appearing in Persian miniatures in the visible form of an androgynous being surrounded by an extraordinarily complex calligraphy. In the same way that a marvelous being existed amidst graphic tracings, he imagines the fantastic incarnated in the exteriority (the "dehors") of the Book (the Qur'ān) – in words, in words that generate other words, in ideas and images, in his own name (Khatibi, whose verbal root KH-T-B means "to declaim out loud," and therefore comes to imply making a speech, "oratory," and, in Islamic parlance, both "sermon" and "preacher"[9]). His digressions and impatience with the divine text that caused him to be called to order by the voice of the Archangel, he tells us, led him to confront the question of his own name with relation to the "hierarchy of angels and praying men." Later, drunk on the divine word, in a trance, mounting heavenward through the absolute binaries of the Holy script

cleaving heaven from earth, good from evil, woman from man ["séparant
le ciel de la terre, le bien du mal, la femme de l'homme"], he glimpsed
God. And, at this moment, he himself was the Book ["A ce moment, il fut
le Livre"] (44).

> Then, Allah multiplied himself in the beads of his ninety-nine
> attributes, and he himself wore one of them. He still believed. Having
> become one and many, his name spread outside, everywhere where
> other gods and other texts signaled him.

> [Alors, Allah se multiplia dans le chapelet de ses quatre-vingt-dix-
> neuf attributs, et lui-même en portait un. Il croyait encore. Devenu un
> et multiple, son nom se ramifia au-dehors, partout où d'autres dieux,
> d'autres textes lui faisaient signe.]   (44)

He set off into the world, following the trace of his fictions. As he leaves
Islam and crosses the threshold into "real life," he finds himself under
"the dominion of a death that was wholly individual" (45) – the death of a
disbeliever who sets out to write himself, outside the Qur'ān. "Outside
the Book, that which he spoke was a novel experience … Yes, those
moments were terrifying and exhilarating. To turn against the Unique
and the Name, to oppose their story with his own, not merely reversed –
his story was already upset – but by a thought from the void that engulfed
his powers" ["Il parlait, hors du Livre, en une expérience nouvelle… Oui,
ces moments furent terribles et enthousiasmants. Se retourner contre
l'Unique et le Nom, leur opposer son récit, non point à l'envers – son récit
était déjà bouleversé – mais par une pensée du vide, qui engloutissait ses
forces"] (45). Though he had grown up under "the Unique [Allah] and the
Name," under the injunction of the Qur'ān that there be only one God
and that his name shall be Allah, as a child born from language itself (11),
who was an adopted child in his mother Arabic and who adopted in turn
another language (French), the asymmetry of his double tongue, of
speech and writing, created "from that instant the scenario of the dou-
bles" (11). He discovered bilingualism as an enabling force, for the bilingual person enjoys supernatural powers: he speaks the language of the
other within, being of that other: "Speaking to you in your own language, I am you without being you, effacing myself in your traces." The
bilingual is freed from the bonds of a single language, divided in two,
educated, as he says, "in thoughts of the void" (11).

Thus, he forsook the Book and plunged into the abyss of thought. He
gave himself over to the play of the unconceived-of ["le jeu de l'inconçu"],
fixed his attention on the beauty of the visible, on beauty itself, belonging

to no one. He came to imagine himself as being "a detour of a being, an affective decentering of the language, one voice among other voices. Yes, simple movement with no progress assured; thoughts so minimal, so fragile" ["un détour d'être, un désaxement émotif de la langue, voix parmi d'autres. Oui, un simple cheminement, sans aucun progrès assuré; pensées si minimes, si fragiles"] (45–46).

The propinquity of the episode above, coming as it does just before the episode of the black spot, serves as an important commentary on the latter. An androgynous angel, with its indeterminate and miraculous character, is linked to writing (calligraphy), which gives rise in turn to the fabulous tale that substitutes itself for the text of the book. The narrator interests himself more in the marvelous character of the angel and his own encounter with the Qur'ān and the hierarchy of angels and praying men than in the religious content. He is attracted by his own "bookish" name – which is to say, his own potential as source of "divine" narrative –, by other gods and other texts. Setting out into the world is equated with following the trace of his own fictions. Matching his story with that of Islam and Allah – not merely reversing his with theirs – he writes anew out of a void: the space between, the No man's land, the Middleground, the black spot between his eyes and the page. He contemplates the beauty of the empirical, the material, and visible, rather than the invisible of Islamic thought. He becomes a deviate, a "detour of a being," an "affective decentering of the language," and, importantly, only one voice among many. This last remark of the narrator invokes precisely the phenomenon of "leveling," growing out of a profound conviction in the repositioning of all discourses such that they are viewed as operating on the same level.

One comment in particular here amplifies the sense of Khatibi's words from *Maghreb pluriel*, which I cited earlier, namely: "a thought that does not draw its inspiration from its own poverty is always elaborated with the object of dominating and humiliating; a thought that is not *minority, marginal, fragmentary and incomplete* is always a thought of ethnocide" (18). Imagining himself as a "detour of a being," an "affective decentering of the language," a simple progression that moves forward uncertainly, one single voice among many, whose very thoughts are "so minimal, so fragile," betrays a sense of his own poverty upon which he builds, a building guided by a humility born out of marginality, fragmentation, uncertainty, and the minimal, out of spiritual indigence, destitution, and want. But is it not precisely the state of a human being who has attempted to shed the ideological accoutrements of pre-conceived ideas and the drive towards ascendency over others? Is it not like the monastic divestiture undertaken before entering the life of the spirit, but, here, in the context of one who prepares to enter a state of linguistic spirituality? While poverty may in other instances be a source of meanness, it also holds the positive potential of eliciting empathy and understanding, and it is doubtless in this sense that Khatibi refers to it.

In speaking later of the religious and cultural discourse of his own childhood, the narrator says that he was born in the mouth of an invisible god (i.e., Allah), which renders him unable to recite the whole chain of names and sounds of his native speech. When he tries to do so, the chain destroys itself, like a speech impediment, "and then comes back reversed even to the extent of stammering. At that moment I lose my words, and I confuse the languages in which I utter them" (48–49). The confusion between languages and the inability to distinguish words allude, on the surface, to his bilingual mixture of French and Arabic. But the mention of limitations placed on his "native speech," which he cannot wholly recite, seems to refer also to the control and blockage that comes about from the imposition of Islamic discourse. He alludes to the latter's dominant nature:

> In my country (?) [the question mark appears in the original], there takes place a ceremony of response without a question being asked: proverbial speech, empty maxims, an unpronounceable ritornello. It spells out this: There is no God but Allah. In giving yourself to my name, was it not called for to recite: There is no name but my name. To bless myself in your turn, in this face to face encounter.

> [Dans mon pays (?), il existe une cérémonie de la réponse sans question: parole proverbiale, maximes vides, ritournelle de l'imprononçable. Epelle ceci: Il n'y a de Dieu qu'Allah. En t'adonnant à mon nom, ne convenait-il pas de te répéter: Il n'y a de nom que mon nom? Pour me bénir à ton tour, dans ce face à face.]   (91)

The question mark that Khatibi interjects after the reference to his country appears to underscore the fact that the space between, which he occupies, is an "other" country, his true country. Within the geographical boundaries of his country of political and social residence, the discourse of Islam offers only answers that brook no questions, ritualistic, purified speech, emptied of any content not in praise of Allah. Against this Holy book, the narrator counters with his own book, with everything that his own beliefs and convictions as well as his own writing offer in contradistinction.

Khatibi speaks at length about the richness, inexhaustibility, and redemptive qualities of the *bi-langue* flowing out of its contestatory maneuvering, but one cannot for one moment forget its vulnerability to becoming reappropriated by the dominant discourse. By being and speaking from elsewhere, the sets of expectation in Islamic and European readerly or discursive modes that operate to naturalize (render intelligible) the text and the author's discourse by bringing them into relation with known models of order, are outmaneuvered.[10] My own analysis of *Amour bilingue*, to the degree it seeks to explicate, tends unavoidably towards an act of recuperation. It proceeds only so far, however, before it runs aground on imponderables, contradiction, the existence of opposing orders of being and speaking in the selfsame text. But that ultimate impossibility of recuperation is the very point of my attempt to illustrate, to perceive, the character of Khatibi's narration of impossibility.

The anonymous conventionalizing and silent authorities legislating the discourse of Islam and the French language, which share and propagate within their differing cultural hegemonies a common world and a common fund of knowledge, are unable to secure the text here. Khatibi's text, like his discourse, lies outside or beside the norm. It confounds the expectations of the Western readers brought up on conventional narratives, for example, in a way similar to that introduced by the "new novels" of such writers as Alain Robbe-Grillet and Claude Simon in the 1950s and 1960s in France, but with a difference. The works of the new novelists still kept within a cultural sphere whose artefacts and fragments were drawn from objects recognizable to French readers. That is far from the case with Khatibi, for most of his readers run up against cultural elements that are at a remove and grossly unfamiliar – to name just a few: the manifold and usually indirect allusions to Islam, the Book (the Qur'ān), the importance of naming, and the traditional role of the Arab woman. In short, the vision of the world and the values inhering in Khatibi's narrative, are distinctly unfamiliar to most European readers. Their unfamiliar nature is re-enforced owing to the fact that Khatibi's narrative does not seek to develop a focal point or communicate anything so consistently comprehensible as a fund of knowledge to which we might have recourse to make the unfamiliar intelligible. Khatibi telescopes time and space, things and events, and points of view in a "mosaic-like, chromatic form of writing" that breaks the contract of conventional fiction.[11]

The tactic underlying Khatibi's work resembles strongly the technique of defamiliarization conceptualized by the Russian formalist critic Victor Shklovsky – a technique that removes objects from the automatism of perception in order to jolt us into taking notice even though the object may not be fully, if at all, comprehensible. There is a difference, of course, owing to the fact that, with regard to the European readers, the defamiliarized of Khatibi is to some degree culturally induced through the unfamiliar nature of the non-Western object. Nonetheless, the effect is similar in function. "An image," Shklovsky says, "is not a permanent referent for those mutable complexities of life which are revealed through it; its purpose is not to make us perceive meaning, but to create a special perception of the object – *it creates a 'vision' of the object instead of serving as a means for knowing it.*"[12] Art, for Shklovsky, is a special sort of perception, therefore, that gives value to every object.

For Khatibi that purpose of art is doubly underscored by viewing art and cultural expression through the focus of the *bi-langue* and endowing it with the power, as Shklovsky puts it (12), "to impart the sensation of things as they are perceived and not as they are known" (or, in the case of Maghrebian culture, misconstrued, I might add, through exotic distortion or cultural bias). The tactic, as used by Khatibi, destroys the habitual social and political associations conveyed by the traditional narrative/language. This tactic, moreover, is not unlike that employed by such riddles as "What is black and white and red all over?" that are based on the deflection of standard word meaning, puns, sound alikes, etc. Khatibi's glossophilic verbal play, to which we have alluded, re-enforces the effect of defamiliarization by subverting conventional lexical connotation and interrelating words and concepts through association that escapes the comprehension of European readers and heightens the opacity of the text.

The *bi-langue*, androgyny, the double, and the magical real

One observes two faces of Khatibi's *bi-langue*: the face of the double that analogizes the writing space of the postcolonial author forging a parallel or alternate language within (in this instance) French,[13] and the closely related face of oppositionality. The *bi-langue* operates under the sign of the androgyne, that sex described by Aristophanes in Plato's *Symposium*, as "a distinct sex in form as well as in name, with the characteristics of male and female." The androgyne was sprung from the moon, which partakes equally of the sun (the male) and the earth (the female). The strength of the androgynes was prodigious, Aristophanes relates, and they challenged the very gods. To weaken them, Zeus cleaved them into two parts, female and male, which, out of desire, ever after have sought to find the other half and embrace it. Aristophanes draws a moral in saying that love serves simply as the name for the whole that one desires and pursues.[14] The whole for Khatibi is the co-existence and interpenetration of opposites that yield leveling and equalization of all discourse.

In conjunction with his discussion of "impure purity" (his demand for pure love but fascination with prostitutes), Khatibi's narrator speaks of his obsession with the androgyne as coming from his bewitchment since childhood with "this duplicity... of body and language" (29–30). The desire "To translate the impure into the pure, prostitution into androgyny" ["Traduire l'impur dans le pur, la prostitution dans l'androgynie"] (*AB*, p. 30) guided his travels throughout the world (30). His obsession with the *bi-langue* parallels, moreover, his fascination with the marginalized, doubling character of ventriloquists, albinos, cripples, "all these bizarre types that teem in my real, my very real, phantasmagorias" ["toutes ces espèces bizarres qui grouillent dans mes fantasmagories réelles, bien réelles"] (*AB*, pp. 30–31). He even learned braille and the languages of the handicapped so he could communicate with them. He speculates that he may be capable of writing only for bilingual handicaps (*AB*, p. 31).

At one point, the narrator speaks (in the third person) of his fleeting dreams, comprised of fragments, "Devastated memory, telescoped and lacerated words, shattered ... a thought under construction in an order without foundation. Marvelous thought, vigil of the non-said, thought of the void that kept him awake as he slept" ["Mémoire dévastée, paroles télescopées, déchirées, partant en morceaux ... une pensée en construction dans un ordre sans fondement. Merveilleuse pensée, vigile du non-dit, pensée du vide qui le tenait éveillé dans le sommeil"] (*AB*, p. 15). The state he describes evokes Hermagoras' rhetorical category of adoxis that exists without relation to the ruling doctrine (*doxa*). It is a state ruled by the non-said, by processes and figures like synesthesia, which fuses different senses ("unheard-of thought" ["pensée inouïe"] *AB*, p. 28) and the oxymoron ("impure purity" – "pure impure," *AB*, p. 29; "Ritualistic wandering" ["Errance rituelle"] *AB*, p. 37); by the indeterminate: "sleeping but not sleeping, dreaming but not dreaming, so that he might approach the unsayable" ["dormant ne dormant pas, rêvant ne rêvant pas, pour qu'il s'approchât de l'indicible?"] (AB, p. 16). The unsayable – approached in the *bi-langue*, which is neither one nor the other of the narrator's two languages, but in-between – becomes his language proper. Providing the atmosphere for the unsayable is the description of time and place without precise limits ["sans limite précise"] (AB, p. 17). The French language undergoes radical transformation, driven by the narrator's "passion for the untranslatable" ["passion de l'intraduisible"] (AB, p. 73).

The androgyne in *Amour bilingue*, more specifically, the cleaved state of the androgyne, figures the double in postcolonial writing as posited by Khatibi, as well as the phenomenon of a type of North African magical realism itself, a state in which two diametrically opposed ontologies – the supernatural world of unreason and the natural world of reason and logic – cohabit, a multipartite space of oppositionality that repositions everything by giving the lie to binary either/or reasoning ruled by universal absolutes. The deconstructive movement of Khatibi's text that gives rise to this state throws into doubt the certainty of the Sign, of identity and origin. The magical realist aspect of Khatibi's *bi-langue* lies in its replay of the desire and pursuit of the whole by the two sexes once making up the androgyne, through the search for the complementary existence of anti-nomical orders – supernatural/natural – that constitute the whole. Just as language (the *bi-langue*) spills over the boundaries of the real, so events and objects transgress/transcend the boundaries of conventional representation. Natural objects become animate in Khatibi's world – the night writes the narrator and watches him dozing (AB, p. 9); the sea becomes language ("Scansion, cadence from wave to wave" ["Scansion, cadence de vague en vague"] (AB, p. 13); "flowers, trees and crystals love me enough to take me by the hand … [and] he let himself be meditated by the flowers, as if, joining himself to their marvelous blooming… he took root in the thought of their roots" ["les fleurs, les arbres et les cristaux m'aiment suffisamment en me tenant la main… il se laissait méditer par les fleurs, comme si, se joignant à leur éclosion si féerique… il s'enracinait dans la pensée de leurs racines"] (AB, p. 64). He communes with the elements as he swims in the sea.

> He entered the night, eyes half closed. He needed still more stars, more asteroids around him; he needed still more brillance, the full force of the night, that astral breath, that exorbitant vision. Drunk, he gave himself utterly to the Ocean, offering up his thoughts even to the substance of the night. He sprang forth, transfigured, into the

unconceived. Superabundant joy! These were radiant visions: he saw himself above the water, mounted on a solar horse. Visions that brought him back to the earth, to the light, and to the beloved night.

[Il entra dans la nuit, les yeux mi-clos. Il lui fallait encore plus d'étoiles, plus d'astres autour de lui; il lui fallait plus de fulgurance, toute cette force nocturne, ce souffle astral, cette vision exorbitante. Grisé, il se donna entièrement à l'Océan, offrant ses pensées à la substance de la nuit même. Il surgit, transfiguré, dans l'inconçu. Joie surabondante! Ce furent des visions radieuses: il se voyait au-dessus de l'eau, sur un cheval solaire. Visions qui le ramenèrent à la terre, à la lumière, à la nuit aimée.]   (14)

The natural becomes a mode of transfiguration and the external is confounded with the beloved. He is moved by desire and ejaculates into the Ocean. This interaction (intercourse) between the sensate and the non-sensate, the animate and the inanimate, results in a perceptual and sexual interpentration of orders – the intrusion of the supernatural into the natural, that marks Khatibi's narrative.

The narrative frequently turns hallucinatory:

Just such a call [from the archangel – a winged and androgynous angel] had brought him face to face, very soon, with the place of his name in the hierarchy of angels and praying men. Later, he became drunk over that holy reading. One evening, he fell into a trance. He climbed the steps of the Book, spelling it out word by word; and separating the sky from the earth, the good from the bad, woman from man, he rose into the heavens. He then opened the invisible doors. He turned all the pages of the Book, devouring them with his eyes. Suddenly, he saw God. At that moment, he was the Book.

[Un tel rappel [d'"un ange… ailé et androgyne," 44] l'avait confronté, très tôt, à la question de son nom, dans la hiérarchie des anges et des hommes en prière. Plus tard, il fut grisé par cette lecture divine. Un soir, il était tombé en transes. Il gravit les marches du Livre, l'épelant mot à mot; et séparant le ciel de la terre, le bien du mal, la femme de l'homme, il monta au ciel. Il ouvrit alors les portes invisibles. Il tourna toutes les pages du Livre, les dévorant des yeux. D'un coup, il vit Dieu. A ce moment, il fut le Livre.]   (44)

Such hallucinatory images often derive, as here, from an involved play on words that calls forth a chain of associations – the reference to the Book, for example, which simultaneously alludes to the Qur'ān and turns on an autobiographical allusion to Khatibi's own (linguistic) self.

But the fantastic that erupts into the midst of the real is attributable not only to hallucination. The layering of events renders a similar effect. Later in the narrative, the narrator in the guise of the third-person protagonist ("he") loses control of his car, skids off the road, and falls asleep next to it, only to awaken in the middle of a wheat field. This event is fused with a car accident in which the narrator ("I") is involved and ends up in a field of wildflowers. And in yet a third version intertwined with these, the narrator has no accident but continues to drive to the sea where he takes a night swim. Upon this latter version the narrator overtly layers another story of a visit to Caracas – "There, right in the middle of the ocean, I must recount to you – so wet your fingers to turn the pages – a story that happened to me one evening on another beach, in Caracas" ["C'est-là, en pleine mer, que je dois te raconter – mouille tes doigts pour tourner les pages – mon histoire sur une autre plage à Caracas. C'était le soir"] (82).

In Caracas he "did the town" with a lame companion who taught him "to walk on one leg and with a dance-like step. A dance of drunkenness, it was, of poetry and of revolution sweeping across the entire continent" ["Il m'apprenait à marcher sur un seul pied et sur un pas de danse. Danse d'ivresse, voyons, de poésie et de révolution en marche à travers tout le continent"] (82). He laments the death of his companion and plunges into a Joycean rush of description that ends with a song he heard in Caracas entitled "Punto y raya":

> Entre tu pueblo y el mío
> hay un punto y una raya
> La raya dice: no hay paso
> El punto, vía cerrada.
> Y así entre todo los pueblos,
> raya y punto, punto y raya
> Con tantas rayas y puntos
> el mapa es un telegrama
> Caminando por el mundo
> se ven rios y montañas,
> se ven selvas y desiertos,
> pero no puntos ni rayas
> Porque esas cosas no existen,
> sino que fueron trazadas
> para que mi hambre y la tuya
> esten siempre separadas.

Between your town and mine
there is a point and a line
The line says: there is no passage
The point, road closed.
     And thus between all the towns
line and point, point and line
With so many lines and points
the map is a telegram
     Wandering through the world
one sees rivers and mountains
one sees meadows and deserts
but no points and lines
     Why do these things not exist
except that we might be laid out
so that my desire and yours
are always separated.

(My translation)

The layering of episodes or planes of existence is much like the dance of his own narrative; it is the dance of the *bi-langue*. Points and lines, that, while both offering closure in the song, suggest diacritical orders based on difference (like the components of Morse code) – are these not further suggestive of the two types of order that are brought into contiguity in the *bi-langue*: the systematized order of convention (dot), the open-ended order of the supernatural or non-conventional (dash)?

The protagonist learns, we are told, that all languages are bilingual, "oscillating between the spoken part and another, that affirms itself while destroying itself in the incommunicable" ["Il avait appris que toute langue est bilingue, oscillant entre le passage oral et un autre, qui s'affirme et se détruit dans l'incommunicable"] (*AB*, p. 27). Khatibi posits his creation of a postcolonial language expressive of his desires and concerns on this midground, on the paradox of a language balanced between the communicable and the incommunicable. Samuel Beckett, too, was preoccupied with this paradoxical midground. He once stated to Georges Duthuit that it is the very absence of relation "between the artist and the occasion" that he wished to make the subject of his art. It is up to the modern artist, he proposed, "to make of this submission, this fidelity to failure, a new occasion, a new term of relation, and of the act which, unable to act, obliged to act, he makes an expressive act, even if only of itself, of its impossibility, of its obligation."[15] Like the Beckettian narrator who experiences failure in face of the language, the postcolonial writer *à la* Khatibi makes of that failure the basis for a new idiom. Except that, contrary to Beckett, namelessness (the impossibility of a name) is not primarily the source of pain, but rather the source of fascination and salvation as well – "What fascinated him [the narrator–protagonist] was, as suggested by the no-name, that utopia and that void, which, effacing their sources, aspired to that grace of the unnameable, that charm of the forgotten. He admired that stupifying illusion that fought off the real" ["Ce qui le fascinait, c'étaient, par l'attrait du sans-nom, cette utopie et ce vide qui, effaçant leurs sources, se voulaient être cette grâce de l'innommable, ce charme de l'oubli. Il admirait cette stupéfiante illusion qui luttait contre le réel"] (*AB*, p. 34). Elsewhere he says, "Thus, I name myself in two languages by unnaming myself; I unname myself in reciting myself. Speaking in this no-name sense, the body revels in rupture and outbursts" ["Or, je me nomme à deux langues en m'y innommant; je m'y innomme en me récitant. Parlant selon cette direction du sans-nom, le corps jouit par rupture, par déchaînement"] (*AB*, p. 89). The language he comes to speak is a "language of dislocation" – "I was born without leaving a trace, I went mad without irrationality, irrational from day to day. Such an eccentric movement. I lived against my name, I loved against myself, in order that nothing might remain of my lucrubations" ["Je naissais sans laisser de trace, je devenais fou sans déraison, déraisonnable au jour le jour. Mouvement si excentrique. Je vivais contre mon nom, j'aimais contre moi-même, afin que rien ne reste de mes élucubrations"] (90). The *bi-langue* locates him elsewhere, in that gap he spoke of; it dislocates him, endows him with being without trace, craziness without madness, allows him to move ahead off center ("eccentric"), in an antinomical realm where he enters into tension with his very being – opposing himself to his name, loving in spite of himself, devoted to the strange project of ridding himself of his dark ravings,[16] the dark ravings perhaps that constitute his enunciations (his name suggesting the act of declaiming, oratory), his utterances of "self." The *bi-langue* would thus afford an escape, an entry into other dimensions of self that contain inconsistencies, contradiction, unexplored realms that unname him, for unnaming is to multiply, to evade, to escape recuperation by outside forces (was not it Whitman who said, "Do I contradict myself? So I contradict myself. I am vast and I contain multitudes"?).

The process of "unnaming" holds special value for Khatibi. He speaks of giving to the woman several names, such that she suffered from a loss of name. "She appeared, on her part, to delight in that loss of name, to draw new strength from it" ["Elle semblait, de son côté, jouir de cette perte de nom, y puiser de nouvelle forces"] (*AB*, p. 32). The loss of name (official identity) is accompanied by the corollary of loss of speech: "As soon as she was unnamed, she relapsed into childhood and stuttered astonishingly. Story without end and a very strange time, with its extraordinarily happy moments" ["Sitôt innommée, elle retombait dans l'enfance et un étonnant bégaiement. Histoire sans fin et période très étrange, avec ses grands moments heureux"] (32). The French "histoire" may be translated as "history" also. Moreover, the original elides "histoire" and "période." "Period," which in English may mean either a historical time or the sign of punctuation, in French emphasizes historical time of a defined (punctuated) duration. The fall of the woman back into childhood and her stammering are accompanied by a loss of history (her past) as well as entry into a time (or story) for which there exists no closure. The inference we might draw would be that loss of name and of speech frees one from the contingencies of social and linguistic systems – a liberated state carrying the possibility of "extraordinarily happy moments."

Autocriticism and the *bi-langue* as woman

Khatibi's narrative exemplifies the type of highly self-conscious writing of the authors I am studying – a trait familiar in the work of many other postcolonial authors who set out to break from the habits of traditional writing in order to forge a new idiom. More than most of these writers, however, Khatibi, in *Amour bilingue*, rarely steps out of the role of autocritic to assume that of story-teller. Rather, story-telling for him does not leave off being anything so much as a commentary on language and writing. The following phrase, that comes after a long digression (*AB*, pp. 41–91) occasioned by the description of a swim in the sea during which he is pulled into a whirlpool, is symptomatic: "And I have a tendency – I tend to the unheard of – to consider all the vicissitudes that I have recounted more or less happily (ocean and whirlpool) as a chain of utterances that can never dissociate themselves" ["Et j'ai tendance – je tends à l'inouï – à considérer toutes ces péripéties que j'ai racontées avec plus ou moins de bonheur (mer et tourbillon), à la manière d'une chaîne de vocables qui n'arrivent pas à se dissocier"] (*AB*, p. 91).

Early in the narrative, the narrator asks the woman about the city where she was born. As she speaks of it, he comes to feel that it becomes less real, less distinct, existing only in and protected only by her words, that, "once abandoned by words, that city would fall into ruins" ["son image se réduisait alors à cette parole, seule capable, à ces moments, de l'évoquer et de la protéger. Il constatait: abandonnée par les mots, cette ville tomberait en ruine"] (20). Khatibi reminds us that everything in his narrative takes on material substance through words alone. Furthermore, words intermingled, of the two languages they speak, produce an antinomical world where the real and the fantastic, the represented and imagined exist side by side – a sort of rhetorical magical realism.

In the opening words of his Epilogue, which I have cited – "The story fell joyously that autumn: the leaves, the leaves of paper, all that very real enchantment of my summer" – Khatibi typically mixes the ostensibly representational (his story about a love-affair with a woman) and the purely inward-directed narrative, such that the empirical autumn comes to double the writerly. Following this sentence, he speaks directly about his narrative: "To say now that this story is untouchable, that it is organized in the *bi-langue* by a double figure of reading, would be very mysterious" ["Dire maintenant que ce récit est intouchable, qu'il est organisé dans la bi-langue par un double chiffre de lecture, serait très mystérieux"]. But a double figure of reading does occur and it is indeed very mysterious (enigmatic), whereby the woman becomes the *bi-langue* and the external is linked inseparably to the internal. "If someone asked me," he continues, "'Is your story a new new novel [*nouveau nouveau roman*]? Or, better, a bi-new new novel?,' I'd reply that the novel never wanted much to do with me. We don't have the same history [story]" ["Si l'on me demandait: 'Votre récit est-il un nouveau nouveau roman? Ou mieux, un bi-nouveau nouveau roman?' je répondrais que le roman n'a jamais voulu de moi. Nous ne sommes pas de la même histoire"]. The conventions of the novel, in origin a Western genre, do not answer to his needs. As he clues us in more than once: though ostensibly taking up the novel form, he is writing an "other-literature" engendered by an "other-thought."

For hardly a moment does Khatibi allow us the unalloyed luxury of the illusion that the characters are anything but fictional creatures of language, paper beings (*êtres de papier*), as they have been called,[17] the media to convey the problematics of language and writing. The woman he speaks of and with whom he has an extended love affair is indeed language itself. At one moment, he speaks of the *bi-langue*:

> The *bi-langue* divides, gives rhythm to separation, while all unity has been since time immemorial uninhabited. The *bi-langue*! The *bi-langue*! Herself a character in this story, pursuing her quest across continents,

beyond my translations. The strange, foreign woman that you were, that you are in my language, will be the same in hers, a little more, a little less than my love for you.

[La bi-langue sépare, rythme la séparation, alors que toute unité est depuis toujours inhabitées. La bi-langue! La bi-langue! Elle-même, un personnage de ce récit, poursuivant sa quête intercontinentale, au-delà de mes traductions. L'étrangère que tu fus, que tu es dans ma langue, sera la même dans la sienne, un peu plus, un peu moins que mon amour pour toi.]   *(AB,* p. 109)

Apart from the love "story," the few anecdotes interspersed in his text re-enforce his illustration of what he wishes to say about language and writing. The following anecdote is typical:

One day I had met a multilingual stutterer. Curiously he collected dictionaries: it was touching! And, yes, if you do not comprehend that my language clashed within yours and that it stuttered within it, you will understand neither my disorders nor my stammering (real or feigned) that would allow you to get wrapped up in this story, I mean, to tie it up and mail it to its double destination.

[Un jour, j'avais rencontré un bègue plurilingue. Il collectionnait si curieusement les dictionnaires: c'était touchant! Eh oui, si tu ne comprends pas que ma langue s'est désaccordée dans la tienne et qu'elle y bégaie, tu n'entendras ni mes désordres ni mes balbutiements (réels ou simulés) pour t'emballer dans ce récit, je veux dire le ficeler et l'envoyer par la poste à sa double destination.]   (74)

This most cursory of allusions, condensed into three brief sentences, serves without pretense as a jumping off to his own thought. He address-es a "you" *(tu)* which is ambiguous – it could be the woman or a reader, ostensibly a French interlocutor. The multilingual man with a stammer could also be the narrator himself, who offers us dissociative phrases and constructions throughout the narrative. Might he not be referring to French as the language he stammers and mumbles, replete with traces of his mother tongue? Other such examples of dissociation appear in phras-es such as this one in which he describes himself looking upon himself being looked upon: "Seated, I saw myself seen by the night" ["Assis, je me voyais vu par la nuit"] *(AB,* p. 74). Ultimately, this dissociative motif comes to inform Khatibi's relationship with language itself, which takes on formidable force as a determinant of she who utters, and with writing as a determinant of she who writes.

Language gave me over to the totality of words, the *bi-langue* to their division within me: love, jealousy, disaster [themes he continuously comes back to]. This story, I swear, seeks me out and loves me more than I would have thought. And surely, I think less and less, ever since the end of the story is born each time in the last sentence. Henceforth, I am called to work under the sway of a law even more strange. There where I decide to speak, a phrase infallibly plants itself in front of me. It [she] watches me, sleeps, awakens at the end of my sleepless nights: I spell tremblingly, and from my trembling I don't wish to keep any pact sealed outside of it [her]: that phrase is my sole oath, and so long as it remains indecipherable, fixing me with such intensity in its [her] gaze, I shall be unable to tear myself from of its grasp.

[La langue m'a donné à la totalité des mots, la bi-langue à leur division en moi: amour, jalousie, désastre. Ce récit, je l'avoue, me cherche et m'aime plus que je n'aurais pensé. Et à coup sûr, je pense de moins en moins, dès lors que la fin du récit naît chaque fois à la dernière phrase. Désormais, je suis appelé à travailler sous l'ordre d'une loi encore plus étrange. Là où je décide de parler, une phrase est immanquablement plantée devant moi. Elle me regarde, dort, se réveille au bout de mes nuits blanches: j'épelle en tremblant, et de mon tremblement, je ne veux garder aucun pacte scellé en dehors d'elle: cette phrase est mon seul serment, et tant qu'elle sera indéchiffrable, me fixant avec une telle intensité, je serai incapable de m'arracher à son étreinte.]   (73)

He speaks of himself as carried along by the words. "I am myself a ceremony, a ritual of wandering, an exorcism of the unthought within me" ["Je suis moi-même une cérémonie, un rituel d'errance, un exorcisme de l'impensé en moi"] (74). The dissociation that sets up between the speaker/writer and the word a shifting movement whereby the writer writes and is written, the speaker speaks and is spoken, comes from the bilingual doubling that operates at the very core of this work. The narrator speaks of having entered the *bi-langue*, as he would have a woman, impregnating it with his "shooting pains." In addressing it/her, he says: "I will have transcribed you in your native tongue while ravishing you in mine" ["je t'aurai transcrite dans ta langue natale en te ravissant à la mienne"] (*AB*, p. 113). He refers to the woman/*bi-langue*, to his relationship with her and his mixing of the transcribed language (French) with his own (Arabic).

The woman appears at times as language given physical form. Indeed, at one point he elides language and the woman in this way: "Forever, the sensuous pleasure of your language will be my foreign queen" ["A tout jamais, la volupté de la langue est ma reine étrangère"] (*AB*, p. 71). Elsewhere he describes her as she lies sleeping and he caresses her: "The pleasure of language's body, inundating his obsessions with mutilation. They were caressing each other now, one dreaming oneself in the dream of the other ... The closer he approached her, the more she called him towards the unsayable" ["Jouissance du corps de la langue, inondant ses hantises de mutilation. Ils se caressaient maintenant, se rêvant l'un dans l'autre... Plus il allait vers elle, plus elle l'appelait vers l'indicible"] (*AB*, p. 23). In his allusions to her vertigo (for instance, *AB*, p. 24), one might wonder if it derives from the exhilaration of language breaking convention. He calls her the "daughter of the untranslatable" ["fille de l'intraduisible"] (*AB*, p. 24). "The things themselves invaded her, overflowing on all sides: things speaking for themselves, things for no one – ecstasy of their inconception" ["Les choses mêmes l'envahissaient, la débordant de toutes parts: choses parlantes pour elles-mêmes, choses pour personne – extase de leur inconception"] (*AB*, p. 24). Once again this phrase repeats the idea of language composing itself (cf. p. 3).

The fact that the love object, the woman, is often confounded with language, makes us keenly aware of the processes by which the *bi-langue* functions. The narrator says that "that which I desired in her was reversed in me: love's mirror, they say" ["et ce que je désirais en elle était en moi inversé: miroir d'amour, dit-on"] (*AB*, p. 73), leaving us to scan this thought in terms of language and its reversal, its transformation into a discourse of the other.

Concluding the unconcludable

The *bi-langue* leads to the phenomenon of doubling that forms the basis of the *pensée autre* or other thought. The problem tackled by Khatibi is to bring about the affirmation of difference and of self, and, concurrently, the resolution of the self–other dialectic through the creation of a true discourse that translates them. The narrator asks the question: "what is a bilingual desire that ends in a doubling?" To which he responds: "A double that translates the other without coming back to either the one or the multiple, they say, so they say" ["qu'est-ce un désir bilingue qui se termine doublement? Un double qui traduit l'autre sans revenir ni à l'un ni au multiple, on le dit, on le dit"] (*AB*, p. 119). In other words, bilingualism affords a "translation" of the other, without returning to the point of departure or subsuming the other into the multiple self/other. Réda

Bensmaïa states, in regard to the choice of language within which one writes, that, "it's no longer a question of knowing whether one *must* write in Arabic or in French, if that is necessary or contingent, politically correct or not, but of making emerge in writing and thought a level of 'otherness' (subliminal) that thoroughly nullifies the problematic of dualistic opposition" ["il ne s'agit plus de savoir s'il *faut* écrire en arabe ou en français, si cela est nécessaire ou contingent, politiquement juste ou faux, mais de faire apparaître un niveau autre (infraliminaire) d'écriture et de pensée qui rend profondément caduque la problématique de l'opposition dualiste"].[18] The aim of the *bi-langue* is the creation of a special space of subliminal "otherness" that transcends, as Bensmaïa points out, the question of mere duality, bipolarity, or dialectics.

The pseudo-dialogue of Western ethnocentric discourse has long spoken for the non-Western other of the so-called Third World, fabricating a pseudo-response that "answers" to a speech context defined in terms of Western ideology. Such an intertextual practice operates by means of an allegorizing identity that, as Stephen Tyler puts it, anesthetizes us to the other's difference.[19] The fallacy is to perceive of the other in terms of its likeness to us, as an analogue of our own self, rather than to seek to discover the differences that make up the other.

Implicit in Khatibi's narrative is a dialogical model that rejects the monological model of ethnocentric discourse, which, in seeking to know the other through scientific analysis, constitutes that other in terms of itself, of its ideological grounding. Conversely, Khatibi's dialogical model allows the other to speak for itself as a subject equal to us instead of as an object of knowledge. The difficulties of representing the other inhere in what Adorno views as the irreducible difference existing between external phenomena and our conceptual constructions.[20] Even if we were to replace this conceptualization of other as object of knowledge by the idea of other as subject of discourse, no less do we encounter the problem of how, in speaking for the other, in representing the speech of the other, in conceptualizing the other in terms comprehensible to us, we can avoid the erosion of difference existing between us.

To understand the other, distance between oneself and the other must be preserved – not in a subordinative way, but through an affirmation and acceptance of distance. The approach that would try to establish other as a mirror-image of self, through ideological, paternalistic or sentimental motives, would dispel the distance between self and other, and erode the difference between them that allows dialogue (Kauffmann,

"The Other in Question," p. 179). Michel Serres speaks of the attempt of dialogue to do away with interference or *noise* (those phenomena that interfere with communication[21]). Communication consists of two inter-locutors working to do away with any confusion or interference, to counter any persons or groups who seek to interrupt the communication (Serres, "Platonic Dialogue," p. 67). Thus, when we open a dialogue, we project the existence of a third man whom we try to prevent from enter-ing in. Should we succeed, the dialogue will be successful. Serres locates the true dialectical problem of dialogue, not in the other, who is only a variation of the same, but in the problem of the third man. He proposes that we call that third man, whom we seek to exclude, the demon or "prosopopeia" of noise (*Ibid.*, p. 67).

In the authors I study, the third thing or the *tertium quid*, or the noise that impedes or prevents communication between the two interlocutors (narrator and empirical reader), can be construed, on the one hand, as the European third, on the other, as the Islamic third that is excluded (*tiers exclu*), ideally prevented from misshaping, interfering with, or appropri-ating the communication. These dominant thirds are the demons that must be exorcised so that the postcolonial alternate other might be heard. On the other hand, the excluded third ("noise") is the indispens-able interference without which dialogue would not be possible.[22]

Interestingly, and contrary to Serres' definition of dialogue as the exclusion of a third party in order to facilitate communication, Khatibi does not put communication foremost. In fact, he puts distance between himself and the reader: by maintaining a marked degree of alienness, of strangeness, a plane of difference, by using diverse forms of alien/estranged discourse that is dispersed, hidden or obscured[23], that the reader often finds impossible to interpret. Abdallah Mdarhri-Alaoui sug-gests that, "Khatibi's text mimics mystical writing in the sense that it favors dialogic (I–you) narration while constantly obscuring the sources of utterances in a perpetual decentering that re-enforces the androgy-nous ambiguity of the characters and their grounding in spatial, tempo-ral, and phenomenological terms."[24] This decentering of which Mdarhri-Alaoui speaks, and which results in the disintegration and dis-persion of the narrator and "other" characters, forms the basis for the alien or estranged discourse that marks Khatibi's work and renders it unseizable by the magisterial discourse.

The narrator, in a postmodern vein, replaces the master narratives of the West with a proliferation of those narrative repositionings referred to

in my introduction, which Jean-François Lyotard, using the term of Ludwig Wittgenstein, calls "language games."[25] As I have alluded, such
devices work to delegitimize these master narratives by revising,
through dialogue, the structures they have laid down and, as Wittgenstein suggests, by inventing rules and even altering them as we go
along.[26] The master narratives are replaced in *Amour bilingue* by games of
dialogical invention, glossophilic verbal play, as well as by the little stories and anecdotes told by the narrator. Story-telling holds special importance in Khatibi's bag of narrative devices, as in that of the other authors I
consider – a characteristic, of course, of postmodern writing in general
and of postcolonial narrative in particular, both of which mix genres and
hark back to the orality of language, before the word was technologized.
Oral communication, though managed, is not rigidly fixed, but retains
the potential of change and variation.[27]

From such devices as dialogue invention, language play, and story-
telling results a narrative marked by indeterminacy, variability, and endless permutation.

Contrary to traditional, representational literature of Europe, in
viewing meaning as deriving from language, rather than language as an
instrument to convey a pre-existing "reality," Khatibi posits the "real" as
an effect of linguistic production. Philippe Sollers argues that: "Writing
is not the servant of the real or the economy; it is the force of symbolic
transformation."[28] Sollers' idea accords with Khatibi's assumption
regarding the narrative imagination, his belief in the discontinuity or
divorce between language and the external world in terms of one-to-one
relationships between words and things, which results in "the experience of the being of language," as we infer from Carlos Fuentes' words.[29]

Every new speech act reshapes the identity of the subject in dialogue
such that identity is embedded in language (Maranhão, *The Interpretation
of Dialogue*, p. 19). By being concerned with itself, by putting into focus
language as subjective experience, "the experience of [it's own] being,"
and writing as the "experience of limits" (Sollers, "Réponses"), the dialogical model is admirably suited to convey the material presence of the
postcolonial other.

By such devices and tactics as we have seen in *Amour bilingue* – dialogue
invention, language play, and story-telling – Khatibi fragments the narrative and creates a new narrative world that replaces the old totalistic
universe governed by the master narratives.

I emphasize again, however, the need to distinguish between Serre's theory of dialogue and the implicit dialogical model of Khatibi. As I have indicated, Serre maintains that the holders of dialogue seek to exclude a third person who impedes communication. But Khatibi, in putting forth a new, alternative discourse based on dialogical exchange, does not seek merely to replace European/Islamic discourse by communicating a subject-matter grounded in difference. Rather he calls into question the view of dialogue/discourse as fundamentally communicative in nature. Khatibi's narrator says, "I am aiming at something else in the incalculable, that experience of the unthought-of, which accepts and refuses all categories of thought without nullifying them, nor unifying them, and which ceases to transmit, to communicate whatever may be involved" ["je vise autre chose dans l'incalculable, cette épreuve de l'impensé, qui accepte et refuse toutes les catégories de la pensée, sans les annuler, ni les unifier, et qui cesse de transmettre quoi que ce soit"] (*AB*, pp. 119–20). The *pensée-autre* he seeks renders equalities, equivalences, and dialectical pairs (beloved/lover, angel/demon [*AB*, pp. 119–20]) unclassifiable. "Yes, the end of all hierarchy of that sort was the resolve of that *pensée-autre*, unadorned and explosive" ["Oui, la fin de toute hiérarchie de cette sorte était la fermeté de cette pensée-autre, nue et explosive"] (*AB*, p. 120). By fashioning an alternative discourse based on an "other thought," Khatibi aims at a depositioning of discourse whereby all discourses lose privileged position and are put on the same level.

The *pensée-autre* thus holds the prospect of a new literature. The narrator asks, "Literature? Why not! Let's agree, nothing is to be condemned! An other-literature born from thought no less other, to the very end of time" ["La littérature? Pourquoi pas! rien n'est condamnable, voyons! Une littérature-autre selon une pensée non moins autre, jusqu'à la fin des temps"] (*AB*, p. 131).

The model for postcolonial discourse envisaged by Khatibi translates self and other without fusing them – and exemplifies the *impensé* or *pensée autre* of which Khatibi speaks at length in *Maghreb pluriel*. On page 120 of *Amour bilingue*, he describes the woman in this way: "Not only did she not resemble her parents (where did she come from then?), but in her own language, the home country of her body, she made herself unclassifiable. Other-thought: she envisaged no living place, nor a place of death, and if one might have invoked her absence, I believe that for her this word would have been only mockery, the revenge of a nameless presence" ["Non seulement elle ne ressemblait pas à ses parents (d'où venait-elle donc?), mais dans sa langue même, patrie de son corps, elle se rendait inclassable. Pensée-autre: elle ne vit aucun lieu vivant, ni mort non plus, et si l'on eût invoqué l'absence, je crois que pour elle ce mot n'eût été qu'une dérision, la vengeance d'une présence sans nom"].

He also describes the woman as "the figure of the unfigurable, around which this other-thought unceasingly revolved. As for the unthought-of, she felt only this obsession to differentiate herself, whatever the cost, from any concept that brought her to her knees" ["Elle était la figure de l'infigurable, autour de laquelle tournait et tournait cette pensée-autre. De l'impensé, elle ne sentait que cette hantise de se différencier, coûte que coûte, de tout concept qui la mit à genoux"] (AB, p. 122). We have here the perfect description of an alternate discourse seeking its difference and refusing to be coopted.

To come to an end of my remarks, in Roland Barthes' Postface written for Khatibi's La Mémoire tatouée, which I cited in my introduction, he concludes that Khatibi's originality lies in the fact that he proposes to "rediscover at the same time identity and difference: an identity of such a pure metal, so incandescent, that it obliges us to read it as difference" ["retrouver en même temps l'identité et la différence: une identité telle, d'un métal si pur, si incandescent, qu'elle oblige quiconque à la lire comme une différence"].[30]

Khatibi's theorizing of a new literature rewrites the language of power – whether the secular or religious power of Western societies or the theocratic power of the Islamic faith – by effacing all metanarratives and beginning again. Through a leveling discourse, through the thinking of the "unthought-of" that rejects categories of hegemonic thought "without nullifying them, nor unifying them," the new postcolonial discourse of North Africa theorized by Khatibi is in process of constituting an other-literature out of the shards and laminae of colonialist and neocolonialist discourse. As Khatibi's Tunisian confrère Abdelwahab Meddeb has remarked in his novel Phantasia: "We stride in ancient footsteps. The earth resonates beneath our feet. We move toward uncharted realms."[31] Khatibi, along with Meddeb and other "Third World" authors, moves towards just such realms of liberating discourse.

The phenomenon of making the incommunicable, the unthought-of, the unfinished, the basis of a new discourse is shared by a number of postcolonial writers of the Maghreb – along with Khatibi and Meddeb we must range the Moroccan, Tahar Ben Jelloun, and the Algerian, Assia Djebar – in all of whose discourses, as Barthes says of Khatibi, identity is of such a pure metal that it comes to be read as difference.

The view from underneath: Salman Rushdie's
Satanic Verses

[T]hose of us who did not have our origins in the countries of the
mighty West, or North, had something in common – not, certainly,
anything as simplistic as a unified "third world" outlook, but at least
some knowledge of what weakness was like, some awareness of the
view from underneath, and of how it felt to be there, looking up at the
descending heel.   SALMAN RUSHDIE, *The Jaguar Smile*[1]

Without Contraries is no progression. Attraction and Repulsion,
Reason and Energy, Love and Hate, are necessary to human existence.

From these contraries spring what the religious call Good & Evil.
Good is the passive that obeys Reason. Evil is the active springing
from Energy.

Good is Heaven. Evil is Hell.   WILLIAM BLAKE,
The Marriage of Heaven and Hell[2]

In the scheme of the book I have undertaken to write, which treats
in considerable detail the position of North African Muslim authors who
have adopted French as their writerly language, the introduction of
Salman Rushdie at the end makes us mindful of important similarities
existing with Muslim authors born in Islamic communities elsewhere
and writing in European languages. The situation of Maghrebian
authors attempting in their writings to locate themselves in a space
somewhere outside or apart from that of dominant religious, political,
and social structures of Islamic and European countries, upon which they
nevertheless draw and in the face of which they seek to preserve their singularity, translates fluently to a discussion of the Anglo-Indian Rushdie.

It is important that I locate myself in regard to Rushdie. The material
in this chapter was essentially completed in substance in mid-1988, nearly

a year before the Ayatollah Ruhollah Khomeini issued his *fatwa* on Valentine's Day, 1989, decreeing the death of Salman Rushdie.[3] When later I contemplated including a chapter on Rushdie in the project that has evolved into this book, my initial inclination was to choose another Rushdie narrative to study, in order to obviate any feeling on the part of readers that I was capitalizing on the controversy. I came to realize, however, that precisely those characteristics that brought forth Khomeini's decree were at the core of my own study of the postcolonial writer face to face with authoritarian power.

Also, and even more importantly, while assuming an undeniable oppositional stance in the way I have defined it, the *Satanic Verses* remains a work of fiction that, in drawing upon the riches of European, Islamic, and Hindu tradition, as well as opposing what the author regarded as their totalizing excesses, attempts to bring about a "radical reformulation of language, form and ideas," and insists on our seeing the world "anew," as the word *novel* implies. Therein lies its importance. More specifically, the work of Rushdie, who migrated from his native India and has spoken of himself equally as Indian, Pakistani, and English, presents "a migrant's-eye view of the world," through the creation of "a literary language and literary forms in which the experience of formerly-colonized, still-disadvantaged peoples might find full expression."[4] Far from yielding to my momentary disinclination, I have come to feel that no other work of Salman Rushdie has gone further in the struggle to lessen the hold of the state (or ruling discourses of states) over our minds and means of expression.

I am interested in dealing with the literary and discursive structures, cultural context, and plurality of signification of the *Satanic Verses*, with only passing reference to the so-called "Rushdie Affair," would it be more accurate to call it the Ayatollah Khomeini Affair?, but with the awareness that these same structures and meanings are inseparable from social, religious, and political issues. The spate of books on Rushdie's *Satanic Verses* ranges from intemperate ones such as M. M. Ahsan and A. R. Kidwai's *Sacrilege Versus Civility. Muslim Perspectives on the Satanic Verses Affair*, Shabbir Akhtar's *Be Careful with Muhammad. The Rushdie Affair*, and Richard Webster's *A Brief History of Blasphemy. Liberalism, Censorship and 'The Satanic Verses'* to those that seek to present a balanced view by understanding both sides: Lisa Appignanesi and Sara Maitland's *The Rushdie File*, Daniel Pipes' *The Rushdie Affair*, and Malise Ruthven's *A Satanic Affair: Salman Rushdie and the Wrath of Islam*.[5]

Relatively few critics speak of Rushdie's *Satanic Verses* with an under-standing of the novel as fictional narrative. Many fellow Muslims have castigated him for presenting a distorted view of Islamic history. Even arguments by Muslim critics that presume to examine the literary merit of the *Satanic Verses* turn on non-literary judgments. Ziauddin Sardar criticizes Rushdie as an exponent of "the postmodern genre of magical realism," which "aims at turning history into amnesia" by deliberately and systematically blurring "the boundaries of fact and fiction [to show that] reality is often imagined and imagination often becomes real." Sardar sees behind the *Satanic Verses* "the fictional form of Marxist theorist Jean Baudrillard's theory of semulacurum [*sic*]".[6] These comments of Sardar show, not only ignorance of contemporary thought, but a notable failure to understand the literary dimensions of Rushdie's narrative.

Rushdie's reply to this extra-literary criticism was to the effect that, "The Book is being judged and misjudged by having the historical method applied to what is in fact an imaginative text ... To say that a work of fiction is basically a work of fact in disguise [whose aim] is to distort facts is wrong. The real purpose of fiction is not to distort facts but to explore human nature, to explore ideas on which the human race rests itself."[7] These same critics read Rushdie's book literally, as a factual rather than an imaginative rendering of human nature and the external world. The problem comes in part, as Pipes points out, from the reading of novels (the written word) in the Islamic Middle East, which "tends to be a more programmatic experience than a literary one," for the "traditional sense [holds] that the written word must describe truth; storytelling in the bazaar is one thing, but a published and bound book is quite another" (*The Rushdie Affair*, p. 112). Pipes' point, of course, is that truth is packaged very differently in literary and non-literary forms. Cultural differences enter strongly into the attitudes formed, actions taken, and reactions in regard to the *Satanic Verses*.

Some exceptions among studies of Rushdie's narrative, that read it as literature or with literary understanding are James Harrison's *Salman Rushdie*, Timothy Brennan's *Salman Rushdie & the Third World*, Mark Edmundson's essay "Prophet of a New Postmodernism," and certain essays in D. M. Fletcher's edited collection *Reading Rushdie*.[8] Such works stand out for their relative rarity. The controversy surrounding Rushdie's narrative has elicited numerous thorny questions revolving around issues such as censorship, oppositionality, the ways different cultures read texts, the uses of imaginative literature – all of which to some degree enter into my study. And, though I again insist on the primary concern of this book as being literary, I cede to the observation that one cannot talk literature without engaging issues of cultural, social, and political relevance.

I shall now set out on the last turning of my path.

Locating Rushdie

As Jumpy makes his way to the house of his mistress, Pamela Chamcha, in Rushdie's *Satanic Verses*, he decides that his resentment of his friend Hanif Johnson is primarily linguistic. "Hanif was in perfect control of the languages that mattered: sociological, socialistic, black-radical, anti-anti-anti-racist, demagogic, oratorical, sermonic: the vocabularies of power."[9] But Hanif, to Jumpy's way of thinking, misconceives what is at stake linguistically: "*The real language problem: how to bend it shape it, how to let it be our freedom, how to repossess its poisoned wells, how to master the river of words of time of blood: about all that you haven't got a clue.*[10] How hard that struggle, how inevitable the defeat. *Nobody's going to elect me to anything. No power-base, no constituency: just the battle with the words.*" Jumpy admires, nonetheless, his friend's control of the language. "Language is courage," he reflects, "the ability to conceive a thought, to speak it, and by doing so to make it true" (*SV*, p. 281).

Rushdie's prodigious epic narrative, *The Satanic Verses*, fundamentally involves a linguistic problem on the order of that mentioned by Jumpy – the need to reclaim language, to repossess the wells poisoned by the discourses of power, to invent a discourse for those underneath. As George Steiner and others have so convincingly argued and so well shown, literature in the last 100 years in the West, particularly oppositional literature, has turned more and more away from the world, towards a minimalist discourse, premised on a profound distrust of language as a means to translate or communicate thought and desire, which effectively disengages it from the empirical world by creating a private discourse of sharply narrowed compass. We witness this tendency in the works of such major writers as Mallarmé, Beckett, Duras, and Blanchot. And even to some degree in Khatibi.

Rushdie, in company with certain other postcolonial writers, represents a counter trend leading the narrative away from wordlessness and silence. He creates a narrative at once disarmingly traditional in its emphasis on story-telling and imaginary/poetic invention, and radical in its formal and contextual functioning. In his earlier novel, *Midnight's*

Children, Rushdie introduces the motif of fragmentation in the circumstances of the perforated sheet through whose seven-inch circular hole Dr. Aziz views/experiences isolated parts of the ailing young woman Naseem. The motif reappears as the narrator, Saleem Sinai, speaks of his body cracking[11] and as Amina resolves to fall in love with her husband "bit by bit" (*MC*, pp. 63, 68). This same motif figures in the dilemma and threatened defeat facing the writer, as Jumpy sees it. On the one hand, the Anglo-Indian writer is smitten with what Rushdie has called the Indian disease – the "urge to encapsulate the whole of reality" (*MC*, p. 84)[12] – while, on the other hand, he deals with a language constantly under threat of disintegration, like himself, in its, his, encounter with empirical reality.

Rushdie's characters in the *Satanic Verses*, exhibiting a porousness of being reminiscent of that of Kandar in Kundera's *The Intolerable Lightness of Being*, are, if anything, even more prone to dissolution, shattering, cracking. Around every corner we meet these brittle yet often indomitable beings – Rosa Diamond, a "creature of cracks and absences" (*SV*, p. 130), the glass man in Chamcha's dream (34), and the woman in the asylum whose skin has turned to glass (169). The *Satanic Verses*, Rushdie himself has told us, is written out of the very experience of uprootedness, disjunction, and metamorphosis that characterizes the migrant condition, and that condition can itself serve as a metaphor for humanity at large ("A Pen Against the Sword," p. 52). From such experience also derives the medium of Rushdie's narrative, a narrative incessantly dissolving and recombining into new forms, throwing off shards and fragments which Rushdie the *bricoleur* recombines into new episodes and situations. Everything becomes a pretext for story-telling. We encounter a dynamic rush of narrative in the process of inventing itself, a grotesque and irreverent manner, a use of parody and travesty as regenerative forces seldom wielded with such power and purpose since Sterne and Diderot.

An epigraph, drawn from Defoe's *History of the Devil*, which describes Satan condemned to eternal wandering without abode – "without any fixed place, or space, allow[ing] him to rest the sole of his foot upon" – introduces from the outset the motif of migrancy and vagabondage reflected in the situation of most of the characters we encounter in Rushdie's narrative. As the narrator mentions, they are not, however, nomads for whom the journeying itself becomes home, but migrants, for whom the journey constitutes a necessary evil: "the point is to arrive"

(94). One might say, then, that we find here the motivation, in a Shklovskian sense, that moves the narrative forward: the need to arrive. Whether arrival ever occurs will be a subject for later discussion.

The principals in Rushdie's extravagant miracle play are Gibreel Farishta and Saladin Chamcha, both, like Rushdie, born in Bombay, who achieve success in the world of film, radio, and television – the former a superstar of Indian film, the latter the foremost radio voice of London. Both characters are creatures of false appearance and dissimulation: Gibreel an outsize effigy ubiquitously plastered over billboards throughout Bombay (16); Saladin, a disincarnate voice – the Man of a Thousand Voices and a Voice on radio commercials who breathed verbal life into inanimate objects as diverse as ketchup bottles, garlic-flavored crisps, and carpets (in a radio play, he once interpreted, under a variety of pseudonyms, every part for 37 voices, "and nobody ever worked it out"!, 60). Rushdie's main characters (before their fall, which I shall get to) are role-players: reified, alienated from anything identifiable as verisimilar "real-life" beings. Examples abound: Gibreel is idolized on the screen, but, at close quarters with his female co-star Miss Pimple Billimoria, his breath stinks; Saladin starts out by being a voice-over and, later, in his new television show for children, *The Aliens Show*, he wears a mask and constantly changes guises.

The sudden disappearance of the superstar Gibreel from Bombay is tantamount, the narrator tells us, to "the death of God" (16). His fame has arisen from his roles in popular genre films called "theologicals," in which he played supernal deities of the Indian subcontinent. For his fans, "the boundary separating the performer and his roles had long ago ceased to exist" – he had become for them the "face of the Supreme" (17).

As actors, then, Gibreel and Saladin have become wholly Other – "Masks beneath masks until suddenly the bare bloodless skull" (34). When Gibreel disappears, people speculate whether his fate might not be tied to that of India itself.

In fact, Gibreel and Saladin incarnate the weakness (and, in another light, the strength) of the Indian himself, a migrant and eclectic being without a self he can call his own: "Was not the entire national culture based," Zeeny Vakil explains, "on the principle of borrowing whatever clothes seemed to fit, Aryan, Mughal, British, take-the-best-and-leave-the-rest?" (50). The Indian penchant for transmutation resembles that of the couple played for London television by Saladin and Mimi Mamoulian (his Jewish co-actor) in *The Aliens Show*: invisible creatures constantly undergoing permutation, changing their voices "along with their clothes, to say nothing of their hair, which could go from purple to vermilion between shots, which could stand diagonally three feet up from their heads and vanish altogether; or their features and limbs, because they were capable of changing all of them, switching legs, arms, noses, ears, eyes, and every switch conjured up a different accent from their legendary, protean gullets" (62).

Such is Rushdie's Indian in a Western context, but he reminds us that it is not solely a question of the Indian migrating to the West, for Western culture infiltrates the Indian subcontinent as surely and as insidiously as the invisible poisonous gas emerging from the stacks of Union Carbide, insinuating itself into the lungs and breathing passages of the people of the city of Bhopal (52). Like that poison gas, "Amrika" represents "Power in its purest form, disembodied, invisible. We can't see it," Zeeny's Indian friend George explains, "but it screws us totally, no escape" (56).

The Indian in Rushdie's narrative, even at home, assumes thus the figure of the migrant undergoing constant mutation. The heart of Rushdie's India, Bombay – that impossible city embodying the Indian character – is called by the narrator "a culture of re-makes." It is a postmodern fantasy mimicking the Western metropolis, and the center of the most robust and flamboyant film industry in the world. In such a setting, characters often feel a sense of loss or displacement. When Saladin returns to Bombay from London he is seized by the melancholy feeling that the garden of his youth, with its strange and unknown flora, "had been a better place before he knew its names, that something had been lost which he would never be able to regain" (45). This loss, consequent upon the acquisition of knowledge, stands as a metaphor for Rushdie's Anglo-Indian migrant, departed from a lost paradise, an Eden left behind, victim of a fall.

Rushdie opens his novel with a Miltonic Fall – an Epic Fall – in which his principal characters tumble from the sky after hijackers have blown up the plane that carries them from India over the English Channel. The novel begins suitably with disintegration and fall, accompanied by a process of transmutation heralded by Gibreel Farishta's singing "to be born again" as he tumbles from the "heavens" (3). The narrator describes the topos of fall, the air space – the narrative space, we might add – as a place of change, a "defining location" where everything is possible (5).[13]

He likens the fall to birth, "newness" coming into the world (8). Chapter 2 begins, in fact, with the word "reincarnation."

The metamorphoses, transformations, and permutations that make of the world of Rushdie's narrative a phantasmagorical setting where magic and unfettered change rule, are nowhere better exemplified than in the episodes of Gibreel's stay with the 88-year-old widow, Rosa Diamond, who harbors Gibreel and Saladin after their landing on a snow-covered English beach, and of the incarceration of Chamcha in Part III. The second chapter begins with the traditional Arabic phrase: *Kan ma kan / Fi qadim azzaman*, rendered by the English "It was so, it was not, in a time long forgot." The phrase *Kan ma-Kan* gave its name to a well-known genre of popular narrative poetry in Arabic and provides the opening of many of the older tales of *The Thousand and One Nights*. It became so stereotypical in its usage in a composite sense (like "Once upon a time") that any micro-analysis of its inner semantics in regard to its traditional Arabic usage holds questionable significance.[14] But, for Rushdie, ever mindful of the parts as well as of the whole, the phrase takes on special importance for his narrative, for it suggests an antinomical narrative in which opposites, mutually contradictory propositions, are not only possible but consciously invoked.

The story of Rosa's previous life and loves in Argentina begins, and, as Gibreel listens to it, he feels himself constantly beset with the sensation of tugging at his abdomen. The story turns into the dream of Argentina and plunges him into bizarre visions – of an ostrich racing along the sand of an English beach, of the English marshland changed into pampa, of a pony cart full of Argentine celebrants in the middle of an English village, of himself transformed into Rosa's former lover, Martín de la Cruz. Gibreel reaches the point where he realizes that he has become the prisoner of Rosa, just as he was the prisoner of Mahound in his dream of the Prophet. He discovers that the tugging at his abdomen comes from a shining cord linking his navel to that of Rosa, similar to the cord that linked him to Mahound (and just as later he is bound, imprisoned, "used" as a medium, by Ayesha and, ultimately, by the narrator).

Meanwhile, Chamcha, after his arrest as an illegal immigrant, is carried away in a police van in which the police discover the state of metamorphosis he is undergoing – from that of an ordinary human being into that of an infernal creature with a filthy goatish body, powerful hairy thighs between which is lodged an indecently large sexual organ, and legs which terminate in cloven hooves. He drops dung over the floor of the van, is forced to eat it, and is otherwise humiliated and brutalized by the police. He ends up in the hospital ward of the Detention Centre. There he finds himself surrounded by animal-like beings, mutants of all description, "men and women who were also partially plants, or giant insects, or even, on occasion, built partly of brick or stone; there were men with rhinoceros horns instead of noses and women with necks as long as any giraffe" (171). The manticore (suggested to Rushdie perhaps by Borges' manticore) tells him how they (the immigrant detainees) change: "They describe us ... they have the power of description, and we succumb to the pictures they construct" (168). The "they" who "describe" them are the powers that be, the legislators of the discourse used by the white inhabitants of London, by the Westerners. Their power of description is grounded in a narrative that defines, outlines, and fixes the non-Westerner, turns him into a demonic entity, grotesque and threatening, in need of incarceration in ghettos, detention centers, asylums, and jails.

Another power exists, however, a discursive counterpower. We recall the comments of the narrator himself when he remarks on the effects of the fall from the sky that brings about changes in Chamcha and Gibreel: "What did they expect?" he asks, "Falling like that out of the sky: did they imagine there would be no side-effects? Higher Powers had taken an interest, it should have been obvious to them both, and such Powers (I am, of course, speaking of myself) have a mischievous, almost wanton attitude to tumbling flies." He goes on to speak of the effects of falling, of long plunges, using himself, with ominous prescience, as an example ("In the matter of tumbles, I yield pride of place to no personage"), plunges which inevitably bring about mutations, "not all of them random. Unnatural selections. Not much of a price to pay for survival," he observes, "for being reborn, for becoming *new*" (133; cf. 408–09).

This is not the first time that the narrator has alluded to his mischievousness, his perversity. When he speaks of the city of Jahilia, a city built entirely of sand, whose enemy is water, he vents a devilish desire: in his "wickedness" ("I, in my wickedness"), he imagines a great wave of foaming water swamping the city and reducing it to nothingness (94). Such a detail underscores a seeming purposiveness. Is the narrator not also the creator/enunciator of the "Satanic Verses," for they result ostensibly from the narratorial imperative? Is it not his choice (or that of the author) to unearth heretical (suppressed) material concerning the early life of Muhammad? Is he not fulfilling the role of an *agent provocateur*, like Satan/Shaitan himself, or like someone on an anti-quest who, emulating the doubting angels (92), dares to ask a series of anti-questions in regard to established power? (Human beings are not so easily pacified as angels, however: they have will, we are told, and "To will is to disagree; not to submit; to dissent.") Is he not also the one who chooses the name for Gibreel's dream-image of Muhammad ("*our* mountain-climbing, prophet-motivated solitary," my emphasis; 93) – the personage whom the narrator endows with "the Devil's synonym: Mahound" (93). Mahound was the name used by Christian authors of the *chansons de geste* in the medieval period to refer disparagingly to Muhammad himself, the "medieval baby-frightener" they deemed the false prophet.[15]

Two powers engage in implicit conflict in the *Satanic Verses*. First, the power of institutionalized authority that adjudicates the laws governing traditional Western (European, Anglo-American) and Eastern (Islamic, Arabic, Hindu) magisterial narratives, which in the case of the West has seized control of the sign and represents the postcolonial personage (the migrant) as a figure of alterity, a monster who disrupts the peaceful, law-abiding existence of the London bourgeoisie, and which in the case of the Islamic East rigorously selects and frames the details of the legend on which it bases the life of Muhammad and the jurisprudence (*fiqh*) legislating Islamic society.

The second power is that of the writer/narrator/*agent provocateur*, the bugaboo of established wisdom and belief, he who dissents, who challenges the doxy, who seeks, as Ross Chambers says, "room for maneuver" in a society meant to confine movement and thought, above all, who initiates countermovement and counterthought.[16] This power of the writer/narrator underlies the creation of an anti-narrative, a counternarrative that opposes the authoritarian rule of Western and Eastern house narrative, institutionalized perception and received ideas. It is, to be sure, out of this institutionalized perception that individuals and groups, belonging primarily to the Shi'a sect, perceived Rushdie's novel to be an attack on the orthodox religious faiths of Islam and Hinduism.[17]

How does Rushdie's narrative develop its tactics of opposition? It does so, as I see it, in two interrelated ways: (1) through the antilogical angle of contestation along which his discourse unravels,[18] which calls into question the rhetorical/philosophical predicates underlying conventional discourse and thought; (2) through the perceptual field in which objects and events are viewed, which opposes the immutability and logic of official cultural fields. The first way invokes rhetorical (reasoning) processes; the second way invokes spatial processes, that is, movement within a defined locus.

Logical versus antilogical discourse

Repossessing the poisoned wells of language

Let us first look at the antilogical character of Rushdie's discourse. After the wolf and the manticore attempt to persuade Chamcha to escape the Detention Centre, he is described as having "woke and slept as if the two conditions no longer required to be thought of as opposites, but as states that flowed into and out of one another to create a kind of unending delirium of the senses" (169). Through the power of counterdescription asserted by Rushdie's narrator, the reader enters an antilogical world where eristic processes rule supreme and challenge received ideas of established narrative discourse and authority, East and West. The art or operation of "antilogic" (from the Greek *antilogike*), attributed primarily to the Sophists, describes very well Rushdie's discursive tactics. Antilogic, as G. B. Kerferd defines it for us (and as I cited in my chapter on Ben Jelloun), "consists in causing the same thing to be seen by the same people now as possessing one predicate and now as possessing the opposite or contradictory predicate."[19] It is a technique whereby, by opposing one logos (that is, argument) to another logos, one's opponent is led either to accept both logoi or to abandon the original proposition (Kerferd, "Dialectic, Antilogic and Eristic," p. 63).

Rushdie's discourse introduces contrariety and contradiction, challenging the logical, scholastic contention that a thing cannot be and not not be at the same time. His discourse establishes a parallel in this regard to the preconscious state of Chamcha in which wakefulness and dream coexist. In fact, the narrative, which often attributes its source to Gibreel Farishta's dream, operates according to an oneiric-like logic characterized by emphatic ambiguity. The story of Mahound, in particular, is one of the major dream narratives or theological constructs of Gibreel Farishta, who assumes the role of the archangel Gibreel (Gabriel) and at times appears to be confounded as well with Mahound to whom he is ineluctably connected. Gibreel finds himself in a state of "hovering-above-looking-down," bound by a shimmering umbilical cord to Mahound, who is in a state of listening, of trance (*SV*, p. 110). When Mahound has a vision of being visited by the Archangel, Gibreel feels a voice working his jaw, drawing forth words that appear to emanate from

Mahound himself. In this way, the Archangel Gabriel transmits the verses Mahound will utter in the public assembly of the Grandee Abu Simbel,
acknowledging the pagan goddesses Lat, Uzza, and Menat as angels, in
exchange for the Grandee's recognition of Allah as the Supreme Being.

Later, after wrestling with the Archangel – in the form of the humble
Gibreel – Mahound comes to believe that the previous encounter with
the Archangel was really with Shaitan (Satan) and that the verses uttered
in the poetry tent were satanically inspired and must be repudiated. He
hurries to the House of the Black Stone in the city (the Kaaba in Mecca
houses this most venerated of Muslim objects), where he abrogates "the
foul verses that reek of brimstone and sulphur, to strike them from the
record for ever and ever, so that they will survive in just one or two unreliable collections of old traditions and orthodox interpreters will try and
rewrite their story" (123).

The verses that have come to be known historically in the West as the
satanic verses, originally revealed to Muhammad, followed the present
verses 19–20 of Surah LIII (The Star) of the Qur'ān:

> Have you considered al-Lat and al-'Uzza
> And Manat, the third, the other?   (vv. 19–20)

The satanic verses that have survived in commentaries characterize these
pagan goddesses in the following manner:

> They are the Exalted Birds
> And their intercession is desired indeed.[20]

Verses 19–23 of the official (that is, authorized) version of Surah LIII of the
Qur'ān, which expunge the satanic verses received by Muhammad, read
as follows:

> Did you consider al-Lat and al-'Uzza
> And al-Manat, the third, the other?
> For you males and for Him females? That would be unfair sharing.
> They are but names you and your father names; God revealed no
>   authority for them; they [the worshippers of the idols] follow only
>   opinion and their souls' fancies, though from their Lord there has
>   come to them guidance.   (vv. 19–23)

The satanic verses were profoundly heretical because, by allowing for
the intercession of the three pagan female deities, they eroded the
authority and omnipotence of Allah.[21] But they also held what Maxime
Rodinson feels are damaging implications in regard to the revelation as a

whole,[22] for Muhammad's revelation appears to have been based on his desire to soften the threat to the deities of the people – so much was this the case, the historian al-Tabari tells us, that Muhammad kept repeating it to himself, desiring it, and wishing for it.[23] It was at that moment, with the revelation of the Surah of the Star (LIII), that the Demon spoke through him.[24]

Rushdie's version of what has come to be called the "lapse of Mohammed" or the "compromise with idolatry" was based on the accounts of the Arab historians al-Waqidi and al-Tabari. Daniel Pipes has acutely noted that the vehement protest against Rushdie's book derived in large part from the title, which Muslims found incredibly sacrilegious. For the phrase "Satanic verses" does not come directly from al-Tabari (though the latter attributes the source of the verses to Satan), but from orientalist literature, notably W. Montgomery Watt's *Muhammed. Prophet and Statesman*. Muslims know the omitted verses as the *gharaniq* ("birds") verses. Since the phrase "Satanic verses" is unknown in Islam, and the "verses" of the title was translated into Arabic as *ayat* (which refers solely to the "verses of the Qur'ān"), many Muslims took Rushdie's title to refer to the whole of the Qur'ān as being the work of the Devil. If this is true, and it is indeed plausible, the title resulted in a monumental misunderstanding leading to the condemnation of the author to death (see Pipes, *The Rushdie Affair*, pp. 114–18).

To return to Rushdie's narrative, after Mahound rushes off to abrogate the foul verses, Gibreel reflects on Mahound's new-found conviction: "just one tiny thing that's a bit of a problem here" – namely, that both times it was Gibreel who uttered "both the statement and the repudiation, verses and converses, universes and reverses, the whole thing." The situation is even more complex, however, for, as he acknowledges, "we all know how my mouth got worked" (*SV*, 123): it was Mahound himself up to "his old trick, forcing my mouth open and making the voice, the Voice, pour out of me once again" (123; cf. 112). Thus, presumably, the Voice directing the Prophet is not that of Allah through the intercession of the Archangel Gabriel, but his (the Prophet's) own! The *most* damaging implication here lies in the inference (shared by al-Tabari and Rodinson) that Muhammad's unconscious desire is the source of the verses imputed to the Devil.

From the standpoint of the narrative, not only do the heretical satanic verses provide the basis for the telling of the "full story" of the revelations received by Muhammad at Jahilia (Mecca), but they serve as a privileged metaphor for the terms of Rushdie's oppositional discourse and the poles between which it swings. The attempt by authorities to strike the satanic verses from the record reflects the operation of a magisterial discourse of exclusion that lies at the heart of Islam, indeed of all monotheistic religions, for it is in the nature of magisterial discourses to seek and require protection against the intrusion of external discourses such as those apocryphal verses attributed to Satan.[25] As magisterial discourses, religious scriptures rely on a strictly defined "region of discourse" making them immune to outside discourses. "The only permissible debates will be those concerning external debates" (Lyotard, "On the Strength of the Weak," p. 212), that is, the satanic verses may indeed survive but solely as an outside, unreliable, institutionalized variant, whose terms of opposition are set by the discourse of Islam. In other words, this variant will not be allowed into the inner precinct, the inner region or space of discourse that is the Qur'ān.

Rushdie turns the very reliability of the authorized divine discourse of revelation against itself, however, for by focusing on Mahound as the probable source of the satanic verses, he throws doubt on the reliability of the medium (be it Mahound, be it the spurious archangel Gibreel), and underscores the arbitrariness out of which the authorized version comes. Salman the Persian, a follower of Mahound who serves as his scribe, suggests in Gibreel's dream narrative that Mahound made up the laws first and only afterward received revelations from Gibreel confirming them. To test the arbitrariness of the process, Salman begins to miscribe rules: "So there I was, actually writing the Book, or rewriting, anyway, polluting the word of God with my own profane language." After Mahound discovers his deceit, Salman fears for his life, for "It's his Word against mine" (SV, pp. 367–68).

Discourse, as Rushdie shows in his narrative, is fraught with ambiguities and misunderstanding, owing to the equivocal nature of the sign; it is, as Michel Serres says (and as I have previously cited), integrally bound to its own "slips." Gibreel the archangel "speaks" to Ayesha the butterfly girl by means of tunes of popular hit songs, which she interprets as the divine Word calling her to lead the Titlipur villagers on a miraculous foot pilgrimage across the Indian Ocean to Mecca (497). Even Gibreel is unaware of what the tunes might mean! The signification of language as inferred from Rushdie's narrative is ambivalent and dependent upon translation by/of the Other, who most often makes of it, as Mahound does of the words of the Archangel, a signifier of one's own desires and needs.

All revelation, all recitation, must undergo the hazards and shortcomings of translation, the recasting of the originary language into a different language, a new discourse born out of the supplementarity and "slips" of the former discourse. What is more, as George Steiner asserts,

> Only a small portion of human discourse is nakedly veracious or informative in any monovalent, unqualified sense ... Scarcely anything in human speech is what it sounds. Thus it is inaccurate and theoretically spurious to schematize language as "information" or to identify language, be it spoken or vocalized, with "communication." The latter term will serve only if it includes, if it places emphasis on, what is *not* said in the saying.[26]

Steiner calls into question thus the supposed communicative or informational character of language. Indeed, so far as discourse goes, communication is subordinate to the desire to assert authority.[27]

Shaitan serves a particular role in the whole process of false revelation. The Revelator is cast as Shaitan if the revelation is deemed invalid or heretical, as the Archangel if it is deemed "true." Shaitan resembles Euathalus who, in his debate with Protagoras, is now disciple now antagonist, as the argument requires: the devil loses all identity, all properties, becomes a creature of convenience, of the moment, on whom blame can be shifted if things do not work out; the obverse of Gibreel, who is the amanuensis or mouthpiece of good, Shaitan serves as the amanuensis of evil. And, as Lyotard notes of Protagoras' argument in regard to Euathalus, the future is already worked out "in the manner of a parody, for the discourse Protagoras holds with respect to his disciple is precisely the parody of the magisterial discourse" – that, by reason of the fact that the outcome of the magisterial discourse lies in the advance knowledge of that very outcome owing to the preconceived needs and goals of the Master. Consequently, it matters not whether one wins or loses – forfeit has to be paid in either case (212). The future, the authorized version, is established.

The Devil operates, then, as a rhetorical figure of parody in terms of Rushdie's counterdiscourse, not solely for the story of Mahound but for the entire narrative. He figures the antilogical nature of the world, its ambivalent othersidedness. The state of Satan is the state of variability, metamorphosis, the unrelatability of means to preconceived ends. Characters and situations in flux in the *Satanic Verses*, revealing all their contrariety and contradiction – particularly the migrants and their migrancy – are linguistic markers for an excluded, repressed discourse, an antilogical discourse that parodies the operation of the Master's discourse. Rushdie moves towards the repossession of the poisoned wells of language by such a discourse that constitutes itself on the very basis of its otherness. That is the sense of Rushdie's statement in his essay, "A Pen Against the Sword," to the effect that "the process of reclaiming language from one's opponents" is central to the purposes of the *Satanic Verses*. He goes on in that vein to say that "The very title . . . is an aspect of this attempt at reclamation. You call us devils? it seems to ask. Very well then, here is the devil's version of the world, of 'your' world, the version written *from the experience* of those who have been demonized by virtue of their otherness" ("A Pen Against the Sword," p. 54; author's emphasis). The devil's version involves the remaking and remapping of the English language, as Rushdie indicates in one of his collected essays: "We can't simply use the language in the way the British did . . . it needs remaking for our own purposes" ("Imaginary Homelands," *Imaginary Homelands*, p. 17). In another essay in the same collection, entitled "'Commonwealth Literature' Does Not Exist," Rushdie says, "What seems to me to be happening is that those peoples who were once colonized by the language are now rapidly remaking it, domesticating it, becoming more and more relaxed about the way they use it – assisted by the English language's enormous flexibility and size, they are carving out large territories for themselves within its frontiers" (*Ibid.*, p. 64). This passage manifests Rushdie's interest, found throughout his writings, in the remaking of the colonizers' language to conform to the cultural specificity of formerly colonized peoples.

Perceptual fields culturally construed

Monsters, demons and migrants

Quite apart from the representation of the master Demon, Satan, we find manifestations of the monstrous everywhere in Rushdie's narrative. If we scrutinize these, we discover that they are representations deriving from dominant social and religious structures/strictures – as we might well have suspected, for the very reason that the magisterial discourse wields control of the signs by which such representations are produced. In his reaction against the "liberals'" defense of the *Satanic Verses*, Richard Webster sees Rushdie as reviving the Christian stereotypes that demonize Muslims,[28] while in truth and ironically Rushdie's narrative is precisely about the demonization of marginal peoples (migrants, women) by Islamic and Hindu societies around the world, by Eastern and Western Christian societies, by secular edicts in all these societies.

We recall the manticore's words regarding the "power of description" exerted by the authorities and how they, the detainees in the Detention Centre, more generally the migrants, "succumb to the pictures" the former construct (168). Monstrosity is a perceptual construct, construed culturally. It is the means by which the magisterial discourse at the same time excludes and appropriates outside objects, events, and persons. The migrant, an outsider like Satan, by his or her very oppositionality serves as a figure of complementarity that affirms the system. As we shall see with reference to Rushdie's narrative, the migrant, like Satan, is needed by the system. Rushdie, through the inversion of these same signs (perceptions) of monstrosity, however, succeeds in turning them into supporting elements of a process of leveling that strips the discourse of power of its arbitrary ascendency/primacy.

Let us look first at the figure of the migrant. The scene in the Detention Centre (164ff.) describes the conspiracy of the marginals against the world of "normalcy." Consequent upon his state of monstrousness and the preconditions of that state itself, the migrant and his condition in the *Satanic Verses* meet the criteria called for by the stereotypes of persecution enumerated by René Girard: the existence of a social/cultural crisis threatening the deterioration of social order in general ("organized crime, political agitators, bomb-factories, drugs" are the threats listed by Police Inspector Kinch [*SV*, p. 455], to which we might add the ritualistic serial murders of old women by the "Granny Ripper"); the propinquity of someone seen to have a relationship of culpability with the crisis (the migrant); finally, the presence of someone possessing marks that suggest him/her as victim (foreign appearance and accent). What follows is the laying of responsibility on the victim who is seen to have committed an infraction of the rules of the community, and the ensuing punishment or destruction. This outcome is seen in the trial, conviction, and death of Dr. Uhuru Simba aka Sylvester Roberts; in the vigilante raids on the ghetto residents; and in the jailing of dissidents. Girard observes that the persecuted parties "combine the marginality of the outsider with the marginality of the insider."[29] The interesting conjunction of outside/inside with marginality appears to negate the sense of the latter term. Certainly the migrant betrays this dual character, but rather than inhabiting the margin he is in the midst, fully present if invisible in "normal" circumstances. To invoke the notion of margin or marginals is, in fact, to utilize the language of the dominant group, as we can infer from the observation of Lyotard when he says that "there is no such thing as a margin. What speaks of margins is the Empire that reflects its boundaries, its borders, its marches (regions to be conquered)" ["Il n'y a pas de marge du tout. Ce qui parle des marges, c'est l'Empire qui réfléchit ses bords, ses frontières, ses marches (régions à conquérir)]" ("Sur la force des faibles," p. 6; my translation). As I have observed earlier in this study, in the time of classical Greece there were the Greeks and there were the *metoikoi*, the ones who "changed houses," that is, the foreigners domiciled in Greece who were without civil rights. From *metoikos* was to derive the French term *métèque* coined in the mid-1890s to designate foreigners of Mediterranean origin residing in France, that is, undesirables. Such peoples as the *metoikoi* were prime subjects for scapegoating.

The scapegoat mechanism described by Girard (42) is operative among Rushdie's "marginals." Etymologically, "scapegoat" was intended as a translation of the Hebrew *'azazel, Webster's International* tells us, "as if *'ez 'ozel* goat that departs" (Lev. 16:8). *'Azazel* was probably the name of a demon. The concept serves well, in any case, to define the mechanism operating in the case of Satan: the crisis of a compromising declaration, the availability of a personage with a relationship of culpability with the crisis,[30] the defining marks of a victim that result in responsibility being laid at his doorstep, and his ensuing punishment. (In the case of Chamcha, the marks of the victim reveal themselves in his goatish appearance.) The Devil, in his role of scapegoat, becomes the figure of transference in terms of authoritarian discourse, a linguistic marker for an excluded or repressed discourse of opposition (the satanic verses).

Similar types of authoritarian structure having recourse to the scapegoat mechanism function in the social context of urban Western society and the Islamic and Hindu religious creeds. As Girard points out, the scapegoat presupposes "the innocence of the victims, the collective polarization in opposition to them, and the collective end result (persecution) of that polarization." Moreover, "The persecutors are caught up in the 'logic' of the representation of persecution from a persecutor's standpoint, and they cannot break away" (*The Scapegoat*, p. 39). The inevitability of the "logic" that makes the persecutors unaware of the arbitrariness and evil of their representation results in the scapegoat mechanism serving as an "unconscious mechanism for the representation and acts of persecution" (*Ibid.*, p. 120).[31] Girard underscores in these remarks the arbitrary nature of the collective "logic" that leads to the persecution of the victims.

The representation of the monstrous, contrary to the romantic notion of it as pure invention, begins with a lack of differentiation, for mythological monsters borrow and combine elements of existing forms (*Ibid.*, p. 33). Mimeticism lies at the heart of the character of Satan, who apes the supreme being (*Ibid.*, p. 195). Mimeticism leading to a lack of differentiation also attaches to the migrant figure, the Indian, for instance – that eclectic and inveterate borrower of bits and pieces of other cultures, as Zeeny describes him. The Indians as well as other migrants in London or anywhere else in the Western world (North Africans in France, Latin Americans and Haitians in the United States) hold the potential to be victims, for they combine the trait of outsider with the necessary quality of insider, which, through the absence of difference, makes them potentially associable with the "crime" (social or religious) to be expiated.

The motif of the glass man figures the migrants' vulnerability. The glass man appears in Chamcha's dream during his first return journey to India. That man, a "bizarre stranger," begs Chamcha to help release him from his prison of skin. Chamcha breaks the glass and tries to pick off the broken shards but chunks of flesh come away with it. Back in Bombay, Zeeny tells him that they have finally "cracked" his "shell," that is, gotten back to his Indianness. But he says, "Well, this is what's inside... An Indian translated into English-medium... when you have stepped through the looking-glass you step at your peril. The mirror may cut you to shreds" (*SV*, p. 58).

The man with a glass skin suggests the transparency and emptiness of the stereotypical figure of the migrant (cf. 169) who to those outside (the Westerners) is seen through or returns their reflection, a sign of his deference and faithful emulation of them. But, however faithfully he may emulate them, he passes unseen except at a time of crisis. Nevertheless, he always presents to the Westerner a source of uneasiness and a potential threat. In all his "characterless plurality" (250), the "third-world" migrant *is* the devil/scapegoat of Western society.

The most developed example of the migrant is that of Chamcha. At one point Jumpy notes the appropriateness of Saladin Chamcha's name: "He was a real Saladin... A man with a holy land to conquer, his England, the one he believed in" (175). After his first return, Chamcha acknowledges his journey home as a mistake, "a mistake to *go home*, after so long, how could it be other than a regression; it was an unnatural journey; a denial of time; a revolt against history; the whole thing was bound to be a disaster" (34). He is, in effect, the glass man of whom he dreams.

The narrator's description of Chamcha, the migrant *par excellence*, establishes a parallel with the function of Satan, for, like Satan, in setting out to make himself English, to remake himself, he would usurp the role of the Creator: such a creature is

> unnatural, a blasphemer, an abomination of abominations. From another angle, you could see pathos in him, heroism in his struggle, in his willingness to risk: not all mutants survive. Or, consider him sociopolitically: most migrants learn, and can become disguises. Our own false descriptions to counter the falsehoods invented about us, concealing for reasons of security our secret selves.   (49)

In this view of the migrant (which, by the shift from the diacritical marker "him" to "us," indicates that the narrator includes himself and the interlocutor), we see him as a man who invents himself, who willingly makes himself the mouthpiece/mimic of the Voice of another social entity – here an Englishman – just as Satan mimicked the Voice of Allah. Like Satan, he may try to use the authorized discourse in order to turn it against itself, but chances to fail either by becoming completely assimilated or by being revealed in all his monstrosity. His tactics, if he seeks survival, must work towards their end without bringing him into open conflict with his opponent. Success lies in subterfuge. For this reason, his eclecticism, criticized by Zeeny as his weakness, also serves as his strength, for he is infinitely capable of adaptation, he has learned to be a successful actor, a resourceful secret agent.

Ironically, as oppression of the ghetto inhabitants worsens, against his volition Saladin becomes the dream-devil, the dream-figure of the migrant quarters, "a being who has crossed the frontier, evading the normal controls, and was now roaming loose about the city. Illegal immigrant, outlaw king, foul criminal or race-hero, Saladin Chamcha was getting to be true" (288).

Rushdie's narrative implies that the structures of authoritarians, devised to protect against disorder that threatens them, create their own demons and devils, such perhaps as Mahound who puts the words of revelation into Gibreel's mouth. One might turn around the contention of Girard, who maintains that Satan is "the one who deceives men by making them believe that innocent victims are guilty" (207), by maintaining that Satan is the symbolic construct of creeds that assign the designation of demonic to anyone whose victimization might contribute to the consolidation and maintenance of their power. Innocence and guilt have little to do with it. Girard, in the eloquent ending to his book, cites the words of the New Testament: "the hour is coming when anyone who kills you will think he is doing a holy duty for God" (Jn. 16:2).

Unhappily, the hour of religious vengeance has struck many times in this century. Before the *fatwa* pronounced against Rushdie, the Egyptian writer, Taha Husayn, had been declared an apostate by al-Azhar University authorities in 1926; the Iranian writer, Ahmad Kasravi, was condemned for his anticlerical views by Khomeini (then an obscure mullah) as being of impure blood (*mahdur ad-damm*) and was assassinated in 1946; the Sudanese theologian, Mahmud Muhammad Taha, was hanged in 1985 for his teachings (*The Rushie Letters,* 88); and the Palestinian cartoonist and satirist, Naji al-'Ali, was assassinated in London in 1987.

Since the *fatwa* against Rushdie, persecution and murder in the name of religion has continued unabated: a death sentence was pronounced against the Nobel Prize-winning Egyptian novelist, Najib Mahfouz, by the blind Sheikh 'Umar 'Abd al-Rahman;[32] the Turkish author, Turan Dursun, was assassinated in 1990 for "defaming" the prophet and "betraying" Islam; the Egyptian writer, Farag Ali Fouda, was assassinated in 1993 in a Cairo suburb; and, in the same year, a *fatwa* was issued for alleged blasphemy by a group of 'Ulama' in Bangladesh against the woman poet, Taslima Nasreen, upon the appearance of her novel *Lajja* ("Shame"). Finally, in the 1990s, numerous writers, journalists, and intellectuals have been murdered by Algerian fundamentalists (including the well-known novelist Tahar Djaout in Algiers for his political views). These are but a few examples of the religious persecution that has occurred.

Similar episodes of religious persecution and murder have taken place in western societies: the assassinations by individuals belonging to Christian fundamentalist sects in the US of doctors who have performed abortions and of abortion-clinic personnel, the desecration of Jewish cemeteries and synagogues and Islamic mosques; the condemnation of Nikos Kazantzakis for his book *The Last Temptation* (1955) by the Greek Orthodox Church; the banning of it by the Roman Catholic Church and American Protestant fundamentalists; and the furious controversy surrounding the appearance of Jean-Luc Godard's 1984 film *Je vous salue, Marie* ("Hail Mary") and Martin Scorsese's 1988 film version of Kazantzakis' book – to name but a few incidents.

Fall/ascent and reversal

Spatial elements hold a special importance in *The Satanic Verses*, particularly the motif of heights: Chamcha and Gibreel fall from 29,000 feet when the plane explodes, the height of Mount Everest, to which numerous allusions are made. Gibreel's high-rise luxury apartment in Bombay is called the "Everest Villas" – the same building from which his jilted lover Rekha Merchant leaps to her death and from which his new lover Alleluia (Allie) Cone falls to hers ("instead of [making] her longed-for solo ascent of Everest," 546). References to heights proliferate: the 8000 meter Himalayan peaks Gibreel counts to stay awake and avoid dreaming on the plane (82); his childhood dream of Satan's fall (91); and Chamcha's dream of quitting Bombay and setting out for a success in London, which results in a nightmare in which he finds himself falling over London Proper (38–39). The path leading from Bombay to London is, in fact, an air-route along which the characters are constantly making their pilgrimages.

Heights are not solely linked to falling, however, for the reverse – climbing, rising – also occurs: most importantly in the case of Muhammad's ascending the mountain (Mount Cone) to receive his revelations (109 *et passim*). The narrator calls him, in fact, the "mountain-climbing" prophet (93). Of course, on a spiritual level the notion of heights is important, for Allah exists "above." Etherial creatures pop up everywhere: angels, the butterflies that surround Ayesha, the ghosts on Everest, and apparitions such as that of Rekha Merchant on her flying carpet.

What is the importance of these opposing motifs of fall/ascent? The narrator tells us that "great falls change people." He links fall to being reborn, becoming "new" (133). One might say, in fact, that rise and ascent cannot occur without fall (or the reverse). Muhammad must come down from the mountain to rise as a Prophet, the slope to the top of Everest descends, and, in the more pragmatic world, stardom or success also brings descent in its train. More generally, rising narrative leads to falling narrative. But what does all of this mean?

In the movement between upper and lower in Rushdie's narrative, boundaries and frontiers are sundered. The characters, most of them actors in the plot, are also actants as narrative devices: their rise and fall enacts the ritual of the fall of Satan and the death of God (16), and, even more profoundly, the cycle of death and life and their ineluctable intermingling. The manifold references to rebirth through death remove the boundary between the absolute and the non-absolute, the unchanging and the ephemeral.

The function of this motif is, in a word, reversal, a phenomenon that conjures up the opposing concepts of truth that Mikhail Bakhtin finds in the contrast between the official feast of the Middle Ages that sanctioned a "truth" that was considered as timeless and invariable, and carnivalesque "truth" that opposed all that was predetermined and considered as unchanging or absolute. The carnivalesque sought the dynamism of ceaseless change, play, and forms without definition. All the symbols attached to the carnival spirit suggest change and renewal, the relative nature of "truths" accepted as authoritative. Underlying carnivalesque truth we find a special type of logic – that of the "inside out" and the "turn-about" (the reversal of which I speak above), of spatial shifting without end (high to low, front to back), of irreverent parody, of travesty and disguise, blasphemy and humbling, recrownings and uncrownings. In just such ways, as Bakhtin shows, the organizers of carnival deconstructed official culture and constructed a type of anti-culture, a new world, a world Bakhtin calls an inside-out world.[33]

Bakhtin stresses the distance between the parody found in medieval carnival and modern parody, which he describes as being negative and formalistic. Folk humor negates but also renews. Outright negation is something that is alien to folk culture (*Rabelais and His World*, p. 11). In this scheme of things, Rushdie must stand somewhere in-between. It seems to me that it would be untenable if not fallacious to argue on the basis of his narrative that he seeks outright negation, for he by no means categorically rejects Western and Eastern cultural forms, but rather the rigidity and claim to absoluteness of the mandates that have established them, and their categorical and canonical denial of alternative forms of action and belief.

The phenomenon of reversal in Rushdie's narrative is spatial, growing out of the folk tradition of "grotesque realism" of which Bakhtin speaks. Such reversal turns on the principle of degradation, by which the spiritually elevated and the abstract ideals of culture are brought down to the earthly, to the material reality of the body, which, for Rabelais, was wholly positive, grounded in the notion of fertility, growth, abundance, change, and renewal (*Ibid.*, pp. 18–22, and 81–82).

As Rushdie has explained, he sought images that gave form to the opposition existing between various forms of the sacred and secular worlds ("A Pen Against the Sword," p. 54). Reversal lies at the heart of Rushdian narrative. The phenomenon of narrative reversal involved in the *Satanic Verses* and the unofficial inscription of Salman the scribe has its correspondence in several narrative descriptions – most notably and most irreligiously, perhaps, in the episode in which the twelve whores of the brothel, called the Curtain, take on the names and characteristics of the twelve wives of the Prophet. The brothel becomes an "anti-mosque" where the life of the Prophet is re-enacted in a profane setting. The writer-adversary of Mahound, Baal, following whose inspiration the reversal occurs, re-enacts the person of the Prophet himself in becoming the husband of the twelve whores. Upon a confrontation with Mahound, who remonstrates against Baal's blasphemy before the latter is led away to be beheaded, Baal exclaims: "Whores and writers, Mahound. We are the people you can't forgive." Mahound replies, "Writers and whores. I see no difference here" (*SV*, p. 392). The writers and whores he speaks of, of course, are both involved in counterdialogue against the authorized version of the Qur'ān and the legend of the Prophet and his wives.

Many such reversals occur, such as the party thrown by Sisodia on the giant sound stage at the Shepperton film studios, which represents a monstrous alteration of London (422). The narrator himself speaks of the tragedy that will ensue: "A burlesque for our degraded, imitative times in which clowns re-enact what was first done by heroes and kings" (424) – a description that serves to characterize Rushdie's entire carnivalesque narrative.

A particularly significant reversal is that of the roles of Gibreel the archangel and Chamcha the Devil, described as "conjoined opposites, these two, each man the other's shadow" (426). The narrator provides an interesting commentary on this contrast/complementarity of the two principal characters. Gibreel, he suggests, betrays the urge to remain "*continuous* – that is, joined to and arising from his past," whereas "Saladin Chamcha is a creature of *selected* discontinuities, a *willing* re-invention," who leads a revolt against history. Consequently, the former is "true," the latter "false." But, the narrator asks the question, does not this falsity of self make "possible in Chamcha a worse and deeper falsity – call this 'evil' – and that this is the truth, the door, that was opened in him by his fall?" While Gibreel is "'good' by virtue of *wishing to remain*, for all his vicissitudes, at bottom an untranslated man." Immediately, however, the narrator points up the weakness of this contrast, which rests "on an idea of the self as being (ideally) homogeneous, non-hybrid, 'pure' – an utterly fantastic notion!" The truth perhaps is "that evil may not be as far beneath our surfaces as we like to say it is. – That, in fact, we fall towards it *naturally*, that is, *not against our natures*" (427). In this conjoining of good and evil in the human individual, we see the resolution (or the rejection) of the Manichaean/Zoroastrian binary concept of the struggle of good and evil. The ideas of Rushdie recall rather those of William Blake, who had an influence on his perception of the multivalent nature of human character and action.

Bakhtin's view of the social, political, and religious dimension of Rabelais' writing suggests a parallel in the writing of Rushdie. Like Rabelais he sets out to counter the official version of events, strives to see them in a different light, from the point of view of migrants, marginals, and the oppressed (Rabelais conveyed the view of the common people of the marketplace). To do so, Rushdie calls upon all the resources of language – its popular forms such as story-telling and proverbs, its potential for puns and language-play – to level official half-truths and expose the narrow dictates of the ruling authorities (cf. Bakhtin, *Rabelais and His World*, p. 439). But Rushdie's narrative, far from insisting on the overturn or overthrow of official discourse and its replacement by another doxy, functions through such tactics as that of reversal to bring about an *equalization* of the type exemplified in the Scandinavian folk-tale of the wood-cutter who spies a troll burying a treasure under a tree in the forest. In exchange for sparing the troll's life, the woodcutter marks an "x" on the tree and exacts from him the promise not to efface the mark. He then leaves to fetch a shovel to dig up the treasure. When he returns, he finds all the trees in the forest bearing an "x."

Hence, for Rushdie, reversal functions not to destroy but to level differences, such that things are revealed in their full relative character. No one truth or order prevails. Norms, established privilege, prohibitions, tautological systems, completedness – all leading to hierarchizing differences – are bracketed, placed in suspension. We find ourselves in a magic, postmodern, carnivalesque world where a new discourse prevails, a discourse of hesitation, contradiction, and incompletedness, carrying, as Bakhtin said of the grotesque (as opposed to the classic) image of man, the scoriae of its birth and development (*Ibid.*, p. 25).

This process of leveling, by which equalization is brought about, is, I believe, the primary tactical move of Rushdie's narrative in countering dominant discourses. It is also, as I see it, one of the fundamental differences between the phenomenon of the fantastic in literature and what has come to be called magical realism, with which Rushdie appears to have definite affinities. Roger Caillois, in speaking of the fantastic, sees it as manifesting "a scandal, a tear, an unwonted and nearly insufferable irruption in the real world" ["un scandale, une déchirure, une irruption insolite, presque insupportable dans le monde réel"].[34] Caillois thus fastens on the problem of the fantastic, involving the sudden and unexpected intrusion of the supernatural into the midst of the "natural," empirical world. On the contrary, in magical realism the supernatural is not presented as problematic by the narrator (the reaction of the reader is another question), for it is integrated into the perceptual frame of the narrative.[35] Owing to the fact that several postcolonial authors, whose works manifest the phenomenon of magical realism such as we conceive of it here, *do not* hierarchize two "opposing" world views – the authoritarian (colonial) view of reality and a non-authoritarian (postcolonial) view – but "equalize" the difference between them, they reject thereby a system of values that in the West has frequently argued for the inferiority of non-Western thought. Consequently, as Emil Volek, in speaking of the magical realism of Alejo Carpentier, argues, "the essence of this apparently 'artistic' liberation is profoundly *democratic* and in principle *revolutionary*" ["la esencia de esta emancipación aparentemente 'artística' es profundamente *democrática* y en principio revolucionaria"].[36] The word "democratic" conveys the sense of my notion of "leveling" (though the term I have preferred to use to characterize the texts discussed is "oppositional," as distinct from "revolutionary").

In Rushdie's narrative, two totally different levels of reality share the stage: the empirical world of reason and logic (Western society ruled in large part by experimental science and consumerism) and the supernatural/spiritual world (of Islam and Hinduism as well as of Rushdie's anti-logical discourse). But in his world the supernatural functions not as a rupture of a supposed universal coherence, as Caillois calls it (*Anthologie*, I, p. 9), so much as a device to reveal the arbitrariness of that supposed universal coherence. Caillois says: "The narratives of supernatural terror [the fantastic] translate the fright of suddenly seeing the regularity, the order of the world, so painfully established and proved by the methodical investigation of experimental science, cede to the assault of irreconcilable, nocturnal, demonic forces" ["Les récits d'épouvante surnaturelle traduisaient l'effroi de voir soudain la régularité, l'ordre du monde si péniblement établi et prouvé par l'investigation méthodique de la science expérimentale céder à l'assaut des forces irréconciliables, nocturnes, démoniaques"] (*Ibid.*, p. 23). The forces of which he speaks, which bestow order upon an otherwise disorderly and chaotic world, are those of authoritative entities that draw upon the "proofs" of experimental science to validate their ideologically framed constructs. In Rushdie's narrative, one has to differentiate between the empirical world depicted in the novel – the forces of authority (the English government, Islamic doctrine) poised against the demonic (Satan, heretics, the migrants) – and the world of the narrative *itself* where these forces coexist and struggle.

Rushdie's novel violates all kinds of precepts about how the supernatural should be introduced. We are usually told that the writer must begin by creating a believable world, but Rushdie starts off with a far-fetched dialogue between two bizarre characters falling from an exploded airliner. The narrative begins scandalously, for, instead of preparing us for the appearance of the supernatural, the narrator immerses us in it immediately in a sort of defiant gesture indicative of what is to follow. We the readers are bereft of supportive indices that afford us the comfort of anticipation, for, though we may surmise that the two characters are falling to certain death, it is that presumptive proleptic that will be dashed instead.

What is important to note in Rushdie's narrative is that the supernatural episode at the beginning, as well as other such apparitions of the supernatural, which uncategorically contradict the laws of the (Western) reader's world, give no pause at all to the characters. That aspect of the narrative alerts us to the fact that its focalization is not characteristically Western but non-Western. In the face of the irruption of the supernatural in the midst of a recognizable reality, the Western reader is left with a choice similar to that suggested by Todorov: to accept the events as hallucinatory (in which case the laws of his world are not threatened) or to accept the strange occurrences as "real," in which case she encounters a reality that is governed by principles unfamiliar to her. For Todorov, the fantastic exists in the reader's hesitation between these two possibilities.[37]

Amaryll Beatrice Chanady suggests replacing the term "hesitation" by antinomy. Antinomy, from *anti + nomos*, that is, "against the law," denotes the contradiction between two apparently equally valid principles or between inferences correctly drawn from such principles. It is a fortunate term for a discussion of magical realism, because, in bringing us back to Sophist antilogic, it suggests the existence in the selfsame text of two conflicting principles ("codes," she calls them) of apparently equal validity, neither of which can be accredited alongside the other (*Magical Realism*, p. 12), but neither of which, on the other hand, rules supreme. The resolution of the mutual incompatibility of these terms (natural/ supernatural; real/surreal) depends on the point of view: from that of the authoritarian, one brooks no opposition; from that of the non-authoritarian, one may well accept the coexistence of these principles brought about by the leveling function of Rushdie's narrative. Chanady cites Irène Bessière, who, in speaking of Jacques Cazotte's *Le Diable amoureux*, says, "the interest of the text is to present, from the beginning, the natural order and the supernatural order... in order to deconstruct them simultaneously and institute uncertainty in regard to all signs, before re-establishing *in fine* their complementary coexistence" ["Or l'intérêt du texte est de poser, dès son début, l'ordre naturel et l'ordre surnaturel...pour les déconstruire simultanément et installer l'incertitude sur tout signe, avant de rétablir *in fine* leur coexistence complémentaire"].[38] The process at work in Cazotte's narrative as seen by Bessière – namely, that the presentation of the natural/supernatural worlds at the outset results in a deconstructive movement that throws doubt on the certainty of the representation itself (the "sign") and paves the way for the recombination of opposites into a state of complementary coexistence – describes perfectly the opening of Rushdie's narrative and its structural motivation (in the Shklovskian sense), re-enforced by thematic iteration of the need to die in order to be reborn.

We encounter in Rushdie's narrative, then, not a mishmash of Eastern, mystic (Blakean), and religious motifs that confront us with the notion of death in life, but a programmatic set of anti-programmatic narrative imperatives: the death (disempowering) of authoritarian discourses of legitimization, whether Western or Eastern, out of which can emerge a new discourse – a discourse of survival, a discourse for the weak, ignored, unprivileged, unrepresented.

But the new discourse is not one of reconciliation. That is, the natural and supernatural in Rushdie's narrative are never reconciled. The reader has little choice but to conform to the perception of the narrator, which discards the possibilities for rational explanation (by, for instance, attributing the supernatural to hallucination or dream), which can be disposed of, recuperated symbolically. Rather she is forced to accept it as literally occurring. The effect of magical realist texts is to establish the presence of the supernatural from the outset, as Rushdie does, so isolated occurrences of it cannot be explained away, dismissed as symbolic.

Conclusion

Ambivalence lies at the heart of Rushdie's parodic narrative: in the phenomenon of doubling in the case of the renegade version of the Prophet's life, in his repetitive play of names,[39] in the motif of actors, acting, and role-playing, in the uncertainty of the provenance and locus of the events, etc. In regard to the latter, we can never be certain where we are, whether or not events come to us through a "straight" if improbable narrative, whether they result from the dream of the characters, whether the characters and events are dreamt Borgesian-like by some other power in the way that Gibreel seems not only to dream the Prophet, but also to be dreamt by the Prophet, or whether, finally, we are ourselves located within the psyche of a deranged character given over to fits of delusion, for, indeed, at the end, Gibreel's "condition" is diagnosed as schizophrenia.

The ending of the *Satanic Verses* reveals a doubleness that reflects the states of failure and survival exemplified by the principal characters: the usurpation of the prospective usurper and his discourse, in the first case, the fabled return to origins and preservation of self, in the second. At one point the narrator cites Frantz Fanon's words regarding the oppressed: "The native is an oppressed person whose permanent dream is to become the persecutor" (353). Such a pessimistic view of the victim switching roles with the hangman grows out of simple substitution through which no change is effected. In the first instance, Gibreel, as others in the narrative, becomes corrupted by power, lured by what he sees as the unalloyed battle between the forces of good and evil, which he contrasts with "the moral fuzziness of the English" in a city where sharp distinctions between "imperative oppositions were drowned beneath an endless drizzle of greys" (354).

One comes, in Gibreel's case, to the realization that the real villain of the piece *is* power – the simple reversal (not leveling) of hierarchical differences between the oppressor and the oppressed, who are joined by fate as surely as Gibreel and Mahound by their umbilical cord. Such is the trap of the dominant discourse. The Imam, striking a refrain on the words of Mikhail Bakunin about the dangers of sitting down to table with power, tells Bilal: "to be raised in the house of power is to learn its ways, to soak them up, through that very skin that is the cause of your oppression. The habit of power, its timbre, its posture, its way of being with others. It is a disease, Bilal, infecting all who come too near it" (*SV*, p. 211).

Gibreel, who begins as an archangel, proceeds through a satanic conversion, and ends as victim of his own doubleness. Chamcha also has his difficulties. He, who had tried so hard to pursue the good, finds himself as having become the embodiment of sin, the incarnation of evil. He, who had "dedicated himself with a will bordering on obsession to the conquest of Englishness," finds himself thrust back among his own people

(256–57). At the end he suffers from an enervating world-weariness. When Gibreel rubs the brass lamp left to Chamcha by his father and, instead of drawing forth a Djinn, pulls out a revolver he has hidden there, Chamcha reflects: "The true Djinns of old had the power to open the gates of the Infinite, to make all things possible, to render all wonders capable of being attained; how banal, in comparison, was this modern spook, this degraded descendant of mighty ancestors, this feeble slave of a twenti-eth-century lamp" (546). After Gibreel kills himself, Chamcha "could no longer believe in fairy-tales. Childhood was over" (547).

I asked earlier, in regard to the migrant, whether he could return. With Zeeny's "re-entry" into Chamcha Saladin's life, "the process of renewal, of regeneration," we are told, is completed. "His old English life, its bizarreries, its evils, now seemed very remote, even irrelevant, like his truncated stage name" (534). Zeeny tells him that he can now stop act-ing. We note important signifiers of change or rebirth: the name Cham-cha is dropped, an Urdu name meaning "spoon," whose colloquial usage signifies a sycophant, a type who, under independence, supported the status quo;[40] his Englished name that indicated his willingness to con-quer Englishness through obsequiousness reverts to the birth name of Salahuddin, recalling the great Muslim warrior who fought against the Crusaders; the world according to Zeeny promised to be "solid and real" instead of a theatrical or cinematic representation; finally, as an indicator of the end of (Western, Medieval Christian) story-telling, the name Muhammad now appears instead of Mahound.

On the other hand, the question of return may be moot. The migrant, whose point, we have been told, "is to arrive" (94), is perhaps not all that different after all from the desert nomad who has no real destination, for the journey itself is the object, the fact that shapes his existence (Rushdie, "On Adventure," *Imaginary Homelands*, p. 225); the notion of destination, end, is a fiction. The migrant is, in a real sense, without location, at least without physical location. As Rushdie has said, to be a migrant is to be free of "the shackles of nationalism."

> The effect of mass migrations has been the creation of radically new types of human being; people who root themselves in ideas rather than places, in memories as much as in material things; people who have been obliged to define themselves – because they are so defined by others – by their otherness; people in whose deepest selves strange fusions occur, unprecedented unions between what they were and where they find themselves. The migrant suspects reality: having

experienced several ways of being, he understands their illusory
nature. To see things plainly, you have to cross a frontier.

("The Location of *Brazil*," *Ibid*., pp. 124–25)

The migrant according to Rushdie is thus a new breed of being, defined
by his otherness, rooted in ideas and memories in lieu of location. But,
what is more important, Rushdie sees the state of migrancy as an opening
onto understanding, of the transcient nature of things, particularly institutions and the relations between peoples. It is also true that in crossing a
frontier the migrant never arrives in a place. Edward Said describes
migrants as being *in*, without being *of*, any situation they happen to find
ourselves (cited by Rushdie, "On Palestinian Identity: A Conversation
with Edward Said," *Ibid*., p. 171). The migrant is, in fact, the double of the
artist who resists, whose imagination puts him beyond the reach of
authority. In speaking of Gilliam's film *Brazil*, Rushdie says,

> This idea – the opposition of imagination to reality, which is also of
> course the opposition of art to politics – is of great importance,
> because it reminds us that we are not helpless; that to dream is to have
> power. And I suggest that the true location of Brazil is the other great
> tradition in art, the one in which techniques of comedy, metaphor,
> heightened imagery, fantasy and so on are used to break down our
> conventional, habit-dulled certainties about what the world is and
> has to be. Unreality is the only weapon with which reality can be
> smashed, so that it may subsequently be reconstructed.

("The Location of *Brazil*," *Ibid*., p. 122)

Dream and artistic creation thus confer power – the power inhering in
imagination that can call into existence unreality and produce extraordinary literary and artistic visions and techniques that burst open convention and instill uncertainty, that make the ordinary and "real"
susceptible to recombination, to restructuration into a new if not higher
reality.

Just as the migrant stands outside, across the frontier from, the material reality surrounding him, and whose standoffishness affords him a
different perspective and an understanding of the situation he finds himself
in, so the resisting artist stands off in his imagination and observes from
afar. Such standoffishness is at the core of the ironic mode, and allied to
the comedic, the fantastic, and those other modes of literary creation that
achieve an "other" perspective, thereby dissolving "reality" in order that
it might be reconstructed.

In such an age as ours when the question of immigration, legal and illegal, heads or nearly heads national agendas, *The Satanic Verses* strikes a positive and optimistic note, for, as Rushdie says, migration

> celebrates hybridity, impurity, intermingling, the transformation that comes of new and unexpected combinations of human beings, cultures, ideas, politics, movies, songs.[41] It rejoices in mongrelisation and fears the absolutism of the Pure. Mélange, hotch-potch, a bit of this and a bit of that is *how newness enters the world*. It is the great possibility that mass migration gives the world and I have tried to embrace it. "The Satanic Verses" is for change-by-fusion, change-by-conjoining. It is a love-song to our mongrel selves.
>
> ("A Pen Against the Sword," p. 52)

Rushdie celebrates here the potential of mass migration, and its great power to effect positive change through social and racial mixing (*métissage*), which comes with the crossing of borders and counters absolutism and hegemonic "purity" through the realization of new combinations of peoples and cultures in a pluralistic world. From *The Satanic Verses* emerges in such instances of appeal a voice that speaks with infinite sympathy and understanding for the underprivileged, for those "looking up at the descending heel" poised to crush them.[42]

The fear of absolutism Rushdie mentions elicits a warning at the close of the *Satanic Verses*, as the narrative speaks through the character Swatilekha – the lives of people are controlled through the "grand narratives," we are told: "these narratives are being manipulated by the theocracy and various political elements in an entirely retrogressive way" (537). We cannot afford to be caught off guard. The literary world was on Valentine's Day, 1989.

Concluding: breaches and forgotten openings

The night asks who am I?
   I am its secret – anxious, black, profound
   I am its rebellious silence
   I have veiled my nature, with silence,
   wrapped my heart in doubt
   and, solemn, remained here
   gazing, while the ages ask me,
   who am I   NAZIK AL-MALA'IKAH, "Who Am I?"

We need an angry generation,
A generation to plough the horizons,
To pluck up history from its roots,
To wrench up our thought from its foundations.
We need a generation of different mien
That forgives no error, is not forbearing,
That falters not, knows no hypocrisy.
We need a whole generation of leaders and of giants.

   NIZAR QABBANI, "What Value Has the People Whose Tongue is Tied?"[1]

These verses of an Iraqi woman and a Syrian man of the immediate post World-War-II generation of Arabian poets who challenged the strictures of Western and Islamic culture, speak of issues taken up by the contemporary Muslim authors we have studied: giving voice to doubt in the face of hegemonic power and calling past tradition and literary and social thought itself into question. Djebar, Ben Jelloun, Khatibi, and Rushdie are inheritors of such early literary and social revolutionaries who struggled under authoritarian rule.

The struggles we have witnessed in the works of the writers studied in the previous chapters take a variety of forms, and, should we have looked at the writing of other postcolonial writers, we would have seen a still greater diversity of literary expression. No closure is possible for this study. The infinite variation of narratives of postcolonial writers from the so-called Third World, and the rich profusion of narrative positionings and repositionings they bring about in relation to conventional narrative, obviate any attempt to postulate any such imaginary construct as *a* (undifferentiated) "postcolonial" mode of writing.

At most I argue that the diverse tactics I have analyzed in the preceding study provide us with an idea of specific ways postcolonial writers (as I have defined the term postcolonial) work towards a leveling of discourses that counters the privileged status of magisterial discourses grounded on arbitrary philosophic and theocratic principles that "authorize" their social, political, economic, and literary domination.

Jacques Derrida, in an interview, speaks of the need to avoid a simple neutralization of binary oppositions of metaphysics that permits us simply to reside within the "closed field" of those oppositions and, consequently, affirms them.[2] I have shown how postcolonial writers are able to go beyond simple neutralization or reversal.

Derrida describes a double gesture or double writing that is multiple in and of itself. This double or multiple register resembles the counter-discourse created from the narrative tactics devised by the authors studied. Derrida insists that it is necessary for us to go through a phase of overturning. To ignore this phase of overturning means that we misconstrue the conflictual, subordinative structure of opposition itself. In such a case, we run the danger of immediately arriving at a state of neutralization that would in effect leave untouched the field of engagement and render the question of opposition moot, thus obviating any effective means of intervention (Derrida, *Positions*, p. 41).

Derrida affirms that entering this phase of overturning or oppositionality means that we still operate within the system we undertake to deconstruct (*Ibid.*, p. 42). The doubling that occurs dislodges, brings low, what was high – the process I have called "leveling" – and gives birth to a new configuration/concept, that can no longer be and never could be part of the previous system (*Ibid.*, p. 42).

This brief description of Derrida's notion of deconstruction serves to describe the phenomenon of double writing this book has studied in the narratives of Djebar, Ben Jelloun, Khatibi, and Rushdie. Though the narratives of these authors often differ markedly in terms of subject and the structuration of that subject, they all work towards a phase of neutralization in which the terms of both the Islamic and European master narratives are deprived of their arbitrary mastery and put on the same level as other discourses. Secondly, from this neutralizing or contestatory process emerges a new "concept," as Derrida calls it, and a differently constituted mode of discourse.

In an effort to offer a tentative conclusion, I shall bring together the characteristics of postcolonial writing according to two perspectives adumbrated by Derrida. First, I shall look back briefly on the conflictual encounter of these postcolonial writings with the essentially logocentric (philosophically based) discourse of Europe and the major sources of juridical doctrine growing out of the Qur'ān and the Sunna, and on the variety of tactics and narrative repositionings that bring about that neutralization Derrida speaks of, which counters the hegemonic ascendency of one discourse or doctrine over another. Secondly, I shall look again at the "new" discourses that emerge from this encounter in terms of their intertextual constitution – how they have drawn on the storehouses of European and Middle Eastern literature and culture as well as on the works of other non-Western writers around the world to create discourses that speak to their own dynamics, perceptions, needs, and interests.

Oppositionality

The writers I have studied hold in common the refusal to be domesticated, as Kateb Yacine has said, and seek to create a new space for their writing in which will germinate a non-totalizing, alternative discourse. They write out of "the very experience of uprooting, disjunction and metamorphosis" (Rushdie) undergone by the postcolonial writers who have remained in their countries of birth as well as by those who have migrated to the West.

I have used the term postcolonial to denote an agonistic position consciously assumed against the controlling norms of hegemonic discourse. The discourses I have analyzed, though resembling one another in their oppositionality and their struggle to create conditions of possibility, differ significantly – not only in terms of their tactical positionings, but in terms of how they view and express "difference."

None of the authors considered attempts to effect a simple poetics of reversal by replacing one power frame by another. By playing with the aleatory nature of language, its proclivity to escape us, each in his or her own way seeks to seize control of the sign and to bring about what Khatibi

terms "translation," that is, the transformation or re-vision and reworking of the foreign linguistic and cultural values of the European tongue
wielded. These foreign values are then reinscribed into a new context of
value reflecting the indivisible union of diverse tongues (the assumed
language, the mother tongue, and, as the case may be, Classical or dialectical Arabic) and of diverse cultures (European, Arabic, Berber, Islamic,
Indian).

Translation comes about from the creation of what Khatibi calls the *bi-
langue* – a language that is rigorously other, that generates a hybrid writing or "écriture métissée." The *bi-langue* is essentially a counterdiscourse;
it operates as a disordering noise, a lapsus, the corrosion, as I have said,
within the engine of system that admits into the confines of the ruling
discourse the strange, the exceptional, and the unknown. It is a para-dis-
cursive structure lodged in the interior of the ruling discourse.

The neutralization of master narratives to which I have referred, by
means of tactics that result in a leveling of dominant, hegemonistic discourses (statist, patriarchal), comes about by the refusal of all privileged
positional (insider) value to those discourses and by the exposure of the
arbitrary nature of the "universal" precepts underlying them. Hence,
they come to be seen as just so many discourses among others, on equal
footing with all other discourses. Insider discourses are in this way dele-
gitimized or, perhaps more accurately, a-legitimized.

The phenomenon of leveling is also at work in the antilogical character of these oppositional works. Their angle of contestation, using
Richard Terdiman's term, is to a large degree rhetorical, taking the form
of an eristic discourse that challenges the authority of received ideas
through an antilogic opposing one reasoned argument (logos) to another
so as to reveal each as equally valid – despite their being contradictory.
The narratives of all four authors move from one predicate to an opposing if not contradictory one, and play off one logos against another.

The new, "translated" discourse, the *bi-langue*, places emphasis on that
which is *not* said in the saying, as George Steiner says (see preceding chapter) – that is, by exposing the arbitrary, preconditioned future offered by
the authorized version, it reveals the presence of an excluded, repressed
discourse of those persons or groups demonized by the master discourse
– women, minorities, migrants, the outsiders and nomads of the "Third
World." The ironic mode characterizes the artistic stance of the authors
we have studied – the fact of standing off and observing from afar – a
stance that, as I have mentioned, goes hand in hand with the parodic, the

comedic, the fantastic, and the magically real – all of which dissolve an imposed "reality" in order that it might be reconstructed in other terms.

Intertextuality

These authors, who are elsewhere with relation to the dominant discourses, inhabit "locations" (to use Rushdie's terms) that are comprised not just of the distanced geographical and psychological places whence they come, but the "elsewhere" of the intertextuality that also marks their writings. Though all narratives take root in preceding works, the source material for postcolonial narratives – in large part consciously derived – tells us a good deal about the types of narrative encountered in the preceding pages.

The notion of intertextuality has much to do with the phenomenon of *métissage* – the bastardized or culturally/artistically/racially mixed or diluted. It bespeaks the interpenetration of cultures, the use made of other ideas and cultural positionings. It inveighs against any notion of a literary or cultural imperialism that rules by exclusivity. Such activity as we have seen in the works of the writers studied is nomadic, in the sense given to that term by Gilles Deleuze and Félix Guattari.[3]

Lisa Lowe reads Deleuze and Guattari's use of the term as a series of nomadic wanderings that traverse a multitudinous network of intersecting plateaus, which each mediate different moments and forms of relation between that which is fragmented and destratified, immobilized and in motion, measured and in unrestrained abundance.[4] Read in this way, it forms the basis of a strategic move in terms of the creation of narrative. The nomadic aspect of the writing of the authors studied lies in the spatial shifting from site to site, from other text to other text, from plateau to plateau that mediates meaning.

The concept of nomadic wandering is elucidated by Ben Jelloun's description of the manner in which he has constructed his narrative and the device of the interpenetration of narrative levels I have discussed, as well as by the metaphoric spatial shift indicated in his narrative when he mentions that we will no longer pass through a series of doors towards the "interior" of the narrative but that "We must at present slip through breaches in the wall, forgotten openings" ["Nous devons à présent nous glisser par les brèches dans la muraille, les ouvertures oubliées"] (*L'Enfant de Sable*, p. 63).

These breaches and forgotten openings metaphorize the passages effected by nomadic wanderings that provide to the phenomenon of intertextuality another dimension (other dimensions), based on displacement, constant shifting of *loci*. We move incessantly from one cultural, social, and literary terrain to another, from one elsewhere to another, out of reach of the delimiting action of master discourses and of a prescriptive, absolutistic master canon.

We also find in the works of the writers examined a multiplicity of hybrid objects and beings, and metaphors of hybridity, that enrich the sense of *métissage*. Such objects and beings are scattered throughout Rushdie's narrative – the goatish humans, the menagerie of human–beast combinations, the glass man, etc. The motif appears in variant form in the many androgynous beings in the narratives of Ben Jelloun, Khatibi, and Djebar – in the figure of the principal character of Ben Jelloun, in the woman/language metaphors of Khatibi, in the sexual congress Khatibi paints between man and the sea, in the shifting relations between male/female and conqueror/conquered in Djebar, particularly in terms of writing and recounting.

The liberal use of the short tales or anecdotal episodes of Middle Eastern folk tradition that we find in the narratives analyzed emphasizes the replacement of the grand narratives of the West by small narrative units that occasion frequent fragmentation and discontinuity. One explicit source text for Ben Jelloun's *L'Enfant de sable* is *The Thousand and One Nights*, which sets the model for story creation that marks the works of postcolonial authors. These authors draw on a vast array of sources, often marginal to Western Europe: African and Middle Eastern writers of the present as well as the distant past; Latin American writers such as Jorge Luis Borges, Carlos Fuentes, and Gabriel García Márquez; Eastern European writers such as Franz Kafka and Milan Kundera; postmodernists such as Italo Calvino and Thomas Pynchon.

The Muslim authors I have discussed by no means draw exclusively on literary texts for their models, but on a multitude of non-written sources, including the visual and other arts – as exemplified in the case of Rushdie whose narratives work refrains of the Bombay film world, Monty Python, films on the order of Gilliam's *Brazil*, and popular culture. These authors do not hesitate to appropriate what is positive and non-hegemonistic in Islamic beliefs and customs, as well as to dip into the wellhead of Greco-Roman–Christian cultural and literary tradition (in Rushdie's case, into the expansive and explosive narrativity of eighteenth-century masters such as Sterne and Diderot, or the mystics such as Blake). In view of the exchange between the writings of the postcolonial authors I have studied and the literature of the Middle East, Europe, and the Americas, I cannot, moreover, emphasize enough the interrelationship between them – compounded on a constant process of appropriation and reappropriation.

The narratives analyzed place emphasis on polyvocal, polysemic discourse, as well as on play. As we have seen, they often make up narrative game rules as they go along. Their discourses are characterized by expansiveness and openendedness, by polyvalence and disjunctiveness. They contrive to distance themselves or disengage themselves from the ideological underpinnings of the master discourse, a precondition for entering into dialogical narration that opens up to the writers the possibility of exchange and empathy.

Another aspect of *métissage* is the introduction of magical realist elements, whose mixture of fantasy and reality expands the traditional realist narrative. Intermixing or *Métissage* appears also in the manner they traverse genres and blend them in such pronounced ways in their works – prose fiction, poetry, historical and mythic narrative, proverbs, songs, religious texts, popular folk-tales, Classical Arabic rhetorical forms, oral speech transcriptions, dialogic and dramatic discourse, and so on.

This mixing of genres puts in mind the pervasive resemblances between postcolonial writing and what is often called postmodern writing, particularly in the ways in which they expand and mongrelize the conventional narrative, in their extensive use of irony, and in the development of a new antiphonal and antinomical rhetoric (a new sophism) briefly discussed in my Introduction. Though important work has been done on this subject, much more might be said of these resemblances that would profit our understanding of the situation of the contemporary non-Western writer living in a world where societies are undergoing unprecedented economic, political, and social change.

This change, in large part owing to the forces of internationalization and multinationalism – what Fredric Jameson sees as underlying systemic change taking place in world capitalism[5] – has strongly impacted the lives of the writers' compatriots and the writer her/himself. More than ever, non-Western writers can and do suggest to, and learn from, each other new tactics devised to counter the totalizing tendency of dominant discourse that more and more works towards the development and imposition of a universal world discourse.

The technocratic, culturally imperial, consumeristic lexicon of such a discourse creeps insidiously into all cracks and crevices of our society and other societies, and works towards the elimination or irrelevancy of eccentric and ethnic discourses – the final elimination of the hydra heads of multiculturalism. It is the PC police at the door. But, being a foolish mix of optimist and stoic, I harbor the belief that small bands of nomads and misfits will hold out and that they will assure that a luddite ghost will continue to exist, ineradicably, as a counterbalance, within the statist machine.

It is, I hope, not unseemly to end a study of four consummate story-tellers with a story of my own. In the late 1980s, I taught a course in comparative literature at the University of Aix-Marseille I, the subject of which was the modern experimental narrative. The class of forty-some was divided nearly equally between Maghrebian students and French students, most of whom had lived in Algeria or were of French-Algerian descent (*pieds-noirs*).

As the last of the narratives to study I chose *Nedjma* by Kateb Yacine, which describes, from the vantage-point of an Algerian, the Algerian War of Liberation and the events leading up to it. For nearly six months the students had grown accustomed to voicing their own views and hearing those of others. The discussion of *Nedjma*, however, exploded into heated argument and at times shouting matches.

After a while, the heated argument and shouting abated. The students expressed their own views and listened to those of others, often diametrically opposed to theirs. If the airing of views did not change underlying differences, most of the students felt they understood them. I say this because many students from both groups told me. In the words of a French woman student, "I never spoke to an Arab about the Algerian War. I never heard the other side until now."

I tell this story because this book is about hearing the other side.

Notes

1. Abdelkebir Khatibi, *Amour bilingue* (Montpellier: Fata Morgana, 1983), 114 ["Un pays retrouvé s'offre pour ce qu'il est, sans clôture et sans totalité"]. An English translation exists, by Richard Howard, *Love in Two Languages* (Minneapolis: University of Minnesota Press, 1990). I English the title of *Amour bilingue,* as has Howard.

2. Abdellatif Laâbi, *Rue du Retour* (London: Readers International, 1989), p. 85. Despite its French title, this is an English translation, by Jacqueline Kaye, of the original, *Le Chemin des ordalies* (Paris: Editions Denoël, 1982).

3. Although Rushdie, in his essay "Good Faith" published in 1990, disclaims being a Muslim, and pronounces therefore his condemnation as an apostate Muslim as inappropriate, in another essay from the same year ("Why I have embraced Islam") he says that he has been finding his way towards an "intellectual understanding of religion, and religion for me has always meant Islam. That journey is by no means over. I am certainly not a good Muslim. But I am able now to say that I am a Muslim." (Both essays appear in *Imaginary Homelands. Essays and Criticism 1981–1991* [London: Granta Books, in association with Viking, 1991].)

4. I shall term these dominant cultural discourses master or magistral discourses, by which I mean the legitimizing discourses of different societies or cultures that determine the way we talk about things and how we represent them discursively. In all societies, as Michel Foucault has reminded us, production of discourse is carefully selected and regulated as well as organized and redistributed following a specific number of procedures, which legislate and control ways of thinking and speaking. These discourses, which rely on institutional support, are logocentric discourses of exclusion that define and delimit what we "know" as "reality."

I shall also speak of master narratives, which are narratives that tell stories that draw upon the assumptions or "myths" underlying various social discourses and which are organized around the totalistic processes flowing from the conjectural unity Fredric Jameson (following Lyotard) sees as linking all knowledge.

See Michel Foucault, *The Archaeology of Knowledge and the Discourse on Language*, trans. A. M. Sheridan Smith (New York: Pantheon Books, 1972), pp. 216, 219. See also Fredric Jameson, Foreword to Jean-François Lyotard, *The Postmodern Condition: A Report on Knowledge*, trans. Geoff Bennington and Brian Massumi (Minneapolis: University of Minnesota Press, 1984), p. ix.

5. Kateb Yacine, "Le rôle de l'écrivain dans un état socialiste," *Anthologie des écrivains maghrébins d'expression française* (Paris: Présence Africaine, 1965), pp. 179–80.

6. The list is long, and includes the novelist and journalist Tahar Djaout, the poet Youssef Sebti, the journalist Saïd Mekbel, the dramatist Abdelkader Alloula, as well as several other authors and intellectuals whose work was considered as anti-fundamentalist. Assia Djebar writes in memory of those assassinated in *Le Blanc de l'Algérie* (Paris: Albin Michel, 1995).

7. In a short story entitled "Le Voltaïque," the Senegalese writer and film-maker Sembène Ousmane describes a group of Africans discussing the origin of facial scarification, who decide to consult the *griots* (the West African story-tellers, the troubadours or *jongleurs* of the bush) – those people, he notes, whom they call the "libraries" [*bibliothèques*] of their country, for having provided them with the key to the long-buried mysteries of their ancestral traditions dating back centuries. *Voltaïque* (Paris: Présence Africaine, 1962), p. 190.

8. Roland Barthes, "Grammaire africaine," *Mythologies* (Paris: Editions du Seuil, 1957), pp. 155–61. See also Guy Ossito Midiohouan, who discusses this question, as well as Barthes' position, in *L'Idéologie dans la littérature négro-africaine d'expression française* (Paris: l'Harmattan, 1986), esp. pp. 21–22.

9. Jean Ziegler, *Main basse sur l'Afrique. La recolonisation* (Paris: Editions du Seuil, 1980).

10. Salman Rushdie, *The Jaguar Smile: A Nicaraguan Journey* (New York: Penguin Books, 1988), p. 12.

11. Edward Said, *Beginnings: Intention and Method* (Baltimore: Johns Hopkins University Press, 1975), p. 5.

12. Abdellatif Laâbi, *Souffles* 18 (March-April 1970), 36.

13. Michel Foucault, *L'Ordre du discours* (Paris: Gallimard, 1971), pp. 10–11.

14. Julio Cortázar, "To Reach Lezama Lima," *Around the Day in Eighty Worlds* (San Francisco: North Point Press, 1986), p. 85.

15. Lucy Stone McNeece, "Decolonizing the Sign: Language and Identity in Abdelkebir Khatibi's *La Mémoire tatouée*," *Yale French Studies* 83 (1993), 15.

16. Tahar Ben Jelloun, *Harrouda* (Paris: Denoël, 1978), p. 21.

17. There is a "hadith" relating to a communal belief in the fact that an "ijma'" of religious scholars ("'ulama'") cannot be in error. While English sources have occasionally depicted the Shari'a as an unbending system of regulations, it is true that neither it nor any system of religious law is such or can be. To be sure, my own source (an anonymous reader) is of the strong belief that Muslim scholars have not developed (or would not be comfortable with) an extension of that notion into a principle of "infallibility."

Moreover, one should note that a fundamental division exists in Islam between the positions and interpretations of the Sunni and Shi'a (Shiites), the latter of whom the non-Shi'a see as having departed from the original Islam in the belief that Ali was a vice-regent of Allah and that his successors are infallible and sinless. See the *Columbia Encyclopedia*, 3rd edition.

18. In my chapter on Salman Rushdie, I shall speak of the differences of the Shi'a legal system in its modes of establishing and interpreting law, by which it accords a much different role to the force of "ijma'." Once again, I must thank my anonymous reader for leading me through these exceedingly complex and many-nuanced issues.

19. See Richard Bjornson, "Cognitive Mapping and the Understanding of Literature," *SubStance* 30 (1981), 51–62.

20. For Michel Foucault, see *L'Ordre du discours*. Also see Pierre Bourdieu, *Ce que parler veut dire: l'économie des échanges linguistiques* (Paris: Fayard, 1982), esp. p. 60, and Richard Terdiman, *Discourse/Counter-Discourse. The Theory and Practice of Symbolic Resistance in Nineteenth-Century France* (Ithaca: Cornell University Press, 1985).
21. Salman Rushdie, *The Satanic Verses* (New York: Viking, 1988), p. 281.
22. Abdelkebir Khatibi, "L'Orientalisme désorienté," *Maghreb pluriel* (Paris: Denoël, 1983), p. 141.
23. For this formulation, see Lyotard, *The Postmodern Condition*.
24. For my ideas regarding dialogue, I have found useful *The Interpretation of Dialogue*, ed. Tullio Maranhão (Chicago: University of Chicago Press, 1990). Of particular interest for me are the essays of C. Jan Swearingen, R. Lane Kauffmann, Jochen Mecke, and Tullio Maranhão.
25. Ludwig Wittgenstein, *Philosophical Investigations*, trans. G. E. M. Anscombe (Oxford: Basil Blackwell, 1968) and *Remarks on the Foundations of Mathematics*, same publisher and translator, 1964. Also see Lyotard, *The Postmodern Condition*, pp. 10 ff.
26. Wittgenstein, *Philosophical Investigations*, para. 84, 39e. See Jochen Mecke's discussion of Wittgenstein's proposition, "Dialogue in Narration (the Narrative Principle)," in Maranhão, *The Interpretation of Dialogue*, pp. 211–12 (193–215).
27. Michel Foucault, "Theatrum Philosophicum," *Language, Counter-Memory, Practice. Selected Essays and Interviews by Michel Foucault*, ed. Donald F. Bouchard; trans. Donald F. Bouchard and Sherry Simon (Ithaca: Cornell University Press, 1977), p. 182. See also my discussion of the Foucauldian notion of language as event, in "Kateb Yacine's *Nedjma*: A Dialogue of Difference," *SubStance* 69 (1992), 36–38 (30–45).
28. Gilles Deleuze and Félix Guattari, *Capitalisme et schizophrénie: L'Anti-Oedipe* (Paris: Editions de Minuit, 1972), p. 125.
29. Homi K. Bhabha, "DissemiNation: Time, Narrative, and the Margins of the Modern Nation," *Nation and Narration*, ed. Homi K. Bhabha (London and New York: Routledge, 1990), p. 312.
30. Bhabha borrows the phrase "homogeneous empty time" from Benedict Anderson (*Imagined Communities. Reflections on the Origin and Spread of Nationalism* [London: Verso, 1983]), who in turn borrowed it from Walter Benjamin ("Theses on the Philosophy of History," *Illuminations: Essays and Reflections*, ed. Hannah Arendt, trans. Harry Zohn [New York: Schocken Books, 1968], pp. 261–64). Anderson used it to characterize the dissemination of the sense/image of a shared (homogenous) experience of community among a collectivity, whose members are often unaware of each other's individual existence. Bhabha extends to "nation" or "nationness" as a social and textual form of relatedness ("DissemiNation," p. 292) the strategies of cultural identity that Anderson applied to "community," while focusing on the temporal dimension or the temporal alienation of the arbitrary sign (p. 311) that figures in the metaphor of nation.

In contrast to Benjamin's concept of "Messianic time," Rushdie interprets the phrase "homogeneous empty time" as referring to the modern concept of time as regulated by clocks. Time in this sense moves forward. And Rushdie cites Benedict Anderson, who envisages "the idea of a sociological organism moving calendrically through homogeneous, empty time [as] a precise analogue of the idea of the nation" (Salman Rushdie, "In God We Trust," *Imaginary Homelands. Essays and Criticism, 1981–1991* [London: Granta Books/New York: Viking, 1991], p. 382). See the interesting discussion by Rushdie of these two temporal concepts in our "clock-ridden" world and their relation to European–Islamic tensions and the writer, pp. 382ff.

31. This notion echoes Jacques Derrida's notion of paronomasia.

32. See my essay, "*Metoïkoi* and Magical Realism in the Maghrebian Narratives of Tahar Ben Jelloun and Abdelkebir Khatibi," *Magical Realism: Theory, History, Community*, eds. Lois Parkinson Zamora and Wendy Faris (Durham, North Carolina: Duke University Press, 1995).

33. The looseness of language suggests, as Homi K. Bhabha says, that "social conditions are themselves being reinscribed or reconstituted in the very act of enunciation, revealing the instability of any division of meaning into an inside and outside" ("DissemiNation," p. 314).

34. Jean-François Lyotard, "Sur la force des faibles," *L'Arc* 64 (1976), 6 (4–12).

35. Jean-François Lyotard, *Instructions païennes* (Paris: Editions Galilée, 1977), p. 47.

36. "Programme de recherche et d'action de l'A.R.C.," *Souffles* 12 (1968). Readers interested in the revolutionary program of *Souffles*, copies of which are difficult to obtain, may consult the "Programme de recherche et d'action de l'A.R.C." reproduced in Marc Gontard, *Violence du texte: La Littérature marocaine de langue française* (Paris/Rabat: L'Harmattan/Société marocaine des éditeurs réunis, 1981), pp. 151–59.

37. James McGuire uses the term *métissage* to refer to Abdelkebir Khatibi's manipulation of language. "Forked Tongues, Marginal Bodies: Writing as Translation in Khatibi," *Research in African Literatures* 23:1 (Spring 1992), 110. See also the work of Edouard Glissant, *Le Discours antillais* (Paris: Editions du Seuil, 1981), pp. 462–63, which is a source book for usage of the term, and two recent studies by Françoise Lionnet: *Autobiographical Voices: Race, Gender, Self-Portraiture* (Ithaca, NY: Cornell University Press, 1989) and *Postcolonial Representations: Women, Literature, Identity* (Ithaca, NY: Cornell University Press, 1995).

38. Salman Rushdie, *East, West. Stories* (New York: Pantheon Books, 1994), p. 211.

39. Abdelkebir Khatibi, *Le Roman maghrébin* (Paris: François Maspero, 1968), pp. 14–15.

40. Bernard Aresu, *Counterhegemonic Discourse from the Maghreb: The Poetics of Kateb's Fiction* (Tübingen: Gunter Narr Verlag, 1993), p. 11.

41. See Abdallah Mdarhri-Alaoui, "Abdelkebir Khatibi: Writing a Dynamic Identity," *Research in African Literatures* 23:2 (Summer 1992), 169.

42. My use of the concept "postmodernism" coincides fundamentally with that set forth by Linda Hutcheon in such works as *A Poetics of Postmodernism: History, Theory, Fiction* (New York and London: Routledge, 1988) and *The Politics of Postmodernism* (New York and London: Routledge, 1989), as well as with the somewhat variant conceptions of Jean-François Lyotard elaborated in a number of texts. For a useful overview of the varied understandings of the term, see Allan Megill's essay, "What Does the Term 'Postmodern' Mean?" *Annals of Scholarship*, special issue on "Modernism and Postmodernism," 6:2–3 (1989), 129–51.

43. A. Valbueno Briones, "Una cala en el realismo mágico," in *Cuadernos americanos* 166:5 (September–October 1969), 236.

44. Lyotard speaks of this phenomenon of "bricolage" in regard to postmodern architecture in *The Postmodern Explained*, trans. Don Barry et al. (Minneapolis: University of Minnesota Press, 1993), p. 76.

45. Ross Chambers, *Room for Maneuver. Reading (the) Oppositional (in) Narrative* (University of Chicago Press, 1991), p. 45.

46. See my article, "Alienation in Samuel Beckett: The Protagonist as Eiron," *Perspectives* 1, 2 (November 1975), 62–73.

47. See Albert Memmi, *Portrait du colonisé. précédé du Portrait du Colonisateur*. Preface by

Jean-Paul Sartre (Paris: J. J. Pauvert, 1957); *Portrait d'un juif* (Paris: Gallimard, 1962); and *L'Homme dominé* (Paris: Gallimard, 1968). For Frantz Fanon, see *Peau noire masques blancs* (Paris: Editions du Seuil, 1952) and *Les Damnés de la terre*. Preface by Jean-Paul Sartre (Paris: François Maspero, 1961).

48. See Françoise Lionnet's discussion of *anamnesis* in *Autobiographical Voices*, p. 223. Michel Beaujour, in speaking of *anamnesis*, conceptualizes it as a form of metempsychosis, as a special memory that is both ancient and modern, whose operation replaces or effaces events of an individual's life by his or her recall of an entire culture (*Miroirs d'encre* [Paris: Seuil, 1980], p. 9; cited by Lionnet, *Autobiographical Voices*, p. 225). The similarity with Jung's theory of the archetypes of the collective unconscious are apparent.

49. Assia Djebar, *Femmes d'Alger dans leur appartement* (Paris: Editions des femmes, 1980), p. 184.

50. Roland Barthes, Postface to Abdelkebir Khatibi, *La Mémoire tatouée* (Paris: Union Générale d'Editions, série 10/18, 1971).

51. Jean-François Lyotard, *La Guerre des Algériens: écrits 1956–1963*, ed. Mohammed Ramdani (Paris: Galilée, 1989), p. 38. See the essay by Georges Van Den Abbeele, "*Algérie l'intraitable*: Lyotard's National Front," *Passages, Genres, Differends: Jean-François Lyotard*, a special issue of *L'Esprit Créateur* 31:1 (Spring 1991), 144–57. The citation is from p. 146.

52. Michel de Certeau, *L'Invention du quotiden. I Arts de faire* (Paris: Union Générale d'Editions, 10/18, 1980). English trans.: *The Practice of Everyday Life* (Berkeley: University of California Press, 1984). A long extract translated by Fredric Jameson and Carl Lovitt, "On the Oppositional Practice of Everyday Life," appeared in *Social Text* 3 (Fall 1980), 3–43.

53. Salman Rushdie, *L'Express*, February 24, 1989; Tahar Ben Jelloun, "Politics and Literature: An Interview with Tahar Ben Jelloun," by Thomas Spear, *Yale French Studies* 83 (1993), 42 (30–43).

54. Assia Djebar, *Loin de Médine* (Paris: Albin Michel, 1991; Algeria: ENAG/Editions, 1992).

55. In the case of Khatibi, see Ahmed Rhioui, "Words from a Maddening Quest," *Revue CELFAN/CELFAN Review*, Special issue on Abdelkebir Khatibi. 8:1–2 (November 1988–February 1989), 35.

56. Assia Djebar, *L'Amour, la fantasia* (Paris: Jean-Claude Lattès, 1985; reprinted by Editions Albin Michel, 1995), p. 241. Translated into English by Dorothy Blair, *Fantasia: An Algerian Calvacade* (London: Quartet Books Limited, 1989; Portsmouth, NH: Heinemann, 1993), p. 215.

2 Women's voices and woman's space in Assia Djebar's *L'Amour, la fantasia*

1. Assia Djebar, "Fugitive, et ne le sachant pas," *L'Esprit Créateur* 33:2 (Summer 1993), 133 (129–33). This article has been reprinted in *Vaste est la prison* (Paris: Albin Michel, 1995), 167–72.

2. Assia Djebar, *Femmes d'Alger dans leur appartement* (Paris: Editions des femmes, 1980), pp. 7–8; my translation. *Femmes d'Alger* has been translated into English by Marjolijn de Jager, as *Women of Algiers in Their Apartment* (Charlottesville: University Press of Virginia, 1992).

3. Assia Djebar, "Le point de vue d'une Algérienne sur la condition de la femme musulmane au 20e siècle," *Le Courrier de l'UNESCO*, 28 (August–September, 1975), 25.

4. Assia Djebar, *L'Amour, la fantasia* (Paris: Jean-Claude Lattès, 1985; reprinted in 1995 by Editions Albin Michel, Paris). Dorothy Blair has rendered the French original into English, as *Fantasia: An Algerian Calvacade* (London: Quartet Books Limited, 1989; Portsmouth, NH: Heinemann, 1993). I shall avail myself of her sensitive translation though my occasional modifications of it will be indicated in the text.

5. For the notion of a "space of writing" for postcolonial authors, see Abdelkebir Khatibi, "L'orientalisme désorienté," *Maghreb pluriel* (Paris: Denoël, 1983), p. 141, whom I cite in my Introduction, chapter 1. Also, see my essay, "Writing Double: Politics and the African Narrative of French Expression," *Studies in 20th Century Literature* (Winter 1990), 101–22. The subject of writing in terms of space in Djebar's work (the inside and the outside) was first suggested by Djebar herself in "Du français comme butin," *La Quinzaine littéraire*, 436 (March 16–31, 1985), and has been picked up by several critics. See her interview with Mildred Mortimer, "Entretien avec Assia Djebar, écrivain algérien," *Research in African Literature* 19:2 (Summer 1988), 197–205, and Mortimer's critical studies of Djebar: notably "Language and Space in the Fiction of Assia Djebar and Leila Sebbar," *Research in African Literature* 19:3 (Fall 1988), 301–11; also *Assia Djebar* (Philadelphia: CELFAN Edition Monographs, 1988) and *Journeys: A Study of the Francophone Novel in Africa* (Portsmouth, NH: Heinemann, 1990). For the term "la langue adverse," see the interview of Marguerite Le Clézio, "Assia Djebar: Ecrire dans la langue *adverse*," *Contemporary French Civilization* 19:2 (Summer 1985), 230–44.

6. The oral testimonies we find in *L'Amour, la fantasia* come in large part ("voix de veuve," in particular) from Djebar's conversations and inquiries in 1975 and the summer of 1976 in the mountain region of her youth. They served as the point of departure for her film *La Nouba des femmes du Mont Chenoua* (filmed in 1977–1978), which was awarded the Prix de la Critique Internationale at the Venice *Biennale* in 1979. (Letter to the author from Assia Djebar, May 6, 1997.)

Earlier, during her sojourn in Tunisia in 1958, she had recorded conversations with refugees on the Tunisian–Algerian border, which appear in *Les Enfants du nouveau monde* (Paris: Juillard, 1962; Paris: Union Générale d'Editions, coll. 10/18, 1978; republished in January 1998 by Groupe Actes-Sud, poche BABEL) and in *Les Alouettes naïves* (Paris: Juillard, 1967; U.G.E., coll. 10/18, 1978; Groupe Actes-Sud, poche BABEL, 1997).

7. Jean-François Lyotard, *Instructions païennes* (Paris: Editions Galilée, 1977), p. 47.

8. Alev Lytle Croutier, *Harem. The World Behind the Veil* (New York: Abbeville Press, 1989), p. 17. The author is a Turkish Muslim woman. More specifically, *haram* means "protected" or "forbidden." The word for "unlawful" is *haraam* (elongation of the second vowel); the sacred enclosure in Mecca is the *Haram* (two short vowels), and the womenfolk of the family are the *hariim* (elongated "i"). I thank an anonymous reader of my manuscript who offered these distinctions. It is accurate to point out as well that the view of the harem in Western society has often been distorted and that, like the veil, the custom of the harem preceded Arabic or Muslim civilization (its use is recorded in ancient China, for example). See the work of the Moroccan psychiatrist Ghita El Khayat, *Le Monde arabe au féminin* (Paris: L'Harmattan, 1988), pp. 28–34.

9. There is no inference on Assia Djebar's part that the painfulness of the deflowering of the Algerian woman during her wedding night is increased by infibulation or other forms of female circumcision. The practice of female circumcision that takes places in certain areas of Africa and the Middle East assumes three forms: traditional circumcision refers to the removal of the prepuce of the clitoris; excision consists in the removal of the prepuce, the clitoris, and the labia minora; infibulation involves the

removal of the clitoris, the labia minora, and labia majora, and the suturing of the sides of the vulva to leave only a tiny opening for natural functions. One can hardly imagine what pain a woman who has undergone infibulation must experience during the wedding night, when the sutures are broken open by the penetration of the male penis.

For the practice of female circumcision, see Françoise Lionnet, *Postcolonial Representations: Women, Literature, Identity* (Ithaca, NY: Cornell University Press, 1995), p. 129n (esp. chapter 6). For the forms of circumcision, which I refer to above, Lionnet cites the book of Olayinka Koso-Thomas, *The Circumcision of Women: Strategy for Eradication* (London: Zed Books, 1987), pp. 16–17. Nawal El Saadawi discusses the practice in her book, *The Hidden Face of Eve: Women in the Arab World*, trans. Sherif Hetata (London: Zed Books, 1980), and describes the practice in her novel *Woman at Point Zero*, trans. Sherif Hetata (London: Zed Books, 1983), as does Evelyne Accad in her novel *L'Excisée* (Paris: L'Harmattan, 1982).

While roundly condemning the torturous practice of sexual mutilation of women, Ghita El Khayat also criticizes the Western press for its quickness to condemn such practices but failure to understand how they are deeply rooted in ancestral and cultural customs (*Le Monde arabe au féminin*, pp. 36–43).

The authors I cite above (Lionnet, El Saadawi, Accad, and El Khayat) are Mauritian, Egyptian, Lebanese, and Moroccan, respectively.

Clitoridectomy appears to be a non-Islamic, indeed pre-Islamic custom in Africa. Instances still occur in a variety of places, including areas of Africa and the Middle East, as well as other regions of the world. Critics differ, however, as to the extent and geographical location of the practice of female circumcision.

While agreeing with the critics cited in their condemnation of the practice of excision, Assia Djebar says this about its geographical incidence: " in Algeria, with relation to my own experience, and, as I also know as a historian, in the rest of Algeria, excision has not been practiced. I've never had it in mind in my writings... It's a different matter in Egypt, the Middle East, and in Black Africa... As for Morocco, as well as Tunisia, I am of the opinion that the situation is the same as in Algeria... I don't believe that, among the Moroccan Berbers, excision has been practiced, but there I might be mistaken. For Algeria, I can respond in the affirmative, insofar as the non-practice of that form of mutilation is concerned" ["en Algérie, par rapport à mon expérience, à ce que je sais également comme historienne, dans le reste de l'Algérie, il n'y a pas eu de pratique de l'excision. Je n'y ai personnellement jamais pensée dans mes écrits... Ce qui est différent en Egypte, au Moyen Orient, et en Afrique noire... Pour le Maroc, il me semble que le monde citadin féminin, ainsi qu'en Tunisie, est le même qu'en Algérie... Je ne pense pas que, dans le monde berbère marocain, l'excision ait été pratiquée, mais là, je peux me tromper. Pour l'Algérie, je suis affirmative, quant à la non-pratique de cette mutilation"] (letter to the author, May 6, 1997).

10. Fatima Mernissi, *Beyond the Veil. Male–Female Dynamics in a Modern Muslim Society* (New York: Schenkman Publishing Company, 1975), esp. chapter 8, "The Meaning of Spatial Boundaries" (cited hereafter in the text as *Veil*). Also see Mortimer, *Journeys*, and my essay "Veiled Woman and Veiled Narrative in Tahar Ben Jelloun's *Sandchild*," *boundary 2* 20:1 (Spring 1993), 47–64.

11. *The Koran*. Trans. N. J. Dawood (London: Penguin Classics, 1994), p 248.

12. Germaine Tillion, *Le Harem et les cousins* (Paris: Seuil, 1966), p. 22.

13. Abdelwahab Bouhdiba, *La Sexualité en Islam* (Paris: Presses Universitaires de France, 1975), p. 50. Also see Ghadah al-Samman, "The Sexual Revolution and the Total

Revolution," in *Middle Eastern Muslim Women Speak*, eds. Elizabeth Warnock Fernea and Basima Qattan Bezirgan (Austin/London: University of Texas Press, 1977), pp. 393–99.

14. Abu-Hamid al-Ghazali, cited by Mernissi in *Veil*, p. 83. See also Nawal El Saadawi, *The Hidden Face of Eve*, pp. 99–100. It has been pointed out to me that veiling was a symbol of high status in Roman times (especially in the Eastern provinces ruled by Rome) and only upper-class women were allowed to veil. Veiling and its traditional and contemporary symbolism, as well as its varying acceptance and use in different Islamic cultures, make of it an exceedingly complex issue, of which I treat only the broad outline provided by a few critics.

15. Fatima Mernissi, "Virginity and Patriarchy," in *Women and Islam*, ed. Azizah al-Hibri (Oxford/New York: Pergamon Press, 1982), p. 191. Also see Fedwa Malti-Douglas, *Woman's Body, Woman's Word. Gender and Discourse in Arabo-Islamic Writing* (Princeton University Press, 1991).

16. Tahar Ben Jelloun, *La Plus Haute des solitudes. Misère affective et sexuelle d'émigrés nord-africains* (Paris: Editions du Seuil, 1977).

17. Frantz Fanon, *Sociologie d'une révolution (L'An V de la révolution algérienne)*, 1959 (Paris: François Maspero, 1972), p. 20.

18. *Ibid.*, p. 44. The role of women in the Algerian War of Liberation has been disputed. Some, like Mohammed Harbi ("Les femmes dans la Révolution algérienne," *Les Révoltes logiques*, 11 [Winter 1979–1980], 78–93), have argued that women played a minimal role. Harbi speaks also of how, though they envisaged more freedom at the end of hostilities, Algerian women found themselves precisely where they were before the conflict. Jean Déjeux, who discusses Harbi's contention at length in his short study *Assia Djebar. Romancière algérienne, cinéaste arabe* (Sherbrooke, Québec: Editions Naaman, 1984, pp. 29–32), calls Harbi's words important for the reason that they are demythifying. Both Harbi and Déjeux contend that the accounts of feminine combatants reported in the underground journal *El Moudjahid*, edited by Frantz Fanon, were for foreign consumption (Déjeux, *Assia Djebar*, p. 31). Whose is the reliable account? '

Monique Gadant gives greater emphasis to the involvement of Algerian women in the national War of Liberation, while agreeing with Harbi that such involvement, far from winning them rights previously denied them, left their social and political situation essentially unchanged. Monique Gadant, ed., *Women of the Mediterranean* (London: Zed, 1986), Introduction, p. 2.

19. The sexual exploitation of women in Islamic society has been discussed by several authors, including Fadela M'Rabet, *La Femme algérienne* (Paris: François Maspero, 1964) and *Les Algériennes* (1967); Evelyne Accad, *Veil of Shame: The Role of Women in the Contemporary Fiction of North Africa and the Arab World* (Sherbrooke: Naaman, 1978) and *Sexuality and War. Literary Masks of the Middle East* (New York University Press, 1990); and Ghita El Khayat, *Le Monde arabe au féminin* (Paris: L'Harmattan, 1988). See also Ben Jelloun's chapter on "Une sexualité conçue par et pour l'homme," *La Plus Haute des solitudes*, pp. 57–97 (esp. pp. 57–59).

20. Interview by Marie-Françoise Lévy, in her article "L'espace du dedans," *Le Monde*, May 28–29, 1978.

21. Winifred Woodhull, *Transfigurations of the Maghreb. Feminism, Decolonization, and Literatures* (Minneapolis: University of Minnesota Press, 1993), p. 16. See her quote from Lacheref, p. 21. See also, H. Adlai Murdoch, "Rewriting Writing: Identity, Exile and Renewal in Assia Djebar's *L'Amour, la fantasia*," *Yale French Studies* 83 (1993), 78–80; 84

(pp. 71–92). In *Sexuality and War*, Evelyne Accad sees sexuality as central to the motivations involved in war.

22. Marguerite Duras, "Ecrire," in *L'Esprit Créateur* 30:1 (Spring 1990), 6. Duras was born and brought up in Indo-China, the daughter of an impoverished (and fatherless) European family. Her novel *L'Amant* (1984), which won the Prix Goncourt, as a thinly veiled autobiography recounts her childhood and adolescence in Indo-China. In her study of women's autobiography, Françoise Lionnet points out how the five women writers she writes of (Maya Angelou, Marie Cardinal, Marie-Thérèse Humbert, Zora Neale Hurston, and Maryse Condé) all focus ambivalently on metaphors of death (as well as of disease or madness and silence) as the basis of their attempt at writing the self. (Only the first three succeed in reaffirming life through the potential of writing as a freeing force.) *Autobiographical Voices: Race, Gender, Self-Portraiture* (Ithaca: Cornell University Press, 1989), pp. 20–21.

23. Maurice Blanchot, *L'Entretien infini* (Paris: Gallimard, 1969), cited and glossed by Jacques Derrida in "Survivre," *Parages* (Paris: Galilée, 1986), pp. 149–50 (my translation). An English translation of "Survivre" ("Living On: *Border Lines*") by James Hulbert may be found in Harold Bloom et al. (eds.), *Deconstruction and Criticism* (New York: The Seabury Press, 1979). The passage I translated appears on page 104.

24. Michel Serres, "Platonic Dialogue," *Hermes: Literature, Science, Philosophy*, eds. Josué V. Harari and David F. Bell (Baltimore: Johns Hopkins University Press, 1982), p. 67.

25. *Les Alouettes naïves*, p. 162, and *La Nouba des femmes du mont Chenoua*, Radio-Télévision algérienne, 1978. See Déjeux, *Assia Djebar*, pp. 53–54; also Réda Bensmaïa, "La *Nouba des femmes du mont Chenoua*. Introduction à l'oeuvre fragmentale," *Les 2 Ecrans* 17 (Algeria, October 1979).

26. Murdoch, *Rewriting Writing*, p. 72. The author explores the divided desire of the colonized subject, whose writing signifies at once subjection to cultural alienation and its subversion. That very alienation allows the inscription of identity. He sees the textual and cultural *métissage* of the colonial subject as figures for his ambiguities and disjunctures (92).

27. Anne Donadey, "Assia Djebar's Poetics of Subversion," *L'Esprit Créateur* 33:2 (Summer 1993), 107–17. For Gérard Genette's epigraphic categories, see *Seuils* (Paris: Editions du Seuil, 1987), p. 7. For Luce Irigaray's theory of mimicry, see *Ce sexe qui n'en est pas un* (Paris: Minuit, 1977), pp. 65–82.

28. The story of the silver spoon as an object passed down through the generations parallels one recounted to me by Assia Djebar, whose mother inscribed in Arabic the Andalusian songs of the Noubas she had heard as an adolescent in music notebooks which were, regrettably, destroyed by French soldiers. She retells the story of "this passage of transmission" ["ce trajet de transmission"] by her mother ("bearer of this ancestral legacy" ["porteuse de ce legs ancestral"]) in her 1993 essay, "Fugitive, et ne le sachant pas" and, later, in her autobiographical novel, *Vaste est la prison*, pp. 167–72.

29. Djebar's research into women's history, coming in part from her training as a historian and her experience in 1958 interviewing Algerian refugees on the Algerian–Tunisian border, as well as from her interviews and inquiries in 1975 and 1976 in the mountainous region where she was born, would provide much material for her novels, such as *L'Amour, la fantasia* and *Vaste est le prison*, as well as for her films, *La Nouba des femmes du mont Chenoua* (1978) and *La Zerda et les chants de l'oubli* (1982).

30. Fedwa Malti-Douglas says that the voice of the woman in classical and modern Arabo-Islamic discourse is inextricably linked to the body and sexuality, whether she

speaks through the body as in classical discourse or in reaction to it as in modern discourse. *Woman's Body, Woman's Word. Gender and Discourse in Arabo-Islamic Writing*, p. 10.

31. Woodhull acknowledges the source of these comments as contained in a paper by Anne Donadey Roch, "Writing the Trace: Assia Djebar's *L'Amour, la fantasia* as a Bilingual Palimpsest," delivered at a meeting of the Modern Language Association in December 1990.

32. See, for example, R. Lane Kauffmann, "The Other in Question: Dialogical Experiments in Montaigne, Kafka, and Cortázar," in *The Interpretation of Dialogue*, ed. Tullio Maranhão (Chicago: University of Chicago Press, 1990), pp. 179–80.

33. Assia Djebar, "Fugitive, et ne le sachant pas," 133. She says that the story of the captive Zoraidé is "the metaphor for the Algerian women who write today, among which I count myself" (130).

34. Simone Rezzoug, "Ecritures féminines algériennes: histoires et société," *Maghreb Review* 9:3–4 (May-August 1984), 89. See also Donadey, who cites Rezzoug and builds on her premise ("Assia Djebar's Poetics of Subversion," p. 109).

35. Luce Irigaray, *Ethique de la différence sexuelle* (Paris: Editions de Minuit, 1984), pp. 23, 46.

36. See my article, "Maximin's *L'Isolé soleil* and Caliban's Curse," *Callaloo*, special issue on Guadeloupe and Martinique, edited by Maryse Condé, 15:1 (1992), 124–25 (119–30).

37. Stephen A. Tyler, "Ethnography, Intertextuality and the End of Description," *American Journal of Semiotics* 3:4 (1984), 83–98.

38. Edouard Glissant, *Le Discours antillais* (Paris: Editions du Seuil, 1981), p. 462. My translation. I have borrowed from the English translation of J. Michael Dash the term "cross-cultural relationship" to translate Glissant's term *Relation*. Edouard Glissant, *Caribbean Discourse. Selected Essays* (Charlottesville: The University Press of Virginia, 1989).

39. Françoise Lionnet, *Autobiographical Voices*, p. 5. Also, see her discussion of the etymology and extended meaning of the word *métis*, pp. 14–15.

40. Tzvetan Todorov, "A Dialogic Criticism," *Raritan* 4:1, 64–76; Theodor Adorno, *Negative Dialectics*, trans. E. B. Ashton (New York: Seabury, 1973). Cited by Kauffmann, "The Other in Question," p. 160.

3 Tahar Ben Jelloun's *Sandchild*: voiceless narratives, placeless places

1. Tahar Ben Jelloun, *L'Enfant de sable* (Paris: Seuil, 1985), p. 178. I cite this work in my text by page number only. Ben Jelloun's work has been translated into English by Alan Sheridan as *The Sand Child* (New York: Harcourt Brace Jovanovich, 1987).

2. Jorge Luis Borges, *Labyrinths. Selected Stories & Other Writings*, eds. Donald A. Yates and James E. Irby; trans. Donald A Yates et al. (New York: New Directions, 1964), p. 22.

3. Jacques Derrida, "Living On: *Border Lines*," trans. Harold Bloom, et al., in *Deconstruction and Criticism* (New York: Seabury Press, 1979), p. 76; hereafter cited in my text as "Living On."

4. Abdelwahab Bouhdiba writes, "it is to be strongly feared that liberation which would be purely sexual would come about to the detriment of economic and social liberation. Sexuality in that case would only be a subterfuge, a flight from the responsibilities incumbent on Arab consciousness that grapples with the redoubtable problems of poverty, ignorance, sickness, of underdevelopment, that is to say, of independence and survival." Despite the concerns of Bouhdiba, given the inextricable

ties between sexuality and social and political problems, it seems to me that this fear is ungrounded. See *La Sexualité en Islam* (Paris: Presses Universitaires de France, 1975), p. 292; hereafter cited in my text as Bouhdiba. Also see Ghadah al-Samman, "The Sexual Revolution and the Total Revolution," *Middle Eastern Muslim Women Speak*, eds. Elizabeth Warnock Fernea and Basima Qattan Bezirgan (Austin and London: University of Texas Press, 1977), pp. 393–99.

5. Evelyne Accad sees Jelloun to be far from liberating, if not outright chauvinistic, in his thought. She bases her opinion on a reading of *La Nuit sacrée* (Paris: Seuil, 1987), in which she sees the female protagonist as freeing herself by fulfilling all the male sexual fantasies. *Sexuality and War: Literary Masks of the Middle East* (New York: New York University Press, 1990). *La Nuit sacrée*, ostensibly a continuation of *L'Enfant de sable*, strongly contrasts with it in terms of structure and content. I feel, as do some other commentators, that Ben Jelloun, after failing to receive the Prix Goncourt for *L'Enfant*, wrote *La Nuit* specifically to appeal to the Goncourt jury, the general public, and the popular press. This cynical strategy appears to have tempered his work. *La Nuit* is a work notably inferior, in my opinion, to *L'Enfant*. In succeeding narratives such as *Jour de silence à Tanger* (1990), *Les Yeux baissés* (1991), *L'Homme rompu* (1994), and *Le Premier Amour est toujours le dernier* (1995), while continuing to explore the major motives of his work (exile and uprootedness, the tension between two cultures, and women's situation in Islam), Ben Jelloun has reverted to a more traditional narrative structure.

6. See Anouar Abdel-Malek, "Orientalism in Crisis," *Diogenes* 44 (Winter 1963), 103–40; Edward W. Said, *Orientalism* (New York: Pantheon Books, 1978); and Roberto Fernández Retamar, *Caliban and Other Essays*, trans. Edward Baker (Minneapolis: University of Minnesota Press, 1989).

7. The question has been raised as to whether the perspective according to which Middle Eastern women are oppressed in speech and conduct is not a Western and in particular a Western feminist perspective. One critic maintains that the little research that has emerged on these women's lives, written from *within* by women who have become assimilated into the behavioral norms and expectations of the societies involved, shows that, while they may be silent and/or absent from the *public* life of these "societies," their role within the (enclosed) life of the home is far from silent. Indeed, that may often be the position of the husband.

The key word is "assimilated," for assuredly the women authors/commentators I draw upon, and who have to a large extent been educated in Western higher institutions of learning, have for personal reasons or because of their particular familial, social, and educational situation, escaped assimilation. Though they have been born and reared in Maghrebian and Middle Eastern societies and have, like Djebar, often involved themselves deeply in the religious fabric of their societies, they have challenged precisely those behavioral norms and expectations that they encountered in their youth or that governed their ancestral households. Moreover, in so doing, they have often drawn on and "corrected" their own perspective through the testimony of uneducated non-Western women in Muslim and Arab countries, that is, women without formal education much less Western education (see, e.g., Fernea and Bezirgan's *Middle Eastern Women Speak* or Djebar's work that was heavily informed by her interviews of Muslim women during the Algerian War of Liberation).

It appears to me that these differing perspectives reflect the contrast between the traditional view of women as opposed to the rather widespread reaction against that view, tempered, I will agree, by a broadened frame of reference encompassing knowledge of international norms in a changing world.

Whatever perspective one chooses to emphasize, what must be stressed is that the status of women varies enormously from one country to the next. The situation of women in Morocco, as compared with, say, Iraq or Syria (where the status of professional women is, by "Western" standards, quite advanced), differs greatly. Once again, we must guard against overgeneralized comparisons by recognizing significant regional and social variations.

8. Malek Alloula, *The Colonial Harem*, Theory and History of Literature, vol. 21 (Minneapolis: University of Minnesota Press, 1986).

9. See the description by Nancy K. Miller of the male gaze in De Staël's *Corinne*, in *Subject to Change: Reading Feminist Writing* (New York: Columbia University Press, 1988), pp. 164ff.

10. Stephen Heath, "Difference," *Screen* 19:3 (Autumn 1978), 51–112, esp. 62. For a North African woman's view of veiling, see Fatima Mernissi, *Beyond the Veil. Male–Female Dynamics in a Modern Muslim Society* (New York: Schenkman Publishing Company, 1975), pp. 83ff. For other Western considerations of the gaze, see Sigmund Freud, "The Uncanny," in *The Standard Edition*, vol. 17 (London: Hogarth Press, 1963), pp. 219–52; Luce Irigaray, *Speculum of the Other Woman*, trans. Gillian G. Gill (Ithaca: Cornell University Press, 1985), pp. 47–48; Sarah Kofman, *The Enigma of Woman: Woman in Freud's Writings*, trans. Catherine Porter (Ithaca: Cornell University Press, 1985), pp. 82–89, 178–90; Jacques Lacan, *Ecrits* (Paris: Seull, 1966) and *Le Séminaire*, Book XX *Encore* (Paris: Seuil, 1975).

11. Michel Foucault, "Theatrum Philosophicum," in *Language, Counter-Memory, Practice. Selected Essays and Interviews by Michel Foucault*, ed. Donald F. Bouchard; trans. Donald F. Bouchard and Sherry Simon (Ithaca: Cornell University Press, 1977), p. 174. See also Foucault's description of event in *L'Ordre du discours* (Paris: Gallimard, 1971), pp. 59ff.

12. Jorge Luis Borges, "The Sect of the Phoenix," in *Labyrinths*, p. 103. This volume also contains the other stories to which Ben Jelloun alludes: "The Garden of Forking Paths," "The Circular Ruins," and "The Zahir." English translations in my text of phrases rummaged by Ben Jelloun from Borges' stories are drawn from the New Directions volume.

13. The tale of "Abu al-Husn and his Slave-Girl Tawaddud" concerns a rich and influential citizen of Baghdad, who, being without issue for a long time, has a son named Abu al-Husn. The son, after the death of his father, squanders his wealth and finds himself left with only a slave girl of unequaled beauty, knowledge, wisdom, and eloquence of speech. She tells her master to offer her to Harun al-Rashid, the Commander of the Faithful, for 10,000 dinars. When Tawaddud (whose name means "gaining the love of another, love") tells the latter of her knowledge and skills, he agrees to pay the price demanded, provided she answers correctly questions from the most learned men of the day whom he summons to the palace. Each advances questions which she correctly answers. In turn she asks them questions that they find themselves unable to answer. She demands as her due their clothes. She does the same with the master game players and musicians whom she bests. The Caliph, ravished by her exploits, grants her purchase price tenfold and gives her leave to request a boon. She asks to be restored to her master. The Caliph does so and makes Abu al-Husn one of his permanent "cup-companions."

Scheherazade comments: "Marvel, O King, at the eloquence of this damsel and the hugeness of her learning and understanding and her perfect excellence in all branches of art and science" Anon. "Abu al-Husn and his Slave-Girl Tawaddud," in *The Book of the Thousand Nights and a Night*, trans. Richard F. Burton, 17 vols. (London: Burton Ethnological Society, n.d. [1884–1886]), Tales 436–462, v, pp. 189–245. Burton cites John Payne's translation. He notes also that Edward William Lane (*The Thousand and One Nights*, 3 vols. [London, 1838–1841]), like many other translators, omits this tale. Burton cites Lane's reasoning: "as it would not only require a volume of commentary, but be extremely tiresome for most readers." Burton comments: "Quite true; but it is valuable to Oriental Students who are beginning their studies, as an excellent compendium of doctrine and practice according to the Shafi'i School" (p. 189, n1). The original sources for the French translation of Antoine Galland, *Les Mille et une nuits* (1704–1717), which introduced to the European public the famous collection of stories, contained some 250 nights, among which that of Tawaddud was not included.

Tawaddud, who is mentioned by the Blind Troubadour (174), bears resemblances to Ahmed/Zahra. Ahmed's father, like Abu al-Husn's father, finds difficulty in engendering a male offspring. That similarity is slight, however. Of much greater importance is the depiction of woman as vanquisher of man, and the reversal of roles. Her demand that the learned men be stripped of their (masculine) dress, just as their knowledge has been stripped of its supposed superiority, introduces once again the theme of castration, as well as a return to a state of Edenic pristinity in which the female (Eve) dominates. While Tawaddud's state is that of a slave, her name and actions denote a gift of mastery.

14. Tzvetan Todorov, "Les hommes récits," *Poétique de la prose*, Collection Poétique (Paris: Editions du Seuil, 1971), pp. 78–79.

15. Jorge Luis Borges, "Mágias parciales del Quijote", in *Otras inquisiciones* (1952), *Obras completas* (Buenos Aires: Emecé Editores, 1974), 668–69. English translation by James E. Irby, "Partial Magic in the *Quixote*" in *Labyrinths*, p. 195.

16. In regard to this astounding and amusing spoof, I want to thank Lucille Kerr for calling it to my attention. One might add that Borges' deception foreshadows an iconoclastic impulse in postmodern narrative to recast and reinvent past narratives, whether of the stature of *The Thousand and One Nights* or *The Iliad*. It surely reflects as well a shift in philosophical/artistic thinking among many modern artists and writers. In this regard, the French new novelists come to mind as well as the reading of their work by Roland Barthes in such critical studies as his *Essais critiques* (Paris: Seuil, 1964).

17. See David Pinault, *Story-Telling Techniques in the Arabian Nights* (Leiden/New York/Köln: E. J. Brill, 1992), p. 171.

18. Françoise Douay-Soublin has kindly called to my attention the rhetorical categories of Hermagoras, contained in fragments preserved in Saint Augustine's *Rhetorica* (*quae supersunt*). One observes the recent re-entry into contemporary speech of the term *doxa* to denote common opinion, for which Roland Barthes must be acknowledged. (He uses the term in several of his works.) I have cited in my text G. B. Kerferd's description of "antilogic" in "Dialectic, Antilogic and Eristic," *The Sophistic Movement* (Cambridge University Press, 1981). Lyotard's ideas of paralogism are found throughout his work.

19. Fredric Jameson, Foreword to Jean-François Lyotard, *The Postmodern Condition: A Report on Knowledge* (Minneapolis: University of Minnesota Press, 1984), p. xix.

20. Jacques Derrida, *L'Ecriture et la différence* (Paris: Seuil, 1967), p. 421.

21. When, as Lyotard gives as an example, we try to present something that is not presentable, we find that we make presentation give way (suffer). *The Inhuman:*

Reflections on Time, trans. Geoffrey Bennington and Rachel Bowlby (Stanford University Press, 1991), p. 125.

22. The square, not named, is Jemaa el Fna (the "meeting of the dead") – best appreciated, as a guidebook tells us, while wandering through it in the afternoon, mingling with idle spectators from the quarters of Marrakesh and peoples from the surrounding hills, who come to marvel at and listen to the incredible variety of entertainers – story-tellers such as we see in the *Sandchild*, snake charmers with their woven baskets of cobras, jugglers, actors, acrobats, and strolling performers, who, together with the spectators, transform the square into a scene of bustling and marvelous activity. *Morocco* (Paris: Hachette World Guides, 1966), p. 307.

23. Roland Barthes, "Ce que je dois à Khatibi," Postface to Abdelkebir Khatibi, *La Mémoire tatouée* (Paris: Union Générale d'Editions, 1979).

24. George Steiner, *After Babel. Aspects of Language and Translation* (New York and London: Oxford University Press, 1975), p. 181.

25. George Steiner, *Language and Silence* (New York: Atheneum, 1982), p. 254.

4 "At the threshold of the untranslatable": *Love in Two Languages* of Abdelkebir Khatibi

1. The quotation in the title to this chapter is drawn from the French ("aux marges de l'intraduisible") appearing in two works of Abdelkebir Khatibi, both published in 1983: *Amour bilingue* (Montpellier: Fata Morgana, 1983; reprinted by Editions EDDIF Maroc [Casablanca, 1992]), p. 11 (hereafter cited as *AB*) and *Maghreb pluriel* (Paris: Denoël, 1983), p. 183.

2. This essay also appears under the title of "Incipits" in *Du bilinguisme*, ed. Jalil Bennani, et al. (Paris: Denoël, 1985), pp. 171–203.

3. See Eric Sellin, "Khatibi's Passion for Language(s)," *Revue CELFAN/CELFAN Review*, special issue on Abdelkebir Khatibi. 8:1–2 (Nov. 1988–Feb. 1989), 50. See Abdelwahab Meddeb, *Talismano* (Paris: Christian Bourgois Editeur, 1979).

4. See Plato, *Cratylus*, in *The Works of Plato*, vol. III (London: Henry G. Bohn, 1850), pp. 283–395. Cratylus, who maintains that names derive from the inherent characteristics of a person or object, sustains his naturalist theory against his opponent Hermogenes who argues that names derive from a conventionally agreed upon nomination (the conventionalist theory). Genette proposes yet a third position held by Socrates and located somewhere between those of Cratylus and Hermogenes. See Gérard Genette, "L'éponymie du nom," in *Mimologiques. Voyage en Cratylie* (Paris: Seuil, 1976).

5. See Khatibi's *La Mémoire tatouée* (Paris: Union Générale d'Editions, 10/18, 1971), esp. pp. 205ff., and Lucy Stone McNeece, "Decolonizing the Sign: Language and Identity in Abdelkebir Khatibi's *La Mémoire tatouée*," *Yale French Studies* 83 (1993), 12–29.

6. Abdelkebir Khatibi, "Lettre – Préface" to Marc Gontard, *Violence du texte. La Littérature marocaine de langue française* (Paris: L'Harmattan, 1981), p. 9.

7. Michel Serres, *Le Parasite* (Paris: Grasset, 1980), p. 22.

8. Jacques Derrida, "La loi du genre," *Glyph* 7 (1980), 178 (176–210).

9. I thank one of my discerning and helpful readers who pointed out to me the verbal suggestion of Khatibi's name.

10. For the notion of naturalization, see Jonathan Culler, *Structuralist Poetics. Structuralism, Linguistics and the Study of Literature* (Ithaca, New York: Cornell University Press, 1975), pp. 136ff.

11. Abdallah Mdarhri-Alaoui, "Abdelkebir Khatibi: Writing a Dynamic Identity," in *Research in African Literatures* 23:2 (Summer 1992), 169.

12. Victor Shklovsky, "Art as Technique," in *Russian Formalist Criticism. Four Essays*, trans. with an Introduction by Lee T. Lemon and Marion J. Reis (Lincoln: University of Nebraska Press, 1965), p. 18 (author's italics). Shklovsky's essay appeared in 1917.

13. On the question of parallel languages, George Steiner cites Mallarmé, who spoke of "alternate languages, purer, more rigorous, [that] flourish at increasing distances from or below the surface of common discourse." George Steiner, *After Babel. Aspects of Language and Translation* (New York and London: Oxford University Press, 1975), p. 181.

14. Plato, *The Symposium*, trans. W. Hamilton (Harmondsworth, Middlesex: Penguin Books Ltd., [1951] 1962), pp. 59–65.

15. Samuel Beckett and Georges Duthuit, *Three Dialogues*, III. "Bram Van Velde," *Transition Forty-Nine* 5 (December 1949). Reprinted in *Samuel Beckett: A Collection of Critical Essays*, ed. Martin Esslin (Englewood Cliffs, NJ: Prentice-Hall, 1965). *Transition*, p. 103; Esslin, p. 21.

16. The French word "élucubrations" is translated in English as "lucubrations" – a rather unusual word I have retained owing to the suggestiveness of its etymological roots (from the Latin *lucubration < lucubratio*, meaning study by night, work produced at night, from lucubratus, past participle of *lucubrare*, to work by lamplight, akin to Latin luc- lux – Webster's). In English it has come to mean laborious study, but its origin carries interesting nuances for Khatibi's nightwork narrative.

17. Oswald Ducrot and Tzvetan Todorov, *Dictionnaire encyclopédique des sciences du langage* (Paris: Editions du Seuil, 1972), p. 286.

18. Réda Bensmaïa, "Traduire ou 'blanchir' la langue: *Amour bilingue* d'Abdelkebir Khatibi," Hors Cadre 3 (1985), 190 (187–207).

19. Cited by R. Lane Kauffmann, "The Other in Question: Dialogical Experiments in Montaigne, Kafka, and Cortázar," in *The Interpretation of Dialogue*, ed. Tullio Maranhão (University of Chicago Press, 1990), p. 185.

20. Theodor W. Adorno, *Negative Dialectics*, Part 2, "Negative Dialectics: Concept and Category" (New York: The Continuum Publishing Co., 1973), pp. 133–207.

21. Michel Serres, "Platonic Dialogue," *Hermes. Literature, Science, Philosophy*, eds. Josué Harari and David F. Bell (Baltimore: Johns Hopkins University Press, 1982), p. 66.

22. Gadamer describes dialogue as an exchange in which the interlocutors seek a third entity that eludes their comprehension (cited by Kauffmann, "The Other in Question," p. 187).

23. Cf. Mikhail Bakhtin, as cited by Tzvetan Todorov, *Mikhail Bakhtin. The Dialogical Principle*, trans. Wlad Godzich (Minneapolis: University of Minnesota Press, 1984), p. 74.

24. Abdallah Mdarhri-Alaoui, "Abdelkebir Khatibi: Writing a Dynamic Identity," p. 171.

25. Jean-François Lyotard, *The Postmodern Condition: A Report on Knowledge*, trans. Geoff Bennington and Brian Massumi (Minneapolis: University of Minnesota Press, 1984), pp. 10ff.

26. See Jochen Mecke, "Dialogue in Narration (the Narrative Principle)," in Maranhão, *The Interpretation of Dialogue*, pp. 211–12 (195–215). For Wittgenstein, whom Mecke cites, see Ludwig Wittgenstein, *Philosophical Investigations*, trans. G. E. M. Anscombe (Oxford: Basil Blackwell, 1968), para. 84, 39e.

27. See Walter J. Ong, *Orality and Literacy. The Technologizing of the Word* (London: Methuen, 1982).

28. Philippe Sollers, "Réponses," *Tel Quel* 43 (Autumn 1970), 76.

29. Carlos Fuentes, "A Harvard Commencement," in *Myself with Others. Selected Essays* (New York: The Noonday Press, Farrar, Straus and Giroux, 1990), p. 71 (199–214).

30. Roland Barthes, Postface, "Ce que je dois à Khatibi," Khatibi, *La Mémoire tatouée*, pp. 213–14.

31. Abdelwahab Meddeb, *Phantasia* (Paris: Editions Sindbad, 1986), p. 45. I have used the translation of Eric Sellin in his relevant and stimulating essay, "Obsession with the White Page, the Inability to Communicate, and Surface Aesthetics in the Development of Contemporary Maghrebian Fiction: The *mal de la page blanche* in Khatibi, Farès, and Meddeb," *International Journal of Middle East Studies*, 20 (1988), 171 (165–73).

5 The view from underneath: Salman Rushdie's *Satanic Verses*

1. Salman Rushdie, *The Jaguar Smile: A Nicaraguan Journey*. 1987 (New York: Penguin Books, 1988), p. 12. Rushdie is speaking here, of course, of non-Western peoples of diverse origins, beliefs, and ways of looking at and interpreting the world about them, but who hold in common knowledge of past or present oppression, whether from within or without.

2. William Blake, "The Argument," *The Marriage of Heaven and Hell* in *The Portable Blake*, ed. Alfred Kazin (New York: Penguin Books, 1981), p. 250.

3. See *The Rushdie File*, ed. Lisa Appignanesi and Sara Maitland (London: Fourth Estate Limited, 1989), p. 84. It must be understood that in the case of Salman Rushdie and the Imam Khomeini the *fatwa* was issued according to the Shi'a legal system, which differs from the Sunni legal system in its modes of establishing and interpreting law and accords a much different role to Ijma'. A Shi'a legal scholar is called a *mujtahid*, someone who has the right to make independent judgments on matters of legal interpretation. It was precisely on that basis that Khomeini issued the *fatwa* against Rushdie, while the Sunni legal establishment informed him that he was not permitted to do so.

4. The citations in this paragraph come from Salman Rushdie's essay "A Pen Against the Sword. In Good Faith," *Newsweek*, February 12, 1990, 52. This same essay appeared earlier in England in *The Independent on Sunday* edition of February 4, 1990.

5. M. M. Ahsan and A. R. Kidwai, eds., *Sacrilege Versus Civility: Muslim Perspectives on the Satanic Verses Affair* (Markfield, Leicester: The Islamic Foundation, 1991); Shabbir Akhtar, *Be Careful with Muhammad. The Rushdie Affair* (London: Bellew Publishing, 1989); Richard Webster, *A Brief History of Blasphemy. Liberalism, Censorship and 'The Satanic Verses'* (Southwold, Suffolk: Orwell Press, 1990); and more temperate books: Lisa Appignanesi and Sara Maitland, eds., *The Rushdie File* (London: Fourth Estate Limited, 1989); Daniel Pipes, *The Rushdie Affair: The Novel, the Ayatollah, and the West* (New York: Carol Publishing Group, 1990); and Malise Ruthven, *A Satanic Affair: Salman Rushdie and the Wrath of Islam* (London: The Hogarth Press, 1991).

6. Ziauddin Sardar, "The Rushdie Malaise: A Critique of Some Writings on the Rushdie Affair," *Muslim World Book Review* 10:3 (1990), 3–17; cited in Ahsan and Kidwai, *Sacrilege Versus Civility*, p. 279.

7. Salman Rushdie, Note, *Far Eastern Economic Review*, March 2, 1989.

8. James Harrison, *Salman Rushdie* (New York: Twayne Publishers, 1992); Timothy

Brennan, *Salman Rushdie & the Third World: Myths of the Nation* (Basingstoke: Macmillan, 1989); Mark Edmundson, "Prophet of a New Postmodernism: The Greater Challenge of Salman Rushdie," *Harper's Magazine* (December 1989), 62–71; D. M. Fletcher, ed., *Reading Rushdie: Perspectives on the Fiction of Salman Rushdie* (Amsterdam/Atlanta, GA: Editions Rodopi B.V., 1994).

9. Salman Rushdie, *The Satanic Verses* (New York: Viking, 1988), p. 281. Hereafter cited in the text as *SV*.

10. Rushdie uses with irony the phrase "river … of blood," expressed by the politician Enoch Powell. The phrase reappears in Jumpy's verses mocked by Hanif Johnson.

11. Salman Rushdie, *Midnight's Children* (New York: Alfred A. Knopf, Inc., 1980), p. 65. Cited in the text as *MC*.

12. Timothy Brennan argues that it is from the perspective of the urge to encapsulate the whole world that Rushdie carries forward his rejection of linearity, by presenting images of fragmented reality reflected in the deliberate breaking of continuity in his narrative. Ganesh, with his elephantine figure and the embodiment of *elephantiasis*, is for Brennan the perfect paradigm for India's national configuration. *Salman Rushdie and the Third World. Myths of the Nation*, pp. 116–17.

13. Rushdie's acute sense of a "defining location" guides his commentary on Terry Gilliam's film, *Brazil*, in his essay "The Location of *Brazil*," in *Imaginary Homelands. Essays and Criticism, 1981–1991* (London: Granta Books, 1991), pp. 118–25.

14. This usage is pointed out to me by one of the helpful readers of my manuscript.

15. See Ian Richard Netton, *Text and Trauma: An East–West Primer* (Richmond, Surrey: Curzon Press, 1996), p. 26. As an important purpose of his book, Netton emphasizes the necessity of examining ("unpacking") the semantic, linguistic, and cultural connotations of Arabic words, particularly those employed in the Qur'ān.

16. Ross Chambers, *Room for Maneuver: Reading (the) Oppositional (in) Narrative* (University of Chicago Press, 1991). Roland Barthes, in *Critical Essays*, trans. Richard Howard (Evanston: Northwestern University Press, 1972), distinguishes between the writer and the author, the former being the voice of authority, the latter an inducer of ambiguity who challenges the former's discourse (p. 145). Barthes maintains, moreover, that our times have produced a bastard-type: the author-writer, who gives to society the possibility of experiencing the fantasy of communication bereft of system and institution, of writing without style, of communicating thought that is "pure" (p. 149). Such a dream fantasy is ultimately, as Susan Rubin Suleiman has indicated, a utopian project. *Authoritarian Fictions. The Ideological Novel as a Literary Genre* (New York: Columbia University Press, 1983), pp. 199–200.

17. Ironically, the very slippage inherent in the sign, which Rushdie turns to his own devices and from which flows the ambiguity and ambivalence that mark the wonderful richness of his discourse and free it from rigid monolithic thinking, opens it to the danger of being read in ways he undoubtedly did not intend it to be read – not least of all the way the institutionalized, perceptual conditioning of the more conservative adherents to Islam and Hinduism seem with hindsight bound to read it.

Does another, even more subtle, irony exist? The varied and often contradictory interpretations existing in Islam itself are resolved by reference to the saying attributed to Muhammad that "My community will never agree in an error." This is the principle of Ijma' or the agreement of Islam which holds that beliefs held by the majority of Muslims are believed to be true by consensus and that practices held in common through the ages are legitimized and valid. Ijma' has given Islam its catholicity of view, unity with its past, and flexibility in its application (*The Columbia Encyclopedia*, entry under "Islam"). In this respect, Islam seems itself to allow for the co-existence of incompatible, even contradictory, interpretations – a characteristic not unlike (on the surface at least) the type of antinomical thinking found in Rushdie's narratives. Perhaps, in view of the *fatwa*, issued within the sphere of Shi'a legal practice, such an irony (if it is) serves to reflect the breadth and diversity of beliefs and interpretations among the faithful.

18. Richard Terdiman speaks of the angle of contestation of major theoretical discourses of the previous century in *Discourse/Counter-Discourse. The Theory and Practice of Symbolic Resistance in Nineteenth-Century France* (Ithaca: Cornell University Press, 1985).

19. G. B. Kerferd, "Dialectic, Antilogic and Eristic," in *The Sophistic Movement* (Cambridge University Press, 1981), p. 61. Antilogic may also be said to consist "in opposing one logos to another logos" (Kerferd, p. 63); Jean-François Lyotard would define it as relating a "truth" to itself or playing verisimilitude of a statement or assertion against itself so as to dissipate its absoluteness. "On the Strength of the Weak," *Semiotexte* 3:2 (1978), 209. Lyotard's essay appears in another version in French, to which I have had occasion to refer and will again have occasion to refer: "Sur la force des faibles," in *L'Arc* 64 (1976).

20. The full translation in my text of the present (accepted) version of Surah LIII, verses 19–23, is taken from W. Montgomery Watt, *Muhammed. Prophet and Statesman* (Oxford University Press, 1961), p. 60. In *The History of al-Tabari* (Albany, NY: State University of New York Press, SUNY Series in Near Eastern Studies, 1988), Watt and M. V. McDonald translate the "satanic verses" as: "These are the high-flying cranes / verily their intercession is accepted with approval" (p. 108).

21. Rushdie maintains that the verses just quoted, which still exist in the Qur'ān, have, as one of their reasons for rejecting the three goddesses, the fact that *they were female* ("A Pen Against the Sword," p. 54; Rushdie italicizes these words in the original).

22. Maxime Rodinson, *Mohammed*, trans. Anne Carter (New York: Pantheon Books, 1971), p. 106.

23. Cited by Rodinson, *Ibid.*, p. 106. Rodinson's source is the *Annales* of al-Tabari, ed. M. J. de Goeje et al. (Leiden, 1897–1901).

24. I have consulted Maxime Rodinson's *Mohammed*, especially pp. 104–08, as well as W. Montgomery Watt's *Muhammed. Prophet and Statesman*, pp. 26, 60–65. For an account of the passages and episodes of the *Satanic Verses* leading to Rushdie's condemnation by the Ayatollah Ruhollah Khomeini as *mahdur ad-damm* (he of unclean blood) and a *murtad* (a Muslim fallen away from Islam, who has sided with the enemies of Islam), see William J. Weatherby, *Salman Rushdie: Sentenced to Death* (New York: Carroll & Grof Publishers, 1990).

It is fair to point out that some scholars, including the orientalist John Burton of St. Andrews University, have rejected al-Tabari's version of the satanic verses (J. Burton, "Those are the High-Flying Cranes," *Journal of Semitic Studies*, 15:2 [1970], 246–65; cited by Netton, *Text and Trauma*, p. 86). The rejection of this version has, among other reasons, been put down to the fact that Mohammed's previous prophecies would have been called into question. Netton perceives the real blasphemy for the present-day Muslim to be contained in what he saw as an ancient lie reiterated, dressed up in further falsehood and offered to a largely unschooled audience as a literary entertainment (86–87).

25. Michael M. J. Fischer and Mehdi Abedi argue that, owing to Western ignorance of

Islamic hermeneutics, dialectics, and dialogics, the West views the Qur'ān (and Islam) as prescriptive and fraught by monological fixity, while in truth the Qur'ān contains polysemic and ambivalent significations. See Fischer and Abedi, "Qur'ānic Dialogics: Islamic Poetics and Politics for Muslims and for Us," in *The Interpretation of Dialogue*, ed. Tullio Maranhão (The University of Chicago Press, 1990), pp. 120–53 (150–51).

26. George Steiner, *After Babel. Aspects of Language and Translation* (New York and London: Oxford University Press, 1975), p. 229.

27. Pierre Bourdieu, *Ce que parler veut dire. L'économie des échanges linguistiques* (Paris: Fayard, 1982), p. 31 *et passim*. Language is symbolic in the same sense that material possessions are, that is, they signify the consumption of products along lines of class variation. See Bourdieu, *Distinction. A Social Critique of the Judgement of Taste*, trans. Richard Nice (Cambridge, MA: Harvard University Press, 1984), p. 21 *et passim*.

28. Richard Webster, *A Brief History of Blasphemy*, p. 40.

29. René Girard, *The Scapegoat*, trans. Yvonne Freccero (Baltimore: The Johns Hopkins University Press, 1986), p. 25.

30. Rodinson, citing Tabari, alludes to this relationship of culpability: according to Muslim lore, after the archangel revealed the deception of the Devil, "he added as consolation, that [that] was no wonder because the earlier prophets had experienced similar difficulties and for the same reasons" (*Mohammed*, p. 106).

31. Girard, whose own argument betrays the circular self-reference of a dominant discourse – for example: "From the moment we truly understand myths, we can no longer accept the Gospel as yet another myth, since it is responsible for our understanding" (*The Scapegoat*, p. 205) –, would no doubt protest the application of enabling conditions for the scapegoat mechanism to his own ideas. He also insists, tautologically, on what he calls the "false transcendence" of Satan, who, as victim, "is made sacred because of the unanimous [and explicit] verdict of guilt" (*Ibid.*, p. 166).

32. In 1959, Mahfouz published in serial form in *Al-Ahram* his work later issued in book form in English translation, by Philip Stewart, as *Children of Gebelawi* (or *Children of the Quarter*) (Heinemann, 1981). The serial publication was immediately banned by al-Azhar, although it remained fully available in newspaper article form. It was published as a book in Lebanon without Mahfouz's knowledge or permission in 1967.

Only after the announcement of the Nobel Prize in 1988 was Mahfouz asked about his views on the *fatwa* pronounced against Rushdie. When Mahfouz replied that he supported the freedom of writers, the popular preacher 'Umar 'Abd al-Rahman (then still resident in Egypt) pronounced his death sentence against Mahfouz, saying that, if Mahfouz had not published his *Children of Gebelawi*, Rushdie would never have written the *Satanic Verses*. For this achronological misstep, 'Abd al-Rahman was imprisoned. Upon his release he went to the Sudan where he managed to get an entry visa to the US. The further history of his activities included his alleged involvement in the Trade Building bombing in New York.

For the account of these events, see Roger Allen, "Najib Mahfouz in World Literature," in *The Arabic Novel Since 1950*, Mundus Arabicus, vol. V (Cambridge, MA: Dar Mahjar Publishing, 1992), 121–41.

33. Mikhail Bakhtin, *Rabelais and His World*, 1965, trans. Hélène Iswolsky (Bloomington: Indiana University Press, 1984), p. 11.

34. Roger Caillois, *Anthologie du fantastique* (Paris: Gallimard, 1966), I, p. 8.

35. This distinction accords fully with that of Amaryll Beatrice Chanady, *Magical*

Realism and the Fantastic: Resolved Versus Unresolved Antimony (New York and London: Garland Publishing, Inc., 1985), p. 23. Her thoughtful work, in defining the concept of magical realism – a concept that has proved to be elusive and controversial – makes for the most part clear and useful distinctions that can contribute to our understanding of postcolonial authors such as Rushdie.

36. Emil Volek, "Alejo Carpentier y la narrativa latino-americana actual (dimensiones de un 'realismo mágico')," *Cuaderno hispanoamericanos* 296 (February 1975), 327 (my translation).

37. Tzvetan Todorov, *Introduction à la littérature fantastique* (Paris: Editions du Seuil, 1970), p. 29.

38. Irène Bessière, *Le Récit fantastique: la poétique de l'incertain* (Paris: Librairie Larousse, 1974), p. 57. My translation.

39. See Netton, *Text and Trauma*, p. 33 *et passim*.

40. In "The Empire Writes Back with a Vengeance," *The Times*, July 3, 1982, Rushdie defines the word. He feels that the British Empire could not have succeeded without such collaborators in its colonies. With his usual deft wordplay he draws the two meanings together by telling us that "the Raj grew fat by being spoon-fed" (8).

41. Mark Edmundson calls Rushdie's writing a new and a positive form of postmodernism. He contrasts it with what he regards as the postmodern writing of negativism and demystification, citing Pynchon as an example of these latter. He sees Rushdie's power as lying in sophisticated debunking while at the same time effecting secular renewal that brings with it a sense of the contingency of traditional forms and the possibility of rewriting all existing narratives. Though I disagree with him in Pynchon's case, I find his comments on Rushdie justified and to the point. "Prophet of a New Postmodernism: The Greater Challenge of Salman Rushdie," *Harper's Magazine* (December 1989), 63, 68 (62–71).

42. I say this mindful of some commentators who maintain that Rushdie's background and many years in England make it impossible for him to understand the plight of migrants and "Third-World" peoples, which is essentially the argument of Timothy Brennan, *Salman Rushdie and the Third World*. This argument ignores, I feel, the nature of true dialogue and the conditions of its possibility, as well as Rushdie's sensitivity to issues such as *métissage* that find expression in all of his writings. The issue of *métissage* is driven home with particular force in his formidable novel *The Moor's Last Sigh* (New York: Pantheon Books, 1995).

Concluding: breaches and forgotten openings

1. Nazik al-Mala'ikah, "Who Am I?" and Nizar Qabbani, "What Value Has the People Whose Tongue is Tied," from *An Anthology of Modern Arabic Poetry*, eds. and trans. Mounah A. Khouri and Hamid Algar (Berkeley: University of California Press, 1974), pp. 79 and 189.

2. Jacques Derrida, "Positions. Interview with Jean-Louis Houdebine and Guy Scarpetta," *Positions*, translated and annotated by Alan Bass (University of Chicago Press, 1981), p. 41.

3. Gilles Deleuze and Félix Guattari, *Mille plateaux* (Paris: Editions de Minuit, 1980).

4. Lisa Lowe, "Literary Nomadics in Francophone Allegories of Postcolonialism: Pham Van Ky and Tahar Ben Jelloun," *Yale French Studies*, 1:82 (1993), 46.

5. Fredric Jameson, *Postmodernism, or, The Cultural Logic of Late Capitalism* (Durham, NC: Duke University Press, 1991).

Bibliography

I **Assia Djebar**
Selected works

Alouettes naïves, Les. Paris: Juillard, 1967; Paris: Union Générale d'Editions, 10/18, 1978; Groupe Actes-Sud, BABEL, 1997.

Amour, la fantasia, L'. Paris: Jean-Claude Lattès, 1985; Algiers: Editions EDDIF, 1992; Paris: Albin Michel, 1995. English trans. by Dorothy Blair, *Fantasia: An Algerian Calvacade*. London and New York: Quartet Books Limited, 1989; Portsmouth, NH: Heinemann, 1993.

Blanc de l'Algérie, Le. Paris: Albin Michel, 1995.

"Du français comme butin," *La Quinzaine littéraire* 436 (March 16–31, 1985).

Enfants du nouveau monde, Les. Paris: Juillard, 1962; Paris: Union Générale d'Editions, 10/18, 1978; reprinted in January 1998 by Groupe Actes-Sud, BABEL.

Femmes d'Alger dans leur appartement. Paris: Editions des femmes, 1980. English trans. by Marjolijn de Jager, *Women of Algiers in Their Apartment*. Charlottesville: University Press of Virginia, 1992.

"Fugitive, et ne le sachant pas." *L'Esprit Créateur* 33.2 (Summer 1993): 129–33. This article has been reprinted in *Vaste est la prison*. Paris: Albin Michel, 1995. Pp. 167–72.

Impatients, Les. Paris: Juillard, 1958.

Loin de Médine. Paris: Albin Michel, 1991; Algeria: ENAG/ Editions, 1992.

Nouba des femmes du mont Chenoua, La. Radio-Television algérienne, 1978 (filmed in 1977–1978), awarded the Prix de la Critique Internationale at the Venice *Biennale* in 1979.

Ombre sultane. Paris: J. C. Lattès, 1987.

"Le point de vue d'une Algérienne sur la condition de la femme musulmane au 20e siècle." *Le Courrier de l'UNESCO*, 28 (August–September, 1975): 25.

Soif, La. Paris: Juillard, 1957.

Vaste est la prison. Paris: Albin Michel, 1995.

Zerda et les chants de l'oubli, La. July 1982 (Film).

Interviews and Critical studies on Djebar
Bensmaïa, Réda. "*La Nouba des femmes du mont Chenoua*. Introduction à l'oeuvre fragmentale." *Les 2 Ecrans* 17 (Alger, October 1979).

Déjeux, Jean. *Assia Djebar. Romancière algérienne, cinéaste arabe*. Sherbrooke, Québec: Editions Naaman, 1984.

Donadey (Roch), Anne. "Assia Djebar's Poetics of Subversion." *L'Esprit Créateur* 33.2 (Summer 1993): 107–17.

"Writing the Trace: Assia Djebar's *L'Amour, la fantasia* as a Bilingual Palimpsest." Paper delivered at a meeting of the Modern Language Association, Chicago, December 1990.

Erickson, John. "Woman's Space and Enabling dialogue in Assia Djebar's *L'Amour, la fantasia*." In *Postcolonial Subjects: Francophone Women Writers*. Minneapolis: University of Minnesota Press, 1996. Pp. 304–20.

Le Clézio, Marguerite. (interview) "Assia Djebar: Ecrire dans la langue adverse." *Contemporary French Civilization* 19.2 (Summer 1985): 230–44.

Lévy, Marie-Françoise. (interview) "L'espace du dedans." *Le Monde*, May 28–29, 1978.

Mortimer, Mildred. *Assia Djebar*. Philadelphia: CELFAN Edition Monographs, 1988.

(interview) "Entretien avec Assia Djebar, écrivain algérien." *Research in African Literature* 19.2 (Summer 1988): 197–205.

"Language and Space in the Fiction of Assia Djebar and Leila Sebbar." *Research in African Literature* 19.3 (Fall 1988): 301–11.

Murdoch, H. Adlai. "Rewriting Writing: Identity, Exile and Renewal in Assia Djebar's *L'Amour, la fantasia*. *Yale French Studies* 83 (1993): 71–92.

II Tahar Ben Jelloun
Selected works

Enfant de sable, L'. Paris: Seuil, 1985. English translation by Alan Sheridan, *The Sand Child*. New York: Harcourt Brace Jovanovich, Inc., 1987.

Harrouda. Paris: Denoël, 1978.

Homme rompu, L'. Paris: Editions du Seuil, 1994.

Jour de silence à Tanger. Paris: Editions du Seuil, 1990.

Nuit sacrée, La. Paris: Editions du Seuil, 1987.

Plus Haute des solitudes. Misère affective et sexuelle d'émigrés nord-africains, La. Paris: Editions du Seuil, 1977.

Premier Amour est toujours le dernier, Le. Paris: Editions du Seuil, 1995.

Yeux baissés, Les. Paris: Editions du Seuil, 1991.

Interviews and Critical Studies on Ben Jelloun

Aresu, Bernard, *Tahar Ben Jelloun*. New Orleans, LA: CELFAN Monographs, 1996.

Erickson, John. "Femme voilée, récit voilé dans *L'Enfant de sable* de Tahar ben Jelloun," in *Carrefour de Cultures*. Ed. Régis Antoine. Tübingen: Gunter Narr Verlag, 1993. Pp. 1–10.

"Veiled Woman and Veiled Narrative in Tahar ben Jelloun's *The Sandchild*." *boundary 2* 20.1 (1993): 47–64.

"*Metoikoi* and Magical Realism in the Maghrebian Narratives of Tahar ben Jelloun and Abdelkebir Khatibi," in *Magical Realism: Theory, History, Community*. Eds. Lois Parkinson Zamora and Wendy Faris. Durham: Duke University Press, 1995. Pp. 427–50.

Lowe, Lisa. "Literary Nomadics in Francophone Allegories of Postcolonialism: Pham Van Ky and Tahar Ben Jelloun." *Yale French Studies*, 1.82 (1993): 43–61.

Spear, Thomas. (interview) "Politics and Literature: An Interview with Tahar Ben Jelloun." *Yale French Studies* 83 (1993): 30–43.

III **Salman Rushdie**
Selected works

East, West. Stories. New York: Pantheon Books, 1994.
"The Empire Writes Back with a Vengeance," *The Times,* July 3, 1982.
Imaginary Homelands. Essays and Criticism, 1981–1991. London and New York: Granta
    Books/Viking Penguin, 1991.
Jaguar Smile. A Nicaraguan Journey, The. 1987. New York: Penguin Books, 1988.
Midnight's Children. New York: Alfred A. Knopf, Inc., 1980.
Moor's Last Sigh, The. New York: Pantheon Books, 1995.
(note) *L'Express,* February 24, 1989.
(note) *Far Eastern Economic Review,* March 2, 1989.
"A Pen Against the Sword. In Good Faith." *Newsweek,* February 12, 1990: 52. Appeared
    earlier in *The Independent on Sunday*, February 4, 1990.
Satanic Verses, The. New York: Viking, 1988.

Critical Studies on Rushdie
Ahsan, M. M. and A. R. Kidwai, eds. *Sacrilege Versus Civility: Muslim Perspectives on the
    Satanic Verses Affair.* Markfield, Leicester: The Islamic Foundation, 1991.
Akhtar, Shabbir. *Be Careful with Muhammad. The Rushdie Affair.* London: Bellew
    Publishing, 1989.
Appignanesi, Lisa and Sara Maitland, eds. *The Rushdie File.* London: Fourth Estate
    Limited, 1989.
Brennan, Timothy. *Salman Rushdie and the Third World: Myths of the Nation.* Basingstoke:
    Macmillan, 1989.
Edmundson, Mark. "Prophet of a New Postmodernism: The Greater Challenge of
    Salman Rushdie." *Harper's Magazine* (December 1989): 62–71.
Fletcher, D. M., ed. *Reading Rushdie: Perspectives on the Fiction of Salman Rushdie.*
    Amsterdam/Atlanta, GA: Editions Rodopi B.V., 1994.
Harrison, James. *Salman Rushdie.* New York: Twayne Publishers, 1992.
Netton, Ian Richard. *Text and Trauma: An East–West Primer.* Richmond, Surrey: Curzon
    Press, 1996. Pp. 19–41, 84–89, *et passim.*
Pipes, Daniel. *The Rushdie Affair: The Novel, the Ayatollah, and the West.* New York: Carol
    Publishing Group, 1990.
Ruthven, Malise. *A Satanic Affair: Salman Rushdie and the Wrath of Islam.* London: The
    Hogarth Press, 1991.
Sardar, Ziauddin. "The Rushdie Malaise: A Critique of Some Writings on the Rushdie
    Affair." *Muslim World Book Review* 10.3 (1990): 3–17.
Weatherby, William J. *Salman Rushdie: Sentenced to Death.* New York: Carroll & Grof
    Publishers, 1990.
Webster, Richard. *A Brief History of Blasphemy. Liberalism, Censorship and 'The Satanic Verses'.*
    Southwold, Suffolk: Orwell Press, 1990.

IV **Abdelkebir Khatibi**
Selected works

Amour bilingue. Montpellier: Fata Morgana, 1983. Reprinted by Editions EDDIF Maroc
    (Casablanca, 1992). English translation by Richard Howard, *Love in Two
    Languages.* Minneapolis: University of Minnesota Press, 1990.
"Incipits," in *Du bilinguisme.* Eds. Jalil Bennani et al. (Paris: Denoël, 1985). Pp. 171–203.

"Lettre – Préface" to Marc Gontard, *Violence du texte. La Littérature marocaine de langue française*. Paris: L'Harmattan, 1981. Pp. 7–9.

Maghreb pluriel. Paris: Editions Denoël, 1983.

Mémoire tatouée, La. Postface by Roland Barthes. Paris: Union Générale d'Editions, 10/18, 1979.

Roman maghrébin, Le. Paris: François Maspero, 1968.

Critical Studies on Khatibi

Barthes, Roland. Postface, "Ce que je dois à Khatibi," Abdelkebir Khatibi, *La Mémoire tatouée*. Paris: Union Générale d'Editions, 10/18, 1979. Pp. 213–14.

Bensmaïa, Réda. "Traduire ou 'blanchir' la langue: *Amour bilingue* d'Abdelkebir Khatibi." *Hors Cadre* 3 (1985): 187–207.

Erickson, John. "*Metoikoi* and Magical Realism in the Maghrebian Narratives of Tahar ben Jelloun and Abdelkebir Khatibi," in *Magical Realism: Theory, History, Community*. Eds. Lois Parkinson Zamora and Wendy Faris. Durham: Duke University Press, 1995. Pp. 427–50.

McGuire, James. "Forked Tongues, Marginal Bodies: Writing as Translation in Khatibi." *Research in African Literatures* 23.1 (Spring 1992): 107–16.

Mdarhri-Alaoui, Abdallah. "Abdelkebir Khatibi: Writing a Dynamic Identity." *Research in African Literatures* 23.2 (Summer 1992): 167–76.

Revue CELFAN/CELFAN Review, Special issue on Abdelkebir Khatibi. Ed. Eric Sellin. 8.1–2 (November 1988–February 1989): 1–56.

Rhioui, Ahmed. "Words from a Maddening Quest," *Revue CELFAN/CELFAN Review*, Special issue on Abdelkebir Khatibi. 8.1–2 (November 1988–February 1989): 35–38.

Sellin, Eric. "Khatibi's Passion for Language(s)," *Revue CELFAN/CELFAN Review*, Special issue on Abdelkebir Khatibi. 8.1–2 (November 1988–February 1989): 49–55.

"Obsession with the White Page, the Inability to Communicate, and Surface Aesthetics in the Development of Contemporary Maghrebian Fiction: The *mal de la page blanche* in Khatibi, Farès, and Meddeb." *International Journal of Middle East Studies* 20 (1988): 165–73.

V Selected Works Consulted

Abdel-Malek, Anouar. "Orientalism in Crisis." *Diogenes* 44 (Winter 1963): 103–40.

Accad, Evelyne. *L'Excisée*. Paris: L'Harmattan, 1982.

Sexuality and War: Literary Masks of the Middle East. New York University Press, 1990.

Veil of Shame: The Role of Women in the Contemporary Fiction of North Africa and the Arab World. Sherbrooke: Naaman, 1978.

Adorno, Theodor W. *Negative Dialectics*. Trans. E. B. Ashton. New York: Seabury, 1973.

Allen, Roger. "Najib Mahfouz in World Literature," in *The Arabic Novel Since 1950*. Mundus Arabicus, vol. v. Cambridge, MA: Dar Mahjar Publishing, 1992, 121–41.

Alloula, Malek. *The Colonial Harem*. Theory and History of Literature, vol. 21. Minneapolis: University of Minnesota Press, 1986.

Anderson, Benedict. *Imagined Communities. Reflections on the Origin and Spread of Nationalism*. London: Verso, 1983, 1991.

Aresu, Bernard. *Counterhegemonic Discourse from the Maghreb: The Poetics of Kateb's Fiction*. Tübingen: Gunter Narr Verlag, 1993.

Bakhtin, Mikhail. *Rabelais and His World*. Trans. Hélène Iswolsky. Foreword by Krystyna

Pomorska. Prologue by Michael Holquist. Bloomington: Indiana University Press, 1984 (1965).

Balzac, Honoré de, *Comédie humaine*. Ed. Marcel Bouterou. Paris: Gallimard Pléiade, 1954.

Barthes, Roland. *Critical Essays*. Trans. Richard Howard. Evanston: Northwestern University Press, 1972.

"Grammaire africaine," in *Mythologies*. Paris: Editions du Seuil, 1957.

Postface to Abdelkebir Khatibi, *La Mémoire tatouée*. Paris: Union Générale d'Editions, 10/18, 1971.

Beaujour, Michel. *Miroirs d'encre*. Paris: Seuil, 1980.

Beckett, Samuel and Georges Duthuit, *Three Dialogues*, III. "Bram Van Velde." *Transition forty-nine* 5 (December 1949). Reprinted in *Samuel Beckett: A Collection of Critical Essays*. Ed. Martin Esslin. Englewood Cliffs, NJ: Prentice-Hall, 1965.

Benjamin, Walter. *Illuminations: Essays and Reflections*. Ed. Hannah Arendt. Trans. Harry Zohn. New York: Schocken Books, 1968.

Bennani, Jalil, Ahmed Boukous, Abdallah Bounfour, François Cheng, Eliane Formentelli, Jacques Hassoun, Abdelkebir Khatibi, Abdelfettah Kilito, Abdelwahab Meddeb, and Tzvetan Todorov, eds. *Du bilinguisme*. Paris: Editions Denoël, 1985.

Bessière, Irène. *Le Récit fantastique: la poétique de l'incertain*. Paris: Librairie Larousse, 1974.

Bhabha, Homi K. "DissemiNation: Time, Narrative, and the Margins of the Modern Nation," in *Nation and Narration*. Ed. Homi K. Bhabha. London and New York: Routledge, 1990.

Bjornson, Richard. "Cognitive Mapping and the Understanding of Literature." *SubStance* 30 (1981): 51–62.

Blake, William. "The Argument," *The Marriage of Heaven and Hell* in *The Portable Blake*. Ed. Alfred Kazin. New York: Penguin Books, 1981.

Blanchot, Maurice. *L'Entretien infini*. Paris: Gallimard, 1969.

Book of the Thousand Nights and a Night, The. Trans. Richard F. Burton. 17 vols. London: Burton Ethnological Society, n.d. (1884–1886).

Borges, Jorge Luis. *Ficciones*. Trans. A. Kerrigan. New York: Grove Press, 1962.

Labyrinths. Selected Stories & Other Writings. Eds. Donald A. Yates and James E. Irby. Trans. Donald A. Yates, et al. New York: New Directions, 1964.

Otras inquisiciones. 1952. In *Obras completas*. Buenos Aires: Emecé Editores, 1974. English translation by Ruth L. C. Simms. *Other Inquisitions 1937–1952*. New York: Washington Square Press, Inc., 1966.

Boudjedra, Rachid. *La Répudiation*. Paris: Denoël, 1969.

Bouhdiba, Abdelwahab. *La Sexualité en Islam*. Paris: Presses Universitaires de France, 1986 (1975).

Bourdieu, Pierre. *Ce que parler veut dire: l'économie des échanges linguistiques*. Paris: Fayard, 1982.

Distinction. A Social Critique of the Judgement of Taste. Trans. Richard Nice. Cambridge, MA: Harvard University Press, 1984.

Burton, John. "Those are the High-Flying Cranes," *Journal of Semitic Studies*, 15.2 (1970): 246–65.

Caillois, Roger. *Anthologie du fantastique*. Paris: Gallimard, 1966.

Certeau, Michel de. *L'Invention du quotidien*. I *Arts de faire*. Paris: Union Générale d'Editions, 10/18, 1980. English trans.: *The Practice of Everyday Life*. Berkeley:

University of California Press, 1984. A long extract translated by Fredric
Jameson and Carl Lovitt, "On the Oppositional Practice of Everyday Life,"
appeared in *Social Text* 3 (Fall 1980): 3–43.

Chambers, Ross. *Room For Maneuver. Reading (the) Oppositional (in) Narrative.* University of
Chicago Press, 1991.

Chanady, Amaryll Beatrice. *Magical Realism and the Fantastic: Resolved Versus Unresolved
Antimony.* New York and London: Garland Publishing, Inc., 1985.

Cortázar, Julio. "To Reach Lezama Lima," in *Around the Day in Eighty Worlds.* San
Francisco: North Point Press, 1986.

Croutier, Alev Lytle. *Harem. The World Behind the Veil.* New York: Abbeville Press, 1989.

Culler, Jonathan. *Structuralist Poetics. Structuralism, Linguistics and the Study of Literature.*
Ithaca, New York: Cornell University Press, 1975.

Deleuze, Gilles and Félix Guattari, *Capitalisme et schizophrénie: L'Anti-Oedipe.* Paris:
Editions de Minuit, 1972.

Mille plateaux. Paris: Editions de Minuit, 1980.

Derrida, Jacques. *L'Ecriture et la différence.* Paris: Editions du Seuil, 1967.

"La loi du genre," *Glyph* 7 (1980): 176–210.

"Survivre," in *Parages.* Paris: Galilée, 1986. English translation by James Hulbert,
"Living On: *Border Lines,*" in *Deconstruction and Criticism.* Eds. Harold Bloom et al.
New York: The Continuum Publishing Co., 1979 (published under the imprint
of the Seabury Press).

"Positions. Interview with Jean-Louis Houdebine and Guy Scarpetta," *Positions.*
Translated and annotated by Alan Bass. University of Chicago Press, 1981.

Ducrot, Oswald and Tzvetan Todorov. *Dictionnaire encyclopédique des sciences du langage.*
Paris: Editions du Seuil, 1972.

Duras, Marguerite. "Ecrire." *L'Esprit Créateur* 30.1 (Spring 1990): 6.

Erickson, John. "Alienation in Samuel Beckett: The Protagonist as Eiron." *Perspectives*
1.2 (November 1975): 62–73.

"Kateb Yacine's *Nedjma*: A Dialogue of Difference." *SubStance* 69 (1992): 30–45.

"Maximin's *L'Isolé soleil* and Caliban's Curse." *Callaloo,* Special issue on Guadeloupe
and Martinique. Ed. by Maryse Condé. 15.1 (1992): 119–30.

"Writing Double: Politics and the African Narrative of French Expression." Special
issue on African Literature and Politics. *Studies in Twentieth Century Literature* 15.1
(Winter 1991): 101–22.

Fanon, Frantz. *Les Damnés de la terre.* Preface by Jean-Paul Sartre. Paris: François
Maspero, 1961.

Peau noire masques blancs. Paris: Editions du Seuil, 1952.

Sociologie d'une révolution (L'An V de la révolution algérienne). Paris: François Maspero,
1972 (1959).

Fernández Retamar, Roberto. "Caliban." *Casa de la Americas* 68 (September–October
1971). Reprinted in *Calibán y otros ensayos. Nuestra América y el mondo.* La Habana:
Editorial Arte y Literatura, 1979. English translation, "Caliban: Notes Toward a
Discussion of Culture in Our America," in *Caliban and Other Essays.* Ed. and
trans. Edward Baker. Foreword by Fredric Jameson. Minneapolis: University of
Minnesota Press, 1989.

Fernea, Elizabeth Warnock and Basima Qattan Bezirgan, eds. *Middle Eastern Muslim
Women Speak.* Austin: University of Texas Press, 1977.

Fischer, Michael M. J. and Mehdi Abedi. "Qur'anic Dialogics: Islamic Poetics and Politics for Muslims and for Us," in *The Interpretation of Dialogue*. Ed. Tullio Maranhão. The University of Chicago Press, 1990. Pp. 120–53.

Foucault, Michel. *Language, Counter-Memory, Practice. Selected Essays and Interviews by Michel Foucault*. Ed. Donald F. Bouchard. Trans. Donald F. Bouchard and Sherry Simon. Ithaca: Cornell University Press, 1977.

L'Ordre du discours. Paris: Gallimard, 1971.

Freud, Sigmund. "The Uncanny," in vol. 17, *The Standard Edition*. London: Hogarth Press, 1963. Pp. 219–52.

Fuentes, Carlos. *Myself with Others. Selected Essays*. New York: The Noonday Press, 1990; Farrar, Straus and Giroux, 1988.

Gadant, Monique, ed., *Women of the Mediterranean*. London: Zed Books Ltd, 1986.

Genette, Gérard. *Figures III*. Paris: Editions du Seuil, 1972.

"L'éponymie du nom," in *Mimologiques. Voyage en Cratylie*. Paris: Seuil, 1976.

Seuils. Paris: Editions du Seuil, 1987.

Gerhardt, Mia L. *The Art of Story-Telling: A Literary Study of The Thousand and One Nights*. Leiden: E. J. Brill, 1963.

Girard, René. *The Scapegoat*. Trans. Yvonne Freccero. Baltimore: Johns Hopkins University Press, 1986.

Glissant, Edouard. *Le Discours antillais*. Paris: Editions du Seuil, 1981. English translation by J. Michael Dash. *Caribbean Discourse. Selected Essays*. Charlottesville: The University Press of Virginia, 1989.

Gontard, Marc. *Violence du texte: La Littérature marocaine de langue française*. Paris/Rabat: L'Harmattan/Société marocaine des éditeurs réunis, 1981.

Harbi, Mohammed. "Les femmes dans la Révolution algérienne." *Les Révoltes logiques* 11 (Winter 1979–1980): 78–93.

Heath, Stephen. "Difference." *Screen* 19.3 (Autumn 1978): 51–112.

al-Hibri, Azizah, ed. *Women and Islam*. Oxford/New York: Pergamon Press, 1982.

Hutcheon, Linda. *A Poetics of Postmodernism: History, Theory, Fiction*. New York and London: Routledge, 1988.

The Politics of Postmodernism. New York and London: Routledge, 1989.

Irigaray, Luce. *Ce sexe qui n'en est pas un*. Paris: Editions de Minuit, 1977.

Ethique de la différence sexuelle. Paris: Editions de Minuit, 1984.

Speculum of the Other Woman. Trans. Gillian G. Gill. Ithaca: Cornell University Press, 1985.

Jameson, Fredric. Foreword to Jean-François Lyotard, *The Postmodern Condition: A Report on Knowledge*. Minneapolis: University of Minnesota Press, 1984. Pp. vii–xxv.

The Political Unconscious. Narrative as a Socially Symbolic Act. Ithaca: Cornell University Press, 1981.

Postmodernism, or, The Cultural Logic of Late Capitalism. Durham, NC: Duke University Press, 1991.

"Third-World Literature in the Era of Multinational Capitalism." *Social Text* 15 (Fall 1986): 65–88.

Kauffmann, R. Lane. "The Other in Question: Dialogical Experiments in Montaigne, Kafka, and Cortázar," in *The Interpretation of Dialogue*. Ed. T. Maranhão. University of Chicago Press, 1990.

Kerferd, G. B. "Dialectic, Antilogic and Eristic," in *The Sophistic Movement*. Cambridge University Press, 1981. Pp. 59–67.

El Khayat, Ghita. *Le Monde arabe au féminin*. Paris: L'Harmattan, 1988.

Khouri, Mounah A. and Hamid Algar, eds. *An Anthology of Modern Arabic Poetry*. Berkeley: University of California Press, 1974.

Kofman, Sarah. *The Enigma of Woman: Woman in Freud's Writings*. Trans. Catherine Porter. Ithaca: Cornell University Press, 1985.

Koso-Thomas, Olayinka. *The Circumcision of Women: Strategy for Eradication*. London: Zed Books Ltd, 1987.

Laâbi, Abdellatif. *Rue du Retour*. London: Readers International, 1989. Despite its French title, this is an English translation, by Jacqueline Kaye, of the original, *Le Chemin des ordalies*. Paris: Editions Denoël, 1982.

(Editor's note). *Souffles* 18 (March–April 1970).

Laâbi, Abdellatif and Abraham Serfaty. "Programme de recherche et d'action de l'A.R.C." *Souffles* 12 (1968). Reproduced in Marc Gontard, *Violence du texte: La littérature marocaine de langue française*. Paris/Rabat: L'Harmattan/Société marocaine des éditeurs réunis, 1981. Pp. 151–59.

Lacan, Jacques. *Ecrits*. Paris: Editions du Seuil, 1966.

Le Séminaire, Book 20 *Encore*. Paris: Editions du Seuil, 1975.

Lionnet, Françoise. *Autobiographical Voices. Race, Gender, Self-Portraiture*. Ithaca, NY: Cornell University Press, 1989.

Postcolonial Representations: Women, Literature, Identity. Ithaca, NY: Cornell University Press, 1995.

Lyotard, Jean-François. *La Guerre des Algériens: écrits 1956–1963*. Ed. Mohammed Ramdani. Paris: Galilée, 1989.

L'Inhumain. English translation by Geoffrey Bennington and Rachel Bowlby. *The Inhuman: Reflections on Time*. Stanford University Press, 1991.

Instructions païennes. Paris: Editions Galilée, 1977.

"On the Strength of the Weak." *Semiotexte* 3.2 (1978): 204–14.

The Postmodern Condition: A Report on Knowledge. Trans. Geoff Bennington and Brian Massumi. Foreword by Fredric Jameson. Minneapolis: University of Minnesota Press, 1984.

Le Postmodernisme expliqué aux enfants. Paris: Editions Galilée, 1988. English translation with Afterword by Wlad Godzich. *The Postmodern Explained*. Minneapolis: University of Minnesota Press, 1993.

"Sur la force des faibles." *L'Arc* 64 (1976): 4–12.

MacDonogh, S. ed. *The Rushdie Letters. Freedom to Speak, Freedom to Write*. Lincoln: University of Nebraska Press, 1993.

Malti-Douglas, Fedwa. *Woman's Body, Woman's Word. Gender and Discourse in Arabo-Islamic Writing*. Princeton University Press, 1991.

Maranhão, Tullio, ed. *The Interpretation of Dialogue*. University of Chicago Press, 1990.

McNeece, Lucy Stone. "Decolonizing the Sign: Language and Identity in Abdelkebir Khatibi's *La Mémoire tatouée*." *Yale French Studies* 83 (1993): 12–29.

Mecke, Jochen. "Dialogue in Narration (the Narrative Principle)," in *The Interpretation of Dialogue*. Ed. Tullio Maranhão. University of Chicago Press, 1990. Pp. 193–215.

Meddeb, Abdelwahab. *Phantasia*. Paris: Editions Sindbad, 1986.

Megill, Allan. "What Does the Term 'Postmodern' Mean?" *Annals of Scholarship*, Special issue on "Modernism and Postmodernism," 6.2–3 (1989): 129–51.

Memmi, Albert. *L'Homme dominé*. Paris: Gallimard, 1968.

Portrait du colonisé. Précédé du Portrait du Colonisateur. Preface by Jean-Paul Sartre. Paris: J. J. Pauvert, 1957.

Portrait d'un juif. Paris: Gallimard, 1962.

Mernissi, Fatima. *Beyond the Veil. Male–Female Dynamics in a Modern Muslim Society*. New York: Schenkman Publishing Co., 1975.

Le Harem politique. Paris: Albin Michel, 1987. English translation by Mary Jo Lakeland. *The Veil and the Male Elite: A Feminist Interpretation of Women's Rights in Islam*. Reading, MA: Addison-Wesley Publishing Company, Inc., 1991.

"Virginity and Patriarchy," in *Women and Islam*. Ed. Azizah al-Hibri. Oxford/New York: Pergamon Press, 1982.

Midiohouan, Guy Ossito. *L'Idéologie dans la littérature négro-africaine d'expression française*. Paris: l'Harmattan, 1986.

Mille et une nuits. Contes arabes, Les. Trans. Antoine Galland. 3 vols. Paris: Garnier-Flammarion, 1965.

Miller, Nancy. *Subject to Change: Reading Feminist Writing*. New York: Columbia University Press, 1988.

Morocco. Paris: Hachette World Guides, 1966.

Mortimer, Mildred. *Journeys: A Study of the Francophone Novel in Africa*. Portsmouth, NH: Heinemann, 1990.

M'Rabet, Fadela. *Les Algériennes*. Paris, 1967.

La Femme algérienne. Paris: François Maspero, 1964.

Netton, Ian Richard. *Text and Trauma: An East–West Primer*. Richmond, Surrey: Curzon Press, 1996.

Ong, Walter J. *Orality and Literacy. The Technologizing of the Word*. London: Methuen, 1982.

Pinault, David. *Story-Telling Techniques in The Arabian Nights*. Leiden/New York/Köln: E. J. Brill, 1992.

The Symposium. Trans. W. Hamilton. Harmondsworth, Middlesex: Penguin Books Ltd. (1951) 1962. Pp. 59–65.

Plato, *Cratylus*, in *The Works of Plato*, vol. 3. London: Henry G. Bohn, 1850. Pp. 283–395.

Rezzoug, Simone. "Ecritures féminines algériennes: histoires et société." *Maghreb Review* 9.3–4 (May–August 1984).

Rodinson, Maxime. *Mohammed*. Trans. Anne Carter. New York: Pantheon Books, 1971.

El Saadawi, Nawal. *The Hidden Face of Eve. Women in the Arab World*. 1980. Trans. Sherif Hetata. London: Zed Books Ltd, 1988.

Woman at Point Zero. Trans. Sherif Hetata. London: Zed Books Ltd, 1983.

Said, Edward W. *Beginnings: Intention and Method*. Baltimore: Johns Hopkins University Press, 1975.

Orientalism. New York: Pantheon Books, 1978.

al-Samman, Ghadah. "The Sexual Revolution and the Total Revolution," in *Middle Eastern Muslim Women Speak*. Eds. Elizabeth Warnock Fernea and Basima Qattan Bezirgan. Austin: University of Texas Press, 1977. Pp. 393–99.

Sartre, Jean-Paul. *L'Etre et le néant*. Paris: Gallimard, 1943.

Sembène, Ousmane. *Voltaïque*. Paris: Présence Africaine, 1962.

Serres, Michel. *Le Parasite*. Paris: Grasset, 1980.

"Platonic Dialogue," in *Hermes. Literature, Science, Philosophy*. Eds. Josué Harari and David F. Bell. Baltimore: Johns Hopkins University Press, 1982.

Shklovsky, Victor. "Art as Technique," 1917, in *Russian Formalist Criticism. Four Essays*.

Trans. with an Introduction by Lee T. Lemon and Marion J. Reis. Lincoln: University of Nebraska Press, 1965.

Sollers, Philippe. "Réponses." *Tel Quel* 43 (Autumn 1970): 76.

Steiner, George. *After Babel. Aspects of Language and Translation*. New York and London: Oxford University Press, 1975.

Language and Silence. New York: Atheneum, 1982.

Suleiman, Susan Rubin. *Authoritarian Fictions. The Ideological Novel as a Literary Genre*. New York: Columbia University Press, 1983.

al-Tabari. *Annales*. Eds. M. J. de Goeje et al. Leiden, 1897–1901.

Terdiman, Richard. *Discourse/Counter-Discourse. The Theory and Practice of Symbolic Resistance in Nineteenth-Century France*. Ithaca: Cornell University Press, 1985.

Thousand and One Nights, The. Trans. Edward William Lane. 3 vols. London, 1838–1841.

Tillion, Germaine. *Le Harem et les cousins*. Paris: Editions du Seuil, 1966.

Todorov, Tzvetan. "A Dialogic Criticism." *Raritan* 4.1 (1981): 64–76.

Introduction à la littérature fantastique. Paris: Editions du Seuil, 1970.

Mikhail Bakhtin. The Dialogical Principle. Trans. Wlad Godzich. Minneapolis: University of Minnesota Press, 1984.

Poétique de la prose. Paris: Editions du Seuil Poétique, 1971.

Tyler, Stephen A. "Ethnography, Intertextuality and the End of Description." *American Journal of Semiotics* 3.4 (1984): 83–98.

Valbueno Briones, A. "Una cala en el realismo mágico." *Cuadernos americanos* 166.5 (September–October 1969).

Van Den Abbeele, Georges. "*Algérie l'intraitable*: Lyotard's National Front," in *Passages, Genres, Differends: Jean-François Lyotard*, Special issue of *L'Esprit Créateur* 31.1 (Spring 1991): 144–57.

Volek, Emil. "Alejo Carpentier y la narrativa latino-americana actual (dimensiones de un 'realismo mágico')." *Cuaderno hispano-americanos* 296 (February 1975).

Watt, W. Montgomery. *Muhammed. Prophet and Statesman*. Oxford University Press, 1961.

Wittgenstein, Ludwig. *Philosophical Investigations*. Trans. G. E. M. Anscombe. Oxford: Basil Blackwell, 1968.

Remarks on the Foundations of Mathematics. Trans. G. E. M. Anscombe. Oxford: Basil Blackwell, 1964.

Woodhull, Winifred. *Transfigurations of the Maghreb. Feminism, Decolonization, and Literatures*. Minneapolis: University of Minnesota Press, 1993.

Yacine, Kateb. "Le rôle de l'écrivain dans un état socialiste," in *Anthologie des écrivains maghrébins d'expression française*. Paris: Présence Africaine, 1965. Pp.179–80.

Nedjma. Paris: Editions du Seuil, 1956.

Ziegler, Jean. *Main basse sur l'Afrique. La recolonisation*. Paris: Editions du Seuil, 1980.

Index

Abdel-Malek, Anouar, 179n6, 192
Abedi, Mehdi 186–87n25, 195
Accad, Evelyne 69, 175n9, 176nn19, 21,
    179n5, 192
Ackroyd, Roger 30, 94
Adorno, Theodor 65, 124, 178n40, 183n20,
    192
Ahsan, M. M. 130, 184n5, 191
Akhtar, Shabbir 130, 184n5, 191
Algar, Hamid 196
Algeria, colonization–fundamentalism 35,
    149; gender relations, effect on 43–44,
    47, 49; War of Liberation 29, 38, 44,
    54–55, 168, 176n18
al-'Ali, Naji 149
Allen, Roger 187n32, 192
Alloula, Abdelkader 170n6
Alloula, Malek 72, 180n8, 192
amanuensis 29, 38, 56, 61, 143, 173n48
Anderson, Benedict 171n30, 192
androgyny 104, 107, 109, 112–19, 166
antinomy 155, 185–86n17
Appignanesi, Lisa 130, 184n3, 184n5, 191
Aresu, Bernard 26, 172n40, 190, 192
Aristotle 28, 32, 91, 94
Augustin, Saint 181n18
autobiography 12, 39, 63
autocriticism 119–23

Bakhtin, Mikhail 150–51, 153, 183n23,
    187n33, 192
Bakunin, Mikhail 157
Ballard, J. G. 27
Balzac, Honoré de 24, 193
Barrès, Maurice 30
Barthes, Roland x, 32, 33, 94, 128, 170n8,
    173n50, 181n16, 181n18, 182n23, 184n30,
    185n16, 192, 193

Baudrillard, Jean 131
Beaujour, Michel 173n48, 193
Beckett, Samuel 117, 132, 183n15, 193
Ben Jelloun, Tahar 1, 3–4, 8, 13, 19, 21, 24,
    34–35, 43, 66–95, 128, 161, 162–63, 165,
    166, 170n16, 172n32, 173n53, 176nn16,
    19, 178n1, 179n5, 180n12, 182n22, 190
Beni Menacer tribe 53
Benjamin, Walter 171n30, 193
Bennani, Jahil 193
Bensmaïa, Réda 124, 177n25, 183n18, 189, 192
Berkani tribe 52–53
Bessière, Irène 156, 188n38, 193
Bezirgan, Basima Qattan 194
Bhabha, Homi K. 16–17, 171n29, 171n30,
    172n33, 193
Bjornson, Richard 170n19, 193
Blake, William 129, 153, 166, 184n2, 193
Blanchot 52, 70, 71, 80, 90, 132, 177n23, 193
Borges, Jorge Luis 13, 28, 66, 81, 84, 85,
    87–88, 92, 137, 157, 166, 178n1, 180n12,
    181nn15, 16, 193
Boudjedra, Rachid 69, 193
Bouhdiba, Abdelwahab 42, 45, 175n13,
    178–79n4, 193
Boukous, Ahmed 193
Bounfour, Abdallah 193
Bourdieu, Pierre 9, 187n27, 193
Brennan, Timothy 131, 184–85n8, 185n12,
    188n42, 191
bricolage 28, 32, 95, 133, 172n44
Burton, John 186n24, 193
Burton, Richard 87, 180–81n13

Caillois, Roger, 153–54, 187n35, 193
Calvino, Italo 94, 166
Carpentier, Alejo 154
Cazotte, Jacques 156